GEORGE BE

of the world's greatest literary figures. Born in Dublin, Ireland, he left school at fourteen and in 1876 went to London, where he began his literary career with a series of unsuccessful novels. In 1884 he became a founder of the Fabian Society, the famous British socialist organization. After becoming a reviewer and drama critic, he published a study of the Norwegian dramatist Henrik Ibsen in 1891 and became determined to create plays as he felt Ibsen did: to shake audiences out of their moral complacency and to attack social problems. However, Shaw was an irrepressible wit, and his plays are as entertaining as they are socially provocative. Basically shy, Shaw created a public persona for himself: G.B.S., a bearded eccentric, crusading social critic, antivivisectionist, language reformer, strict vegetarian, and renowned public speaker. The author of fifty-three plays, hundreds of essays, reviews, and letters, and several books, Shaw is best known for *Widower's Houses* (1892), *Arms and the Man* (1894), *Mrs. Warren's Profession* (1893), *Caesar and Cleopatra* (1901), *Man and Superman* (1903), *Major Barbara* (1905), *Pygmalion* (1913), *Heartbreak House* (1919), and *Saint Joan* (1923). He was awarded the Nobel Prize for Literature in 1925.

BANTAM CLASSIC · A BANTAM CLASSIC · A BANTAM CLASSIC · A BANTAM CLASSIC · A BANTAM CLASSIC ·

Arms and the Man and John Bull's Other Island

by
George Bernard Shaw

With an Introduction by
Stanley and Rodelle Weintraub

BANTAM BOOKS
NEW YORK · TORONTO · LONDON · SYDNEY · AUCKLAND

ARMS AND THE MAN and JOHN BULL'S OTHER ISLAND
A Bantam Classic Book

PUBLISHING HISTORY
This text reproduces the 1898 edition of *Arms and the Man* and the 1907 edition of *John Bull's Other Island*. Both prefaces have been edited. Spelling and punctuation have not been altered in any way.
Bantam Classic edition / July 1993

"Colonel Frederick Gustavus Burnaby, 1870" is reproduced courtesy of the National Portrait Gallery, London.

ISBN 0-553-21421-7

Published simultaneously in the United States and Canada

Bantam Books are published by Bantam Books, a division of Bantam Doubleday Dell Publishing Group, Inc. Its trademark, consisting of the words "Bantam Books" and the portrayal of a rooster, is Registered in U.S. Patent and Trademark Office and in other countries. Marca Registrada. Bantam Books, 1540 Broadway, New York, New York 10036.

PRINTED IN THE UNITED STATES OF AMERICA

OPM 0 9 8 7 6 5 4 3 2 1

Contents

Introduction

Arms and the Man and *John Bull's Other Island* are the only Bernard Shaw plays that King Edward VII ever saw. He hated the first, loved the second. Misunderstanding both, he never realized that they were variations upon the same theme. While Prince of Wales in 1894, Edward went with his brother, Duke Alfred of Saxe-Coburg and Gotha, to see *Arms and the Man* at the Avenue Theatre in London. To become the sovereign of the insignificant German duchy the year before, Alfred had relinquished his admiral's rank in the Royal Navy. Suspecting that the play, although set in Bulgaria during its war with Serbia, was mocking the incompetence of the British military, both brothers looked increasingly unhappy. Solicitously, theater manager Charles Helmsley went to the royal box to check. "The man is mad! The man is mad!" Helmsley heard the prince say. Afterward, from Buckingham Palace came a more moderate statement: "His Royal Highness regretted that the play should have shown so disrespectful an attitude toward the Army as was betrayed by the character of the chocolate-cream soldier."

The opening scene of a young woman in bed surprised by a soldier entering the room through a window awakened no such delicious recollections for the prince. It had been thirty-three years since he had been an incompetent young cadet at Curragh, near Dublin, and his helpful comrades had introduced a willing young woman into his bed. He was now, courtesy of his mother, the queen, a field marshal with a closet full of splendid uniforms and unearned decorations.

It did not occur to the future king that the play was as much about pathetically underdeveloped countries like Ireland as it was about an obscure Balkan war. However much the play was about impossibly romantic views of war and love, it was also about what Shaw called the predicament of people "redeemed from centuries of miserable bondage... beginning to work out their own redemption from barbarism—or, if you prefer it, beginning to contract the disease of civilisation.... And their attempts at Western civilisation were much the same as their attempts at war—instructive, romantic, ignorant. They were a nation of plucky beginners in every department."

The notebook containing Shaw's first draft has, as setting, "a lady's bedchamber"—but no geography. The characters were equally nameless spoofs on popular melodrama—the Father, the Daughter, the Heroic Lover, the Stranger. His friend Henry Salt suggested the timeless and placeless title "Battlefields and Boudoirs," but Shaw needed a location for his war, and went to Sidney Webb, his most knowledgeable friend, for help. In "two minutes" Webb came up with a suggestion. The Bulgarians had bested the Serbians in a small war in 1885, he said. All Shaw would have to do would be to find the *Annual Register* for that year in the British Museum Reading Room, and fill in the blanks.

Shaw did, first setting the play in Serbia, then shifting it to Bulgaria, making, he told actor Charles Charrington, "absurd alterations in detail for the sake of local color, . . . which will intensify the extravagance of the play." For contrast of personalities and ideas, Shaw made his trespasser into the bedchamber also an intruder of another sort—a Swiss mercenary among the military rabble. "Put a Republican—say a Swiss—into the tyrant-ridden East," Shaw said, describing his strategy, "and there you are." He thought of calling the play, accordingly, "Alps and Balkans," but settled for the Virgilian resonances of *Arms and the Man*—from the first line of the *Aeneid*.

In *Arms and the Man*, Shaw employs the devices of traditional nineteenth-century comic melodrama in order to ridicule the genre. In the rigid class structure of Victorian society, a misalliance across class lines, though absurd, was often the pivot of the plot. Its resolution created the happy ending. In the fluid class structure of an emerging nation, such a crossing of class lines has a happy logic. In *John Bull's Other Island* (1904), Shaw, by exposing the drab reality, mocks the sentimental Irish romance and its stereotypic village characters. The concluding betrothal scene is romantic only for Thomas Broadbent, who masks all hard realities in false sentiment. The connections between the two plays, written a decade apart—one the work of Shaw's apprenticeship and the other the product of his dramatic maturity—are almost certainly unintentional. Yet they show Shaw's remarkable consistency of both strategy and purpose. While the Bulgaria of *Arms and the Man* is not a covert Ireland but rather any nation struggling into civilized modernity, the Ireland of *John Bull's Other Island* also represents more than just Ireland. The seedy parlor in Cornelius Doyle's house is little different from the "library" of the Petkoff house, a pretentious tag for a room with a few dog-eared paperbacks. The social hauteur of Nora Reilly—the lady of the impoverished Irish village—is akin to the pride of Raina Petkoff, daughter of the best family in their obscure part of Bulgaria.

The first act of *Arms and the Man* appears to focus on the military theme—the reality underlying romantic dreams of military glory. The second extracts comic mileage from social themes—class differences that are more apparent than real, the varieties of erotic intrigue, the collision of bourgeois aspirations with local actuality. Bluntschli's "professional point of view" as a soldier, he explains to the hero-worshipping Raina, is "to live as long as we can." The captain keeps chocolate creams in his cartridge case: after all, he is a Switzer. And Major Sergius Saranoff's bravery, Raina learns, comes from having his horse run away with him, resulting in some left-handed courage.

Raina's boast, in Act I, that people of high standing in her country "wash their hands nearly every day," prepares the audience for the satire of the second act. She understands the need for social amenities. When she offers her hand to Bluntschli as a pledge of trust, the Swiss mercenary pulls it away. "I must have a wash first," he explains, and Raina realizes that he is "a gentleman." As a civilized Englishman, Tom Broadbent respects the dignity of his Irish hosts, and announces, "I'd better have a wash first." Raina's father, one of Bulgaria's leading citizens, will scoff that a bath more than once a week is "a ridiculous extreme," boasting, rather, of his "library" of a few broken-backed, coffee-stained paperbacks and his pride in an electric bell that summons the efficient Nicola. And while the pert, sharp-tongued maid, Louka, accuses Nicola of having the soul of a servant and not knowing the way to success in service, she employs her sexual wiles to rise beyond service. In an emerging nation there are few other avenues for an ambitious woman.

In the final act, although all illusions about love, heroism, and an idealized peasantry are exploded, Shaw remains able to furnish a series of audience-pleasing—although ironic—happy endings. Not so in *John Bull's Other Island*, where the peasantry is never idealized, where politics—the equivalent of war in *Arms and the Man*—is always fraudulent, even when the perpetrator of the partisan hypocrisies believes his own rhetoric, and where marriage is divorced from both love and sexual interest. The happy ending is deliberately sour and troubling, however conventionally auspicious—a betrothal without joy, a political triumph without cheer, an outlook without promise for the exhausted land.

Ironically, Irish poet W. B. Yeats had something to do with both *Arms and the Man* and *John Bull's Other Island*. There would always be a friendly rivalry between Yeats and Shaw, each respecting the other Irishman's abilities and vision. Yeats's short play *The Land of Heart's Desire* was the Avenue's curtain raiser. When the companion piece, John Todhunter's *A Comedy of Sighs*, had failed, Shaw rushed *Arms and the Man* to completion. Sitting through rehearsals of the work that was to save his own play, Yeats remained unimpressed. At the opening, he claimed, so was the audience. Like Victoria's sons, they had a feeling that they were being toyed with slyly and even seditiously. The romantic military melodrama was really something else. "The whole pit and gallery," Yeats remembered, ". . . started to laugh at the author, and then, discovering that they themselves were being laughed at, sat there not converted—their hatred was too bitter for that—but dumbfounded, while the rest of the house cheered and laughed."

Failing, like the gallery, to realize that Shaw had written a "serious farce" unlike anything he had experienced, Yeats sat through the opening "with admiration and hatred. It seemed to me inorganic, logical straightness and not the crooked road of life, yet I stood aghast before its energy. . . . Presently I had a nightmare that I was haunted by a sewing-machine, that clicked and shone, but the incredible thing was that the machine smiled, smiled perpetually."

When Yeats began an experimental theater in Dublin, Shaw promised him a new work. "I saw Shaw today," Yeats wrote to Lady Augusta Gregory, his partner in the venture. "He talks of a play on the contrast between the English and Irish character which sounds amusing." Shaw, however, was busy writing *Man and Superman*, and required Yeatsian prompting to put the Irish play on his creative agenda. In 1903 the possibility seemed closer. Yeats wrote in *Samhain*, the Irish Literary Theatre's organ, that Shaw's comedy was likely to be "unlike the plays we write for ourselves," and would deal with "Irish public life and character." A tinge of concern that he might be fostering a Dr. Frankenstein emerged as Yeats's anticipation increased. "Mr Shaw, more than anyone else, has the love of mischief that is so near the core of Irish intellect, and [his play] should have an immense popularity among us. I have seen a crowd of many thousands in possession of his spirit, and keeping the possession [in]to the small hours."

Postcarding Yeats on June 20, 1904, Shaw confessed good-humoredly: "Not a word of the play yet on paper." Then, sketching a recognizably Shavian head erupting with smoke like a pipe bowl, he added, "Seething in the brain." He had actually begun *John Bull's Other Island* three days earlier, and would finish the play in mid-August. W. G. Fay, Yeats's stage manager, confessed his reservations once he read the script. While it was "full of good things," he worried that it required a cast beyond the resources of Dublin. Like *Arms and the Man*, the play was dominated by a businesslike, outspoken outsider. This time the Bluntschli figure, with his own eccentric streak of pragmatic romance, was Broadbent. He would be difficult to cast. Where among Dublin's actors, Fay wondered, would he find someone to play the repellently hearty Englishman?

Next, Yeats cautiously gave the script to J. M. Synge, later notorious as author of *Playboy of the Western World*, which would provoke a riot at its premiere in 1907 for satirizing the gulf between the never-neverland dream and grimy Irish reality. While predicting that *John Bull* "will hold a Dublin audience, and at times move them," Synge was clearly negative. In a singularly imperceptive opinion for a shrewd satirical playwright, he suggested warily to Fay and Yeats that the dialogue of the saintly Father Keegan with an unseen grasshopper, in which Shaw reaches toward the future theater of the absurd, and the hilarious offstage episode of transporting a pig in the recently invented automobile ("The Handy Andy-like scene about carrying the goose") ought to be cut.

The more Yeats thought about the play, the further he distanced himself from his earlier eagerness for production. "The stage Irishman who wasn't an Irishman" amused him, he wrote to Shaw, but what did Dubliners care about English politics, or about contrasts between English and Irish character? The Irish romantic interest, Nora, and her collisions with the bluff Englishman, Broadbent, Yeats conceded, were "altogether a delight." Although the first scenes left him feeling that Shaw "had forgotten Ireland," reading on, "I found in the other acts that it is the only subject on which you are entirely serious. In fact you are so serious that sometimes your seriousness leaps upon the stage, knocks the characters over, and insists on having the conversation all to himself."

The more complimentary Yeats became, the more he revealed his reluctance to stage *John Bull's Other Island*. "You have said things in this play," he wrote, "which are entirely true about Ireland, things which nobody has ever said before, and these are the very things that are most part of the action. It astonishes me that you should have been so long in London and yet have remembered so much." *John Bull* was unlike Shaw's earlier plays, he judged, remembering *Arms and the Man*. "Hitherto you have taken your situations from melodrama, and called up logic to make them ridiculous. Your process here seems quite different, you are taking your situations more from life, you are for the first time trying to get the atmosphere of a place, you have for the first time a geographical conscience."

Tactlessly, Yeats ventured that the play was not "dangerous"—that the Abbey could "play it, and survive to play something else." But Shaw understood that Yeats meant that the comedy wouldn't do. It was, Shaw explained in the preface to *John Bull*, "uncongenial to the whole spirit of the neo-Gaelic movement, which is bent on creating a new Ireland after its own ideal, whereas my play is a very uncompromising presentment of the real old Ireland." While the play was also big and difficult to cast, the insuperable problem was the unflattering view of Ireland. It was one thing to identify Bulgaria as what would now be called a third-world country, finding sardonic comedy in its pretensions, its aspirations, its evasions, its poverty, its ignorance, its pride. But in calling Ireland backward, Shaw saw past the Ireland of poets and dreamers (the returning Larry Doyle is impatient with the "dreaming") to a drab reality that collided with sentimental Celticism. Yeats must have recognized an allusion to a play of his own, performed in 1902, in Doyle's scoffing first-act line, "If you want to interest him"—the average Irishman—"in Ireland you've got to call the unfortunate island Kathleen ni Hollihan and pretend she's a little old woman."

Shaw's Irish peasant, unlike the folkloric one romanticized in every aspiring nation's literature and theater, is the play's Matt Haffigan, whose fate, bluntly explained by Larry Doyle, "is the tragedy of his wasted youth, his stunted mind, his drudging over his clods and pigs until he has become a clod and a pig himself—until the soul within him has smouldered into nothing but a dull temper that hurts himself and all around him. I say let him die, and let us have no more of his like. . . ." Since lines like that were indeed "dangerous" and could lead to disturbances in the theater, Yeats was willing to forgo the premiere and let "that queer elephant" be produced in the safety of London, where it became such a hit that the leaders of the three major political parties went to see it. A special performance had to be staged on March 11, 1905, when its run in repertory at the Court Theatre ended and Edward VII complained that he had not yet seen it.

Sitting in the royal box, the heavyweight king laughed so heartily that he broke the regal chair that the management had rented for the occasion. Although they had earned nothing at the box office and had the cost of the chair to meet as well, the producers offered Shaw the standard royalty for the performance. He returned their check with a facetious note pointing out that the performance was "unauthorized" and his accepting money for it would be "compounding a felony." The event in any case was beyond price. It established Shaw's reputation as the foremost active playwright in the world.

Both plays reflect Shaw's own state of mind at the time of writing. Optimistic, farcical, full of sexual energy, *Arms and the Man* is a romp in which all ends well, the pairs coupling off to live happily ever after. Then sexually active, Shaw wrote the role of Louka for his mistress, Florence Farr, had other women interested in him, had achieved some fame as music critic and as drama critic, and could look forward to a career as a playwright. *Arms and the Man* became his first box office success.

John Bull's Other Island, bleak despite its comedic texture, in which nothing will end as well as it seems, was written after his marriage to an Irish heiress, Charlotte Payne-Townshend, who insisted that their union remain unconsummated. Jealous of any other woman's attentions to him, she tried to retain control over much of his activities, private and public. Shaw felt doomed to a frustrating abstinence from which there could be no escape, and wrote Charlotte's sexual distaste into the role of Nora.

Raina and Louka in *Arms and the Man* are full of life. They are confident of their ability to direct and control their destinies. Both women exude sexual energy and are capable of using their attractiveness to achieve their goals. Raina, frustrated when Bluntschli confides his desire not to bed her but merely to sleep in her bed, determines to have him. Louka, realizing that Sergius, Raina's fiancé, is physically attracted to her, uses her sexual cunning to ensnare him.

Nora and Aunt Judy in *John Bull's Other Island* have had any liveliness, any joy, washed out of them. They are humorless, snobbish, prudish. Resigned to their lot, they watch their futures happen to them. As maiden housekeeper, Aunt Judy at least has some responsibility, some role to play. Nora, the abandoned "heiress," seems destined only to lonely spinsterhood. When Broadbent proposes to her, she cannot even respond positively to the opportunity to escape her emptiness, scorning marriage with, "What is it but heartbreak and disappointment?" Although she expects nothing from marriage, she permits herself in a moment of wretchedness to be cradled in Broadbent's arms. "And how could I let any other man touch me after that?" This episode seems almost a sentimental courtship next to the declaration of the infatuated Sergius to the upstart minx Louka: "I have had you here in my arms, and will perhaps have you there again. . . . If these hands ever touch you again," he challenges, "they shall touch my affianced bride."

In both plays an outsider intrudes into the life of a less developed society. In the earlier, ebullient, play, Bluntschli is a benevolent and able figure. He assists the young nation in solving problems new to it since independence. Once he has helped arrange postwar demobilization, he will return home. In the later, more pessimistic play, Broadbent is far more competent than the villagers realize. Apparently fit only for ridicule, he is actually a malevolent figure. He will "improve" the area by exploiting it, by displacing and impoverishing the tenants and small landowners. Rather than leaving the community once his work is accomplished, Broadbent—or at least his presence—will remain, even if as absent M.P. and absentee landlord.

In *Arms and the Man*, Bulgaria, freed from Turkish rule, is backward but lively, and having successfully resisted Serbian aggression, has a future more significant than its past. Still without Home Rule, the palliative domestic parliament once promised by the late prime minister W. E. Gladstone, Ireland, in *John Bull*, lives on nostalgia and in the past. Even the Bulgarian servant class seizes its chances for upward mobility; with seemingly nothing to aspire toward, the Irish expect to live out their lives as cadgers, idlers, and dreamers. Raina and Louka look forward in their very different ways to becoming great ladies within their social spheres; Nora, defeated in life despite her village status and without the slightest cultural pretensions, will be miserable as a great lady on the ruling island, even as spouse of a Member of Parliament.

Removing Raina from Bulgaria, Bluntschli will enable her to achieve success and satisfaction. She wants Bluntschli, is glad to be free of Sergius, and has some measure of sophistication. Her wit, her charm, and her intelligence will enable her to adjust to life as a prosperous urban matron. Louka has her brazenness and her body as assets, and Sergius's social position will guarantee her acceptability in an aspiring nation where rank remains fluid. In Ireland or abroad, however, Nora will always regret marrying anyone but Larry Doyle. Going to England with Broadbent, whatever his good intentions, which are many, will only guarantee her misery. A lady in Rosscullen, she will be a provincial in London.

The hotel appears as a symbol of civilization and prosperity in both plays. Rosscullen has seventeen pubs in which to drown the melancholy of exploitation, but no hotel. Broadbent will promote shares in a stock company to build a hotel where farms are now mere patches between the stones. Nicola, the ambitious servant in *Arms and the Man*, aspires to run a hotel, and Bluntschli, it turns out, is heir to a string of Swiss hotels—the ultimate in gentility. Broadbent's vision for Ireland is as a setting for that least industrious of industries, tourism. The climate is salubrious, the people servile. The played-out country will become the site of a golf course and hotel for Englishmen; Irishmen will use the servants' entrance, not being able to afford leisure anyway. (Tourism in Switzerland has a harder edge; the industrious Swiss have always turned everything to their advantage.)

Even the major offstage events seem parallel. Sergius Saranoff's heroic headlong charge into the Serbian cavalry occurs when his horse runs away with him. Ten years later the automobile has been invented, and is brought to Ireland by the equally pompous Thomas Broadbent, who transports Haffigan's pig through Rosscullen at road-race speed because the pig's extremities somehow become entangled with the auto's accelerator and brake. Like Major Saranoff's inadvertent exploit, it becomes the talk of the countryside, and propels Broadbent's political ambitions.

It even emboldens his romantic ambitions, just as the earlier feat stirs Sergius's, for Broadbent can become more daring now that he has proved, if accidentally, that his manhood is not all brag. He proves to be an unabashed romantic, although one might have expected that to be the weakness of his business partner, the émigré Larry Doyle, who by contrast fights the Irish propensity to dream life away. Similarly, the pragmatic Switzer, Captain Bluntschli, conceals—badly—his own vein of sentimental romance, although earlier his emotions seemed to run, as Yeats had dreamed of Shaw, by a clockwork mechanism. In both plays the interloper—the alien from another and different world, whether the Swiss or the Briton—exposes the values, the debits, and the credits of the less sophisticated society he encounters. Shaw would later label the formula for his comedy of ideas "the jam that makes the pill go down."

While the military is the institution that binds together the struggling new Bulgaria and furnishes it with an element of pride, its equivalent in a still-downtrodden Ireland is the institution that furnishes only consolation, the Church. The happiest inhabitants of Rosscullen are, like Aunt Judy, content with "a strainless, narrow life," although the discontented evidence symptoms from Nora Reilly's melancholy to Tim Haffigan's drunkenness to defrocked Father Keegan's perception that earthly life is actually hell. The contrast to ambitious, freshly independent Bulgaria is instructive. The Rosscullen folk and their ways suggest the exhaustion of impoverished Ireland; the vitality awakened by freedom in the Petkoffs' Bulgaria suggests what can happen when dependence is replaced by independence.

Religion never enters as a factor in Shaw's Bulgaria, but in his Ireland, faith capitalizes on hopelessness. The glum Father Dempsey can offer nothing as solace in this world but the promise of a better life in the next. The mystical Father Keegan, his vocation denied him on grounds that he is mad, seems a William Blake crossed with St. Francis of Assisi, and may be the most enchanting character in the Shavian canon.

Keegan's fey charm set off a search for his original. One suggestion was a modernist Irish priest whom Shaw knew, Father George Tyrrell, who after twenty years with the Jesuits had published, in 1899, an unorthodox article, "A Perverted Devotion," which criticized aspects of Roman doctrine. By the time Shaw began his play, a campaign was in progress to defrock Tyrrell for heresy. Life followed art, and in 1906, more than a year after the first production of *John Bull's Other Island*, Tyrrell was drummed out of the clergy. Since Keegan lost his collar before Father Tyrrell did, he may not have been the key personality in Shaw's mind. Another possibility is the Whitmanesque former Anglican clergyman and poet Edward Carpenter, who left the Church on his own to follow the simple life of Thoreau and Whitman, dabbled in Eastern religions, pacifism, socialism, and other doctrines anathema to the religious establishment.

Asian religions led Carpenter to metempsychosis, a doctrine Shaw borrowed to furnish Keegan with a metaphor. Keegan listened to the deathbed confession of a Hindu, and relates the man's bleak tale of "unmerited misfortune, of cruel ill luck, of relentless persecution by destiny, which sometimes wither the commonplaces of consolation on the lips of a priest." His misfortunes had been brought upon him, the

Hindu claimed, "by sins committed in a former existence," and to Keegan that helped explain the bitter paradoxes of worldly existence. "This world, sir," he tells Broadbent, "is very clearly a place of torment and penance." And he follows with a litany of the horrors and torments of ordinary life that belie all manner of charity and sanctity and industriousness. "Now, sir," he goes on, "there is only one place of horror and torment known to my religion; and that place is hell. Therefore it is plain to me that this earth of ours must be hell, and that we are all here, as the Indian revealed to me—perhaps he was sent to reveal it to me—to expiate crimes committed by us in a former existence."

Nora refers to the idea, which Keegan apparently has not been keeping to himself, when she tells him, "I was too wicked in a former existence to play backgammon with a good man like you." Piously, Aunt Judy turns such conversation aside with "Whisht, whisht, child!"

Nora's own name suggests a paradox Shaw employed so subtly that, while obvious to his own generation, it appears almost lost today. No other play Shaw had written to that date had failed to call attention in its title to a significant character, whether as a name or a reference. There is a widower in *Widowers' Houses* and feminine arms certainly enfold at least one warrior in *Arms and the Man*. A pirate captain is converted from a life driven by revenge in *Captain Brassbound's Conversion* and the young Napoleon is *The Man of Destiny*. Other plays name names, as in *Candida* and *Mrs Warren's Profession*. But *John Bull's Other Island* is not "Tom Broadbent's Other Island," nor is it, ironically in the extreme, "The Salvation of Nora Reilly."

European translations of Ibsen's controversial and influential *A Doll's House*, first performed in England on the commercial stage in 1889, often simplified its title to *Nora*, obfuscating the symbolism. Shaw named his docile, defeated heroine Nora, one might guess, because she was a polar opposite to the rebellious Nora Helmer, who resists subjugation of her life and personality to a husband who takes it for granted that a wife is helpmate, sex object, and chattel (literally a movable piece of property). Will Shaw's Nora awaken, possibly in alien London, and run away, like her namesake? Since Shaw preferred plays with unfinished endings, like life, we do not have that fifth act.

Shortly before young Winston Churchill's marriage in 1908, it is said that Shaw offered him seats at the premiere of the newest G.B.S. theater piece. "I enclose two tickets for the first night of my new play," Shaw allegedly wrote, "one for yourself and one for your friend, if you have one."

Whether fact or folklore, Shaw denied for years having taunted Churchill. But when he was ninety-four he claimed to recall Winston's retort: "I am sorry I cannot attend for the first night, but I should be glad to come on the second night, if there is one."

Could young Winston have seen himself in Shaw's play? Elected Conservative M.P. from Oldham in 1900 at twenty-five, Churchill was guest of honor in January 1904 at a widely reported dinner given by the Corinthian Club in Dublin. Replying to a toast, he offered an address in what seems to be Broadbentese. "I feel," said Churchill, "as St. Patrick must have felt when he landed to convert the Irish nation. I can only hope that I may have, if not the good fortune St. Patrick had, at any rate some proportion of that good fortune in driving out of Ireland the fiscal frogs and tariff toads." Reports of the address follow the witticism with *"Laughter"* and *"Hear! Hear!"* The impromptu political meeting that opens the fourth act, as well as its rhetoric—and perhaps the entire device of an ambitious young English politician on alien turf in Ireland—may owe its conception to Churchill's Irish visit.

While Shaw took aim, through Broadbent, at salvation through efficiency, he had already dramatized the collision of romanticism with efficiency in *Arms and the Man*, where he had also drawn aspects of some of his characters from life. The attractive, strong-willed Florence Farr, who wanted to play Raina in the 1894 premiere, settled on Louka, who is more like Florence anyway. The efficient soldier of fortune, Bluntschli, is in part Shaw's political ally Sidney Webb, who on the surface evidenced not a molecule of romance, while the braggart soldier, Sergius, seemingly a stock figure borrowed from the commedia dell'arte, is Shaw's friend Sir Robert Cunninghame Graham to the life. A pugnacious adventurer in whose vocabulary *timidity* did not exist, Graham was identifiable to anyone who recalled his oft-quoted exclamation in the House of Commons, "I never explain!" Shaw awards the remark to Sergius.

Sergius is even given the key line in the play, encapsulating its concerns about our compulsion to romanticize the world around us and the realities we must accommodate. "Everything I think," he mourns, "is mocked by everything I do." It was a theme to which Shaw returned in "A Dramatic Realist to His Critics," the clever *New Review* article which is in effect a postscript to *Arms and the Man* (and reprinted here).

Arms and the Man was made into an unauthorized operetta, *The Chocolate Soldier*, which jettisoned the satire for the romance. Shaw, for whom comedy was always a serious business, hated the adaptation.

No one has attempted to make a *Finian's Rainbow* fantasy out of the even funnier *John Bull's Other Island*. The laughter is too grim. As Father Keegan contends, "Every jest is an earnest in the womb of Time."

Rodelle Weintraub
Stanley Weintraub

Arms and the Man

Preface

I turned my hand to play-writing when a great deal of talk about "the New Drama," followed by the actual establishment of a "New Theatre" (the Independent), threatened to end in the humiliating discovery that the New Drama, in England at least, was a figment of the revolutionary imagination. This was not to be endured. I had rashly taken up the case; and rather than let it collapse I manufactured the evidence.

Man is a creature of habit. You cannot write three plays and then stop. Besides, the New movement did not stop. In 1894, Florence Farr, who had already produced Ibsen's Rosmersholm, was placed in command of the Avenue Theatre in London for a season on the new lines by Miss A.E.F. Horniman, who had family reasons for not yet appearing openly as a pioneer-manageress. There were, as available New Dramatists, myself, discovered by the Independent Theatre (at my own suggestion); Dr John Todhunter, who had been discovered before (his play *The Black Cat* had been one of the Independent's successes); and Mr W. B. Yeats, a genuine discovery. Dr Todhunter supplied *A Comedy of Sighs*: Mr Yeats, *The Land of Heart's Desire*. I, having nothing but unpleasant plays in my desk, hastily completed a first attempt at a pleasant one, and called it *Arms and The Man*, taking the title from the first line of Dryden's Virgil. It passed for a success, the applause on the first night being as promising as could be wished; and it ran from the 21st of April to the 7th of July. To witness it the public paid £1777:5:6, an average of £23:2:5 per representation (including nine matinées). A publisher receiving £1700 for a book would have made a satisfactory profit: experts in West End theatrical management will contemplate that figure with a grim smile. . . .

Returning now to the actual state of things, it is clear that I have no grievance against our theatres. Knowing quite well what I was doing, I have heaped difficulties in the way of the performance of my plays by ignoring the majority of the manager's customers: nay, by positively making war on them. To the actor I have been more considerate, using all my cunning to enable him to make the most of his technical methods; but I have not hesitated on occasion to tax his intelligence very severely, making the stage effect depend not only on *nuances* of execution quite beyond the average skill produced by the routine of the English stage in its present condition, but on a perfectly sincere and straightforward conception of states of mind which still seem cynically perverse to most people, and on a goodhumouredly contemptuous or profoundly pitiful attitude towards ethical conventions which seem to them validly heroic or venerable. It is inevitable that actors should suffer more than most of us from the sophistication of their consciousness by romance; and my view of romance as the great heresy to be swept off from art and life—as the food of modern pessimism and the bane of modern self-respect, is far more puzzling to the performers than it is to the pit. It is hard for an actor whose point of honor it is to be a perfect gentleman, to sympathize with an author who regards gentility as a dishonest folly, and gallantry and chivalry as treasonable to women and stultifying to men.

The misunderstanding is complicated by the fact that actors, in their demonstrations of emotion, have made a second nature of stage custom, which is often very much out of date as a representation of contemporary life. Sometimes the stage custom is not only obsolete, but fundamentally wrong: for instance, in the simple case of laughter and tears, in which it deals too liberally, it is certainly not based on the fact, easily enough discoverable in real life, that we only cry now in the effort to bear happiness, whilst we laugh and exult in destruction, confusion, and ruin. When a comedy is performed, it is nothing to me that the spectators laugh: any fool can make an audience laugh. I want to see how many of them, laughing or grave, are in the melting mood. And this result cannot be achieved, even by actors who thoroughly understand my purpose, except through an artistic beauty of execution unattainable without long and arduous practice, and an intellectual effort which my plays probably do not seem serious enough to call forth.

Beyond the difficulties thus raised by the nature and quality of my work, I have none to complain of. I have come upon no ill will, no inaccessibility, on the part of the very few managers with whom I have discussed it. As a rule I find that the actor-manager is over-sanguine, because he has the artist's habit of underrating the force of circumstances and exaggerating the power of the talented individual to prevail against them; whilst I have acquired the politician's habit of regarding the individual, however talented, as having no choice but to make the most of his circumstances. I half suspect that those managers who have had most to do with me, if asked to name the main obstacle to the performance of my plays, would unhesitatingly and unanimously reply "The author." And I confess that though as a matter of business I wish my plays to be performed, as a matter of instinct I fight against the inevitable misrepresentation of them with all the subtlety needed to conceal my ill will from myself as well as from the manager.

The main difficulty, of course, is the incapacity for serious drama of thousands of playgoers of all classes whose shillings and half guineas will buy as much in the market as if they delighted in the highest art. But with them I must frankly take the superior position. I know that many managers are wholly dependent on them, and that no manager is wholly independent of them; but I can no more write what they want than Joachim can put aside his fiddle and oblige a happy company of beanfeasters with a marching tune on the German concertina. They must keep away from my plays: that is all.

There is no reason, however, why I should take this haughty attitude towards those representative critics whose complaint is that my talent, though not unentertaining, lacks elevation of sentiment and seriousness of purpose. They can find, under the surface-brilliancy for which they give me credit, no coherent thought or sympathy, and accuse me, in various terms and degrees, of an inhuman and freakish wantonness; of preoccupation with "the seamy side of life"; of paradox, cynicism, and eccentricity, reducible, as some contend, to a trite formula of treating bad as good and good as bad, important as trivial and trivial as important, serious as laughable and laughable as serious, and so forth. As to this formula I can only say that if any gentleman is simple enough to think that even a good comic opera can be produced by it, I invite him to try his hand, and see whether anything resembling one of my plays will reward him.

I could explain the matter easily enough if I chose; but the result would be that the people who misunderstand the plays would misunderstand the explanation ten times more. The particular exceptions taken are seldom more than symptoms of the underlying fundamental disagreement between the romantic morality of the critics and the natural morality of the plays. For example, I am quite aware that the much criticized Swiss officer in *Arms and The Man* is not a conventional stage soldier. He suffers from want of food and sleep; his nerves go to pieces after three days under fire, ending in the horrors of a rout and pursuit; he has found by experience that it is more important to have a few bits of chocolate to eat in the field than cartridges for his revolver. When many of my critics rejected these circumstances as fantastically improbable and cynically unnatural, it was not necessary to argue them into common sense: all I had to do was to brain them, so to speak, with the first half dozen military authorities at hand, beginning with the present Commander in Chief. But when it proved that such unromantic (but all the more dramatic) facts implied to them a denial of the existence of courage, patriotism, faith, hope, and charity, I saw that it was not really mere matter of fact that was at issue between us. One strongly Liberal critic, the late Moy Thomas, who had, in the teeth of a chorus of dissent, received my first play with the most generous encouragement, declared, when *Arms and The Man* was produced, that I had struck a wanton blow at the cause of liberty in the Balkan Peninsula by mentioning that it was not a matter of course for a Bulgarian in 1885 to wash his hands every day. He no doubt saw soon afterwards the squabble, reported all through Europe, between Stambouloff and an eminent lady of the Bulgarian court who took exception to his neglect of his fingernails. After that came the news of his ferocious assassination, with a description of the room prepared for the reception of visitors by his widow, who draped it with black, and decorated it with photographs of the mutilated body of her husband. Here was a sufficiently sensational confirmation of the accuracy of my sketch of the theatrical nature of the first apings of western civilization by spirited races just emerging from slavery. But it had no bearing on the real issue between my critic and myself, which was, whether the political and religious idealism which had inspired Gladstone to call for the rescue of these Balkan principalities from the despotism of the Turk, and converted miserably enslaved provinces into hopeful and gallant little States, will survive the general onslaught on idealism which is implicit, and indeed explicit, in *Arms and The Man* and the naturalist plays of the modern school. For my part I hope not; for idealism, which is only a flattering name for romance in politics and morals, is as obnoxious to me as romance in ethics or religion. In spite of a Liberal Revolution or two, I can no longer be satisfied with fictitious morals and fictitious good conduct, shedding fictitious glory on robbery, starvation, disease, crime, drink, war, cruelty, cupidity, and all the other commonplaces of civilization which drive men to the theatre to make foolish pretences that such things are progress, science, morals, religion, patriotism, imperial supremacy, national greatness and all the other names the newspapers call them. On the other hand, I see plenty of good in the world working itself out as fast as the idealists will allow it; and if they would only let it alone and learn to respect reality, which would include the beneficial exercise of respecting themselves, and incidentally respecting me, we should all get along much better and faster. At all events, I do not see moral chaos and anarchy as the alternative to romantic convention; and I am not going to pretend I do merely to please the people who are convinced that the world is held together only by the force of unanimous, strenuous, eloquent, trumpet-tongued lying. To me the tragedy and comedy of life lie in the consequences, sometimes terrible, sometimes ludicrous, of our persistent attempts to found our institutions on the ideals suggested to our imaginations by our half-satisfied passions, instead of on a genuinely scientific natural history. And with that hint as to what I am driving at, I withdraw and ring up the curtain.

shedding meretricious glory on robbery, starvation, disease, crime, drink, war, cruelty, cupidity, and all the other commonplaces of civilization which drive men to the theatre to make foolish pretences that such things are progress, science, morals, religion, patriotism, imperial supremacy, national greatness and all the other names the newspapers call them. On the other hand, I see plenty of good in the world working itself out as fast as the idealists will allow it; and if they would only let it alone and learn to respect reality, which would include the beneficial exercise of respecting themselves, and incidentally respecting me, we should all get along much better and faster. At all events, I do not see moral chaos and anarchy as the alternative to romantic convention; and I am not going to pretend I do merely to please the people who are convinced that the world is only held together by the force of unanimous, strenuous, eloquent, trumpet-tongued lying. To me the tragedy and comedy of life lie in the consequences, sometimes terrible, sometimes ludicrous, of our persistent attempts to found our institutions on the ideals suggested to our imaginations by our half-satisfied passions, instead of on a genuinely scientific natural history. And with that hint as to what I am driving at, I withdraw and ring up the curtain.

[illegible]

Arms and the Man

Act One

Night. A lady's bedchamber in Bulgaria, in a small town near the Dragoman Pass, late in November in the year 1885. Through an open window with a little balcony a peak of the Balkans, wonderfully white and beautiful in the starlit snow, seems quite close at hand, though it is really miles away. The interior of the room is not like anything to be seen in the west of Europe. It is half rich Bulgarian, half cheap Viennese. Above the head of the bed, which stands against a little wall cutting off the left hand corner of the room, is a painted wooden shrine, blue and gold, with an ivory image of Christ, and a light hanging before it in a pierced metal ball suspended by three chains. The principal seat, placed towards the other side of the room and opposite the window, is a Turkish ottoman. The counterpane and hangings of the bed, the window curtains, the little carpet, and all the ornamental textile fabrics in the room are oriental and gorgeous: the paper on the walls is occidental and paltry. The wash-stand, against the wall on the side nearest the ottoman and window, consists of an enamelled iron basin with a pail beneath it in a painted metal frame, and a single towel on the rail at the side. The dressing table, between the bed and the window, is a common pine table, covered with a cloth of many colors, with an expensive toilet mirror on it. The door is on the side nearest the bed; and there is a chest of drawers between. This chest of drawers is also covered by a variegated native cloth; and on it there is a pile of paper backed novels, a box of chocolate creams, and a miniature easel with a large photograph of an extremely handsome officer, whose lofty bearing and magnetic glance can be felt even from the portrait. The room is lighted by a candle on the chest of drawers, and another on the dressing table with a box of matches beside it.

The window is hinged doorwise and stands wide open. Outside, a pair of wooden shutters, opening outwards, also stand open. On the balcony a young lady, intensely conscious of the romantic beauty of the night, and of the fact that her own youth and beauty are part of it, is gazing at the snowy Balkans. She is in her nightgown, well covered by a long mantle of furs, worth, on a moderate estimate, about three times the furniture of her room.

Her reverie is interrupted by her mother, Catherine Petkoff, a woman over forty, imperiously energetic, with magnificent black hair and eyes, who might be a very splendid specimen of the wife of a mountain farmer, but is determined to be a Viennese lady, and to that end wears a fashionable tea gown on all occasions.

CATHERINE [*entering hastily, full of good news*] Raina! [*She pronounces it Rah-eena, with the stress on the ee*]. Raina! [*She goes to the bed, expecting to find Raina there*]. Why, where—? [*Raina looks into the room*]. Heavens, child! are you out in the night air instead of in your bed? Youll catch your death. Louka told me you were asleep.

RAINA [*dreamily*] I sent her away. I wanted to be alone. The stars are so beautiful! What is the matter?

CATHERINE. Such news! There has been a battle.

RAINA [*her eyes dilating*] Ah! [*She comes eagerly to Catherine*].

CATHERINE. A great battle at Slivnitza! A victory! And it was won by Sergius.

RAINA [*with a cry of delight*] Ah! [*They embrace rapturously*] Oh, mother! [*Then, with sudden anxiety*] Is father safe?

CATHERINE. Of course: he sends me the news. Sergius is the hero of the hour, the idol of the regiment.

RAINA. Tell me, tell me. How was it? [*Ecstatically*] Oh, mother! mother! mother! [*She pulls her mother down on the ottoman; and they kiss one another frantically*].

CATHERINE [*with surging enthusiasm*] You cant guess how splendid it is. A cavalry charge! think of that! He defied our Russian commanders—acted without orders—led a charge on his own responsibility—headed it himself—was the first man to sweep through their guns. Cant you see it, Raina: our gallant splendid Bulgarians with their swords and eyes flashing, thundering down like an avalanche and scattering the wretched Serbs and their dandified Austrian officers like chaff. And you! you kept Sergius waiting a year before you would be betrothed to him. Oh, if you have a drop of Bulgarian blood in your veins, you will worship him when he comes back.

RAINA. What will he care for my poor little worship after the acclamations of a whole army of heroes? But no matter: I am so happy! so proud! [*She rises and walks about excitedly*]. It proves that all our ideas were real after all.

CATHERINE [*indignantly*] Our ideas real! What do you mean?

RAINA. Our ideas of what Sergius would do. Our patriotism. Our heroic ideals. I sometimes used to doubt whether they were anything but dreams. Oh, what faithless little creatures girls are! When I buckled on Sergius's sword he looked so noble: it was treason to think of disillusion or humiliation or failure. And yet—and yet—[*She sits down again suddenly*] Promise me youll never tell him.

CATHERINE. Dont ask me for promises until I know what I'm promising.

RAINA. Well, it came into my head just as he was holding me in his arms and looking into my eyes, that perhaps we only had our heroic ideas because we are so fond of reading Byron and Pushkin, and because we were so delighted with the opera that season at Bucharest. Real life is so seldom like that! indeed never, as far as I knew it then. [*Remorsefully*] Only think, mother: I doubted him: I wondered whether all his heroic qualities and his soldiership might not prove mere imagination when he went into a real battle. I had an uneasy fear that he might cut a poor figure there beside all those clever officers from the Tsar's court.

CATHERINE. A poor figure! Shame on you! The Serbs have Austrian officers who are just as clever as the Russians; but we have beaten them in every battle for all that.

RAINA [*laughing and snuggling against her mother*] Yes: I was only a prosaic little coward. Oh, to think that it was all true! that Sergius is just as splendid and noble as he looks! that the world is really a glorious world for women who can see its glory and men who can act its romance! What happiness! what unspeakable fulfilment!

They are interrupted by the entry of Louka, a handsome proud girl in a pretty Bulgarian peasant's dress with double apron, so defiant that her servility to Raina is almost insolent. She is afraid of Catherine, but even with her goes as far as she dares.

LOUKA. If you please, madam, all the windows are to be closed and the shutters made fast. They say there may be shooting in the streets. [*Raina and Catherine rise together, alarmed*]. The Serbs are being chased right back through the pass; and they say they may run into the town. Our cavalry will be after them; and our people will be ready for them, you may be sure, now theyre running away. [*She goes out on the balcony, and pulls the outside shutters to; then steps back into the room*].

CATHERINE [*businesslike, her housekeeping instincts aroused*] I must see that everything is made safe downstairs.

RAINA. I wish our people were not so cruel. What glory is there in killing wretched fugitives?

CATHERINE. Cruel! Do you suppose they would hesitate to kill you—or worse?

RAINA [*to Louka*] Leave the shutters so that I can just close them if I hear any noise.

CATHERINE [*authoritatively, turning on her way to the door*] Oh no, dear: you must keep them fastened. You would be sure to drop off to sleep and leave them open. Make them fast, Louka.

LOUKA. Yes, madam. [*She fastens them*].

RAINA. Don't be anxious about me. The moment I hear a shot, I shall blow out the candles and roll myself up in bed with my ears well covered.

CATHERINE. Quite the wisest thing you can do, my love. Goodnight.

RAINA. Goodnight. [*Her emotion comes back for a moment*]. Wish me joy. [*They kiss*]. This is the happiest night of my life—if only there are no fugitives.

CATHERINE. Go to bed, dear; and dont think of them. [*She goes out*].

LOUKA [*secretly, to Raina*] If you would like the shutters open, just give them a push like this [*she pushes them: they open: she pulls them to again*]. One of them ought to be bolted at the bottom; but the bolt's gone.

RAINA [*with dignity, reproving her*] Thanks, Louka; but we must do what we are told. [*Louka makes a grimace*]. Goodnight.

LOUKA [*carelessly*] Goodnight. [*She goes out, swaggering*].

Raina, left alone, takes off her fur cloak and throws it on the ottoman. Then she goes to the chest of drawers, and adores the portrait there with feelings that are beyond all expression. She does not kiss it or press it to her breast, or shew it any mark of bodily affection; but she takes it in her hands and elevates it, like a priestess.

RAINA [*looking up at the picture*] Oh, I shall never be unworthy of you any more, my soul's hero: never, never, never. [*She replaces it reverently. Then she selects a novel from the little pile of books. She turns over the leaves dreamily; finds her page; turns the book inside out at it; and, with a happy sigh, gets into bed and prepares to read herself to sleep. But before abandoning herself to fiction, she raises her eyes once more, thinking of the blessed reality, and murmurs*] My hero! my hero!

A distant shot breaks the quiet of the night. She starts, listening; and two more shots, much nearer, follow, startling her so that she scrambles out of bed, and hastily blows out the candle on the chest of drawers. Then, putting her fingers in her ears, she runs to the dressing table, blows out the light there, and hurries back to bed in the dark, nothing being visible but the glimmer of the light in the pierced ball before the image, and the starlight seen through the slits at the top of the shutters. The firing breaks out again: there is a startling fusillade quite close at hand. Whilst it is still echoing, the shutters disappear, pulled open from without; and for an instant the rectangle of snowy starlight flashes out with the figure of a man silhouetted in black upon it. The shutters close immediately; and the room is dark again. But the silence is now broken by the sound of panting. Then there is a scratch; and the flame of a match is seen in the middle of the room.

RAINA [*crouching on the bed*] Who's there? [*The match is out instantly*]. Who's there? Who is that?

A MAN'S VOICE [*in the darkness, subduedly, but threateningly*] Sh—sh! Dont call out; or youll be shot. Be good; and no harm will happen to you. [*She is heard leaving her bed, and making for the door*]. Take care: it's no use trying to run away.

RAINA. But who—

THE VOICE [*warning*] Remember: if you raise your voice my revolver will go off. [*Commandingly*] Strike a light and let me see you. Do you hear. [*Another moment of silence and darkness as she retreats to the chest of drawers. Then she lights a candle; and the mystery is at an end. He is a man of about 35, in a deplorable plight, bespattered with mud and blood and snow, his belt and the strap of his revolver-case keeping together the torn ruins of the blue tunic of a Serbian artillery officer. All that the candlelight and his unwashed unkempt condition make it possible to discern is that he is of middling stature and undistinguished appearance, with strong neck and shoulders, roundish obstinate looking head covered with short crisp bronze curls, clear quick eyes and good brows and mouth, hopelessly prosaic nose like that of a strong minded baby, trim soldierlike carriage and energetic manner, and with all his wits about him in spite of his desperate perdicament: even with a sense of the humor of it, without, however, the least intention of trifling with it or throwing away a chance. Reckoning up what he can guess about Raina: her age, her social position, her character, and the extent to which she is frightened, he continues, more politely but still most determinedly*] Excuse my disturbing you; but you recognize my uniform? Serb! If I'm caught I shall be killed. [*Menacingly*] Do you understand that?

RAINA. Yes.

THE MAN. Well, I dont intend to get killed if I can help it. [*Still more formidably*] Do you understand that? [*He locks the door quickly but quietly*].

RAINA [*disdainfully*] I suppose not. [*She draws herself up superbly, and looks him straight in the face, adding, with cutting emphasis*] Some soldiers, I know, are afraid to die.

THE MAN [*with grim goodhumor*] All of them, dear lady, all of them, believe me. It is our duty to live as long as we can. Now, if you raise an alarm—

RAINA [*cutting him short*] You will shoot me. How do you know that *I* am afraid to die?

THE MAN [*cunningly*] Ah; but suppose I dont shoot you, what will happen then? A lot of your cavalry will burst into this pretty room of yours and slaughter me here like a pig; for I'll fight like a demon: they shant get me into the street to amuse themselves with: I know what they are. Are you prepared to receive that sort of company in your present undress? [*Raina, suddenly conscious of her nightgown, instinctively shrinks, and gathers it more closely about her neck. He watches her, and adds, pitilessly*] Hardly presentable, eh? [*She turns to the ottoman. He raises his pistol instantly, and cries*] Stop! [*She stops*]. Where are you going?

RAINA [*with dignified patience*] Only to get my cloak.

THE MAN [*passing swiftly to the ottoman and snatching the cloak*] A good idea! I'll keep the cloak; and youll take care that nobody comes in and sees you without it. This is a better weapon than the revolver: eh? [*He throws the pistol down on the ottoman*].

RAINA [*revolted*] It is not the weapon of a gentleman!

THE MAN. It's good enough for a man with only you to stand between him and death. [*As they look at one another for a moment, Raina hardly able to believe that even a Serbian officer can be so cynically and selfishly unchivalrous, they are startled by a sharp fusillade in the street. The chill of imminent death hushes the man's voice as he adds*] Do you hear? If you are going to bring those blackguards in on me you shall receive them as you are.

Clamor and disturbance. The pursuers in the street batter at the house door, shouting Open the door! Open the door! Wake up, will you! *A man servant's voice calls to them angrily from within* This is Major Petkoff's house: you cant come in here; *but a renewal of the clamor, and a torrent of blows on the door, end with his letting a chain down with a clank, followed by a rush of heavy footsteps and a din of triumphant yells, dominated at last by the voice of Catherine, indignantly addressing an officer with* What does this mean, sir? Do you know where you are? *The noise subsides suddenly.*

LOUKA [*outside, knocking at the bedroom door*] My lady! my lady! get up quick and open the door. If you dont they will break it down.

The fugitive throws up his head with the gesture of a man who sees that it is all over with him, and drops the manner he has been assuming to intimidate Raina.

THE MAN [*sincerely and kindly*] No use, dear: I'm done for. [*Flinging the cloak to her*] Quick! wrap yourself up: theyre coming.

RAINA. Oh, thank you. [*She wraps herself up with intense relief*].

THE MAN [*between his teeth*] Dont mention it.

RAINA [*anxiously*] What will you do?

THE MAN [*grimly*] The first man in will find out. Keep out of the way; and dont look. It wont last long; but it will not be nice. [*He draws his sabre and faces the door, waiting*].

RAINA [*impulsively*] I'll help you. I'll save you.

THE MAN. You cant.

RAINA. I can. I'll hide you. [*She drags him towards the window*]. Here! behind the curtains.

THE MAN [*yielding to her*] Theres just half a chance, if you keep your head.

RAINA [*drawing the curtain before him*] S-sh! [*She makes for the ottoman*].

THE MAN [*putting out his head*] Remember—

RAINA [*running back to him*] Yes?

THE MAN.—nine soldiers out of ten are born fools.

RAINA. Oh! [*She draws the curtain angrily before him*].

THE MAN [*looking out at the other side*] If they find me, I promise you a fight: a devil of a fight.

She stamps at him. He disappears hastily. She takes off her cloak, and throws it across the foot of the bed. Then, with a sleepy, disturbed air, she opens the door. Louka enters excitedly.

LOUKA. One of those beasts of Serbs has been seen climbing up the waterpipe to your balcony. Our men want to search for him; and they are so wild and drunk and furious. [*She makes for the other side of the room to get as far from the door as possible*]. My lady says you are to dress at once, and to—[*She sees the revolver lying on the ottoman, and stops, petrified*].

RAINA [*as if annoyed at being disturbed*] They shall not search here. Why have they been let in?

CATHERINE [*coming in hastily*] Raina, darling: are you safe? Have you seen anyone or heard anything?

RAINA. I heard the shooting. Surely the soldiers will not dare come in here?

CATHERINE. I have found a Russian officer, thank Heaven: he knows Sergius. [*Speaking through the door to someone outside*] Sir: will you come in now. My daughter will receive you.

A young Russian officer, in Bulgarian uniform, enters, sword in hand.

OFFICER [*with soft feline politeness and stiff military carriage*] Good evening, gracious lady. I am sorry to intrude; but there is a Serb hiding on the balcony. Will you and the gracious lady your mother please to withdraw whilst we search?

RAINA [*petulantly*] Nonsense, sir: you can see that there is no one on the balcony. [*She throws the shutters wide open and stands with her back to the curtain where the man is hidden, pointing to the moonlit balcony. A couple of shots are fired right under the window; and a bullet shatters the glass opposite Raina, who winks and gasps, but stands her ground; whilst Catherine screams, and the officer, with a cry of* Take care! *rushes to the balcony*].

THE OFFICER [*on the balcony, shouting savagely down to the street*] Cease firing there, you fools: do you hear? Cease firing, damn you! [*He glares down for a moment; then turns to Raina, trying to resume his polite manner*]. Could anyone have got in without your knowledge? Were you asleep?

RAINA. No: I have not been to bed.

THE OFFICER [*impatiently, coming back into the room*] Your neighbors have their heads so full of runaway Serbs that they see them everywhere. [*Politely*] Gracious lady: a thousand pardons. Goodnight. [*Military bow, which Raina returns coldly. Another to Catherine, who follows him out*].

Raina closes the shutters. She turns and sees Louka, who has been watching the scene curiously.

RAINA. Dont leave my mother, Louka, until the soldiers go away.

Louka glances at Raina, at the ottoman, at the curtain; then purses her lips secretively, laughs insolently, and goes out. Raina, highly offended by this demonstration, follows her to the door, and shuts it behind her with a slam, locking it violently. The man immediately steps out from behind the curtain, sheathing his sabre, and closes the shutters. Then, dismissing the danger from his mind in a businesslike way, he comes affably to Raina.

THE MAN. A narrow shave; but a miss is as good as a mile. Dear young lady: your servant to the death. I wish for your sake I had joined the Bulgarian army instead of the other one. I am not a native Serb.

RAINA [*haughtily*] No: you are one of the Austrians who set the Serbs on to rob us of our national liberty, and who officer their army for them. We hate them!

THE MAN. Austrian! not I. Dont hate me, dear young lady. I am a Swiss, fighting merely as a professional soldier. I joined the Serbs because they came first on the road from Switzerland. Be generous: youve beaten us hollow.

RAINA. Have I not been generous?

THE MAN. Noble! Heroic! But I'm not saved yet. This particular rush will soon pass through; but the pursuit will go on all night by fits and starts. I must take my chance to get off in a quiet interval. [*Pleasantly*] You dont mind my waiting just a minute or two, do you?

RAINA [*putting on her most genteel society manner*] Oh, not at all. Wont you sit down?

THE MAN. Thanks. [*He sits on the foot of the bed*].

Raina walks with studied elegance to the ottoman and sits down. Unfortunately she sits on the pistol, and jumps up with a shriek. The man, all nerves, shies like a frightened horse to the other side of the room.

THE MAN [*irritably*] Dont frighten me like that. What is it?

RAINA. Your revolver! It was staring that officer in the face all the time. What an escape!

THE MAN [*vexed at being unnecessarily terrified*] Oh, is that all?

RAINA [*staring at him rather superciliously as she conceives a poorer and poorer opinion of him, and feels proportionately more and more at her ease*] I am sorry I frightened you. [*She takes up the pistol and hands it to him*]. Pray take it to protect yourself against me.

THE MAN [*grinning wearily at the sarcasm as he takes the pistol*] No use, dear young lady: theres nothing in it. It's not loaded. [*He makes a grimace at it, and drops it disparagingly into his revolver case*].

RAINA. Load it by all means.

THE MAN. Ive no ammunition. What use are cartridges in battle? I always carry chocolate instead; and I finished the last cake of that hours ago.

RAINA [*outraged in her most cherished ideals of manhood*] Chocolate! Do you stuff your pockets with sweets—like a schoolboy—even in the field?

THE MAN [*grinning*] Yes: isnt it contemptible? [*Hungrily*] I wish I had some now.

RAINA. Allow me. [*She sails away scornfully to the chest of drawers, and returns with the box of confectionery in her hand*]. I am sorry I have eaten them all except these. [*She offers him the box*].

THE MAN [*ravenously*] Youre an angel! [*He gobbles the contents*]. Creams! Delicious! [*He looks anxiously to see whether there are any more. There are none: he can only scrape the box with his fingers and suck them. When that nourishment is exhausted he accepts the inevitable with pathetic goodhumor, and says, with grateful emotion*] Bless you, dear lady! You can always tell an old soldier by the inside of his holsters and cartridge boxes. The young ones carry pistols and cartridges: the old ones, grub. Thank you. [*He hands back the box. She snatches it contemptuously from him and throws it away. He shies again, as if she had meant to strike him*]. Ugh! Dont do things so suddenly, gracious lady. It's mean to revenge yourself because I frightened you just now.

RAINA [*loftily*] Frighten me! Do you know, sir, that though I am only a woman, I think I am at heart as brave as you.

THE MAN. I should think so. You havnt been under fire for three days as I have. I can stand two days without shewing it much; but no man can stand three days: I'm as nervous as a mouse. [*He sits down on the ottoman, and takes his head in his hands*]. Would you like to see me cry?

RAINA [*alarmed*] No.

THE MAN. If you would, all you have to do is to scold me just as if I were a little boy and you my nurse. If I were in camp now, theyd play all sorts of tricks on me.

RAINA [*a little moved*] I'm sorry. I wont scold you. [*Touched by the sympathy in her tone, he raises his head and looks gratefully at her: she immediately draws back and says stiffly*] You must excuse me: our soldiers are not like that. [*She moves away from the ottoman*].

THE MAN. Oh yes they are. There are only two sorts of soldiers: old ones and young ones. Ive served fourteen years: half of your fellows never smelt powder before. Why, how is it that youve just beaten us? Sheer ignorance of the art of war, nothing else. [*Indignantly*] I never saw anything so unprofessional.

RAINA [*ironically*] Oh! was it unprofessional to beat you?

THE MAN. Well, come! is it professional to throw a regiment of cavalry on a battery of machine guns, with the dead certainty that if the guns go off not a horse or man will ever get within fifty yards of the fire? I couldnt believe my eyes when I saw it.

RAINA [*eagerly turning to him, as all her enthusiasm and her dreams of glory rush back on her*] Did you see the great cavalry charge? Oh, tell me about it. Describe it to me.

THE MAN. You never saw a cavalry charge, did you?

RAINA. How could I?

THE MAN. Ah, perhaps not. No: of course not! Well, it's a funny sight. It's like slinging a handful of peas against a window pane: first one comes; then two or three close behind him; and then all the rest in a lump.

RAINA [*her eyes dilating as she raises her clasped hands ecstatically*] Yes, first One! the bravest of the brave!

THE MAN [*prosaically*] Hm! you should see the poor devil pulling at his horse.

RAINA. Why should he pull at his horse?

THE MAN [*impatient of so stupid a question*] It's running away with him, of course: do you suppose the fellow wants to get there before the others and be killed? Then they all come. You can tell the young ones by their wildness and their slashing. The old ones come bunched up under the number one guard: they know that theyre mere projectiles, and that it's no use trying to fight. The wounds are mostly broken knees, from the horses cannoning together.

RAINA. Ugh! But I dont believe the first man is a coward. I know he is a hero!

THE MAN [*goodhumoredly*] Thats what youd have said if youd seen the first man in the charge today.

RAINA [*breathless, forgiving him everything*] Ah, I knew it! Tell me. Tell me about him.

THE MAN. He did it like an operatic tenor. A regular handsome fellow, with flashing eyes and lovely moustache, shouting his war-cry and charging like Don Quixote at the windmills. We did laugh.

RAINA. You dared to laugh!

THE MAN. Yes; but when the sergeant ran up as white as a sheet, and told us theyd sent us the wrong ammunition, and that we couldnt fire a round for the next ten minutes, we laughed at the other side of our mouths. I never felt so sick in my life; though Ive been in one or two very tight places. And I hadnt even a revolver cartridge: only chocolate. We'd no bayonets: nothing. Of course, they just cut us to bits. And there was Don Quixote flourishing like a drum major, thinking he'd done the cleverest thing ever known, whereas he ought to be courtmartialled for it. Of all the fools ever let loose on a field of battle, that man must be the very maddest. He and his regiment simply committed suicide; only the pistol missed fire: thats all.

RAINA [*deeply wounded, but steadfastly loyal to her ideals*] Indeed! Would you know him again if you saw him?

THE MAN. Shall I ever forget him!

She again goes to the chest of drawers. He watches her with a vague hope that she may have something more for him to eat. She takes the portrait from its stand and brings it to him.

RAINA. That is a photograph of the gentleman—the patriot and hero—to whom I am betrothed.

THE MAN [*recognizing it with a shock*] I'm really very sorry. [*Looking at her*] Was it fair to lead me on? [*He looks at the portrait again*] Yes: thats Don Quixote: not a doubt of it. [*He stifles a laugh*].

RAINA [*quickly*] Why do you laugh?

THE MAN [*apologetic, but still greatly tickled*] I didnt laugh, I assure you. At least I didnt mean to. But when I think of him charging the windmills and imagining he was doing the finest thing—[*He chokes with suppressed laughter*].

RAINA [*sternly*] Give me back the portrait, sir.

THE MAN [*with sincere remorse*] Of course. Certainly. I'm really very sorry. [*He hands her the picture. She deliberately kisses it and looks him straight in the face before returning to the chest of drawers to replace it. He follows her, apologizing*]. Perhaps I'm quite wrong, you know: no doubt I am. Most likely he had got wind of the cartridge business somehow, and knew it was a safe job.

RAINA. That is to say, he was a pretender and a coward! You did not dare say that before.

THE MAN [*with a comic gesture of despair*] It's no use, dear lady: I cant make you see it from the professional point of view. [*As he turns away to get back to the ottoman, a couple of distant shots threaten renewed trouble*].

RAINA [*sternly, as she sees him listening to the shots*] So much the better for you!

THE MAN [*turning*] How?

RAINA. You are my enemy; and you are at my mercy. What would I do if I were a professional soldier?

THE MAN. Ah, true, dear young lady: youre always right. I know how good youve been to me: to my last hour I shall remember those three chocolate creams. It was unsoldierly; but it was angelic.

RAINA [*coldly*] Thank you. And now I will do a soldierly thing. You cannot stay here after what you have just said about my future husband; but I will go out on the balcony and see whether it is safe for you to climb down into the street. [*She turns to the window*].

THE MAN [*changing countenance*] Down that water-pipe! Stop! Wait! I cant! I darent! The very thought of it makes me giddy. I came up it fast enough with death behind me. But to face it now in cold blood—! [*He sinks on the ottoman*]. It's no use: I give up: I'm beaten. Give the alarm. [*He drops his head on his hands in the deepest dejection*].

RAINA [*disarmed by pity*] Come: dont be disheartened. [*She stoops over him almost maternally: he shakes his head*]. Oh, you are a very poor soldier: a chocolate cream soldier! Come, cheer up! it takes less courage to climb down than to face capture: remember that.

THE MAN [*dreamily, lulled by her voice*] No: capture only means death; and death is sleep: oh, sleep, sleep, sleep, undisturbed sleep! Climbing down the pipe means doing something—exerting myself—thinking! Death ten times over first.

RAINA [*softly and wonderingly, catching the rhythm of his weariness*] Are you as sleepy as that?

THE MAN. Ive not had two hours undisturbed sleep since I joined. I havnt closed my eyes for forty-eight hours.

RAINA [*at her wit's end*] But what am I to do with you?

THE MAN [*staggering up, roused by her desperation*] Of course. I must do something. [*He shakes himself; pulls himself together; and speaks with rallied vigor and courage*]. You see, sleep or no sleep, hunger or no hunger, tired or not tired, you can always do a thing when you know it must be done. Well, that pipe must be got down: [*he hits himself on the chest*] do you hear that, you chocolate cream soldier? [*He turns to the window*].

RAINA [*anxiously*] But if you fall?

THE MAN. I shall sleep as if the stones were a feather bed. Goodbye. [*He makes boldly for the window; and his *hand is on the shutter when there is a terrible burst of firing in the street beneath*].

RAINA [*rushing to him*] Stop! [*She seizes him recklessly, and pulls him quite round*]. Theyll kill you.

THE MAN [*coolly, but attentively*] Never mind: this sort of thing is all in my day's work. I'm bound to take my chance. [*Decisively*] Now do what I tell you. Put out the candles; so that they shant see the light when I open the shutters. And keep away from the window, whatever you do. If they see me theyre sure to have a shot at me.

RAINA [*clinging to him*] Theyre sure to see you: it's bright moonlight. I'll save you. Oh, how can you be so indifferent! You want me to save you, dont you?

THE MAN. I really dont want to be troublesome. [*She shakes him in her impatience*]. I am not indifferent, dear young lady, I assure you. But how is it to be done?

RAINA. Come away from the window. [*She takes him firmly back to the middle of the room. The moment she releases him he turns mechanically towards the window again. She seizes him and turns him back, exclaiming*] Please! [*He becomes motionless, like a hypnotized rabbit, his fatigue gaining fast on him. She releases him, and addresses him patronizingly*]. Now listen. You must trust to our hospitality. You do not yet know in whose house you are. I am a Petkoff.

THE MAN. A pet what?

RAINA [*rather indignantly*] I mean that I belong to the family of the Petkoffs, the richest and best known in our country.

THE MAN. Oh yes, of course. I beg your pardon. The Petkoffs, to be sure. How stupid of me!

RAINA. You know you never heard of them until this moment. How can you stoop to pretend!

THE MAN. Forgive me: I'm too tired to think; and the change of subject was too much for me. Dont scold me.

RAINA. I forgot. It might make you cry. [*He nods, quite seriously. She pouts and then resumes her patronizing tone*]. I must tell you that my father holds the highest command of any Bulgarian in our army. He is [*proudly*] a Major.

THE MAN [*pretending to be deeply impressed*] A Major! Bless me! Think of that!

RAINA. You shewed great ignorance in thinking that it was necessary to climb up to the balcony because ours is the only private house that has two rows of windows. There is a flight of stairs inside to get up and down by.

THE MAN. Stairs! How grand! You live in great luxury indeed, dear young lady.

RAINA. Do you know what a library is?

THE MAN. A library? A roomful of books?

RAINA. Yes. We have one, the only one in Bulgaria.

THE MAN. Actually a real library! I should like to see that.

RAINA [*affectedly*] I tell you these things to shew you that you are not in the house of ignorant country folk who would kill you the moment they saw your Serbian uniform, but among civilized people. We go to Bucharest every year for the opera season; and I have spent a whole month in Vienna.

THE MAN. I saw that, dear young lady. I saw at once that you knew the world.

RAINA. Have you ever seen the opera of Ernani?

THE MAN. Is that the one with the devil in it in red velvet, and a soldiers' chorus?

RAINA [*contemptuously*] No!

THE MAN [*stifling a heavy sigh of weariness*] Then I dont know it.

RAINA. I thought you might have remembered the great scene where Ernani, flying from his foes just as you are tonight, takes refuge in the castle of his bitterest enemy, an old Castilian noble. The noble refuses to give him up. His guest is sacred to him.

THE MAN [*quickly, waking up a little*] Have your people got that notion?

RAINA [*with dignity*] My mother and I can understand that notion, as you call it. And if instead of threatening me with your pistol as you did you had simply thrown yourself as a fugitive on our hospitality, you would have been as safe as in your father's house.

THE MAN. Quite sure?

RAINA [*turning her back on him in disgust*] Oh, it is useless to try to make you understand.

THE MAN. Dont be angry: you see how awkward it would be for me if there was any mistake. My father is a very hospitable man: he keeps six hotels; but I couldnt trust him as far as that. What about your father?

RAINA. He is away at Slivnitza fighting for his country. I answer for your safety. There is my hand in pledge of it. Will that reassure you? [*She offers him her hand*].

THE MAN [*looking dubiously at his own hand*] Better not touch my hand, dear young lady. I must have a wash first.

RAINA [*touched*] That is very nice of you. I see that you are a gentleman.

THE MAN [*puzzled*] Eh?

RAINA. You must not think I am surprised. Bulgarians of really good standing—people in our position—wash their hands nearly every day. So you see I can appreciate your delicacy. You may take my hand. [*She offers it again*].

THE MAN [*kissing it with his hands behind his back*] Thanks, gracious young lady: I feel safe at last. And now would you mind breaking the news to your mother? I had better not stay here secretly longer than is necessary.

RAINA. If you will be so good as to keep perfectly still whilst I am away.

THE MAN. Certainly. [*He sits down on the ottoman*].

Raina goes to the bed and wraps herself in the fur cloak. His eyes close. She goes to the door. Turning for a last look at him, she sees that he is dropping off to sleep.

RAINA [*at the door*] You are not going asleep, are you? [*He murmurs inarticulately: she runs to him and shakes him*]. Do you hear? Wake up: you are falling asleep.

THE MAN. Eh? Falling aslee—? Oh no: not the least in the world: I was only thinking. It's all right: I'm wide awake.

RAINA [*severely*] Will you please stand up while I am away. [*He rises reluctantly*]. All the time, mind.

THE MAN [*standing unsteadily*] Certainly. Certainly: you may depend on me.

Raina looks doubtfully at him. He smiles weakly. She goes reluctantly, turning again at the door, and almost catching him in the act of yawning. She goes out.

THE MAN [*drowsily*] Sleep, sleep, sleep, sleep, slee— [*The words trail off into a murmur. He wakes again with a shock on the point of falling*]. Where am I? Thats what I want to know: where am I? Must keep awake. Nothing keeps me awake except danger: remember that: [*intently*] danger, danger, danger, dan—[*trailing off again: another shock*] Wheres danger? Mus' find it. [*He starts off vaguely round the room in search of it*]. What am I looking for? Sleep—danger—dont know. [*He stumbles against the bed*]. Ah yes: now I know. All right now. I'm to go to bed, but not to sleep. Be sure not to sleep, because of danger. Not to lie down either, only sit down. [*He sits on the bed. A blissful expression comes into his face*]. Ah! [*With a happy sigh he sinks back at full length; lifts his boots into the bed with a final effort; and falls fast asleep instantly*].

Catherine comes in, followed by Raina.

RAINA [*looking at the ottoman*] He's gone! I left him here.

CATHERINE. Here! Then he must have climbed down from the—

RAINA [*seeing him*] Oh! [*She points*].

CATHERINE [*scandalized*] Well! [*She strides to the bed, Raina following until she is opposite her on the other side*]. He's fast asleep. The brute!

RAINA [*anxiously*] Sh!

CATHERINE [*shaking him*] Sir! [*Shaking him again, harder*] Sir!! [*Vehemently, shaking very hard*] Sir!!!

RAINA [*catching her arm*] Dont, mamma: the poor darling is worn out. Let him sleep.

CATHERINE [*letting him go, and turning amazed to Raina*] The poor darling! Raina!!! [*She looks sternly at her daughter*].

The man sleeps profoundly.

Act Two

The sixth of March, 1886. In the garden of Major Petkoff's house. It is a fine spring morning: the garden looks fresh and pretty. Beyond the paling the tops of a couple of minarets can be seen, shewing that there is a valley there, with the little town in it. A few miles further the Balkan mountains rise and shut in the landscape. Looking towards them from within the garden, the side of the house is seen on the left, with a garden door reached by a little flight of steps. On the right the stable yard, with its gateway, encroaches on the garden. There are fruit bushes along the paling and house, covered with washing spread out to dry. A path runs by the house, and rises by two steps at the corner, where it turns out of sight. In the middle, a small table, with two bent wood chairs at it, is laid for breakfast with Turkish coffee pot, cups, rolls, etc.; but the cups have been used and the bread broken. There is a wooden garden seat against the wall on the right.

Louka, smoking a cigaret, is standing between the table and the house, turning her back with angry disdain on a man servant who is lecturing her. He is a middle-aged man of cool temperament and low but clear and keen intelligence, with the complacency of the servant who values himself on his rank in servitude, and the imperturbability of the accurate calculator who has no illusions. He wears a white Bulgarian costume: jacket with embroidered border, sash, wide knickerbockers, and decorated gaiters. His head is shaved up to the crown, giving him a high Japanese forehead. His name is Nicola.

NICOLA. Be warned in time, Louka: mend your manners. I know the mistress. She is so grand that she never dreams that any servant could dare be disrespectful to her; but if she once suspects that you are defying her, out you go.

LOUKA. I do defy her. I will defy her. What do I care for her?

NICOLA. If you quarrel with the family, I never can marry you. It's the same as if you quarrelled with me!

LOUKA. You take her part against me, do you?

NICOLA [*sedately*] I shall always be dependent on the good will of the family. When I leave their service and start a shop in Sofia, their custom will be half my capital: their bad word would ruin me.

LOUKA. You have no spirit. I should like to catch them saying a word against me!

NICOLA [*pityingly*] I should have expected more sense from you, Louka. But youre young: youre young!

LOUKA. Yes; and you like me the better for it, dont you? But I know some family secrets they wouldnt care to have told, young as I am. Let them quarrel with me if they dare!

NICOLA [*with compassionate superiority*] Do you know what they would do if they heard you talk like that?

LOUKA. What could they do?

NICOLA. Discharge you for untruthfulness. Who would believe any stories you told after that? Who would give you another situation? Who in this house would dare be seen speaking to you ever again? How long would your father be left on his little farm? [*She impatiently throws away the end of her cigaret, and stamps on it*]. Child: you dont know the power such high people have over the like of you and me when we try to rise out of our poverty against them. [*He goes close to her and lowers his voice*]. Look at me, ten years in their service. Do you think I know no secrets? I know things about the mistress that she wouldnt have the master know for a thousand levas. I know things about him that she wouldnt let him hear the last of for six months if I blabbed them to her. I know things about

Raina that would break off her match with Sergius if—

LOUKA [*turning on him quickly*] How do you know? I never told you!

NICOLA [*opening his eyes cunningly*] So thats your little secret, is it? I thought it might be something like that. Well, you take my advice and be respectful; and make the mistress feel that no matter what you know or dont know, she can depend on you to hold your tongue and serve the family faithfully. Thats what they like; and thats how youll make most out of them.

LOUKA [*with searching scorn*] You have the soul of a servant, Nicola.

NICOLA [*complacently*] Yes: thats the secret of success in service.

A loud knocking with a whip handle on a wooden door is heard from the stable yard.

MALE VOICE OUTSIDE. Hollo! Hollo there! Nicola!

LOUKA. Master! back from the war!

NICOLA [*quickly*] My word for it, Louka, the war's over. Off with you and get some fresh coffee. [*He runs out into the stable yard*].

LOUKA [*as she collects the coffee pot and cups on the tray, and carries it into the house*] Youll never put the soul of a servant into me.

Major Petkoff comes from the stable yard, followed by Nicola. He is a cheerful, excitable, insignificant, unpolished man of about 50, naturally unambitious except as to his income and his importance in local society, but just now greatly pleased with the military rank which the war has thrust on him as a man of consequence in his town. The fever of plucky patriotism which the Serbian attack roused in all the Bulgarians has pulled him through the war; but he is obviously glad to be home again.

PETKOFF [*pointing to the table with his whip*] Breakfast out here, eh?

NICOLA. Yes, sir. The mistress and Miss Raina have just gone in.

PETKOFF [*sitting down and taking a roll*] Go in and say Ive come; and get me some fresh coffee.

NICOLA. It's coming, sir. [*He goes to the house door. Louka, with fresh coffee, a clean cup, and a brandy bottle on her tray, meets him*]. Have you told the mistress?

LOUKA. Yes: she's coming.

Nicola goes into the house. Louka brings the coffee to the table.

PETKOFF. Well: the Serbs havnt run away with you, have they?

LOUKA. No, sir.

PETKOFF. Thats right. Have you brought me some cognac?

LOUKA [*putting the bottle on the table*] Here, sir.

PETKOFF. Thats right. [*He pours some into his coffee*].

Catherine, who, having at this early hour made only a very perfunctory toilet, wears a Bulgarian apron over a once brilliant but now half worn-out dressing gown, and a colored handkerchief tied over her thick black hair, comes from the house with Turkish slippers on her bare feet, looking astonishingly handsome and stately under all the circumstances. Louka goes into the house.

CATHERINE. My dear Paul: what a surprise for us! [*She stoops over the back of his chair to kiss him*]. Have they brought you fresh coffee?

PETKOFF. Yes: Louka's been looking after me. The war's over. The treaty was signed three days ago at Bucharest; and the decree for our army to demobilize was issued yesterday.

CATHERINE [*springing erect, with flashing eyes*] Paul: have you let the Austrians force you to make peace?

PETKOFF [*submissively*] My dear: they didnt consult me. What could *I* do? [*She sits down and turns away from him*]. But of course we saw to it that the treaty was an honorable one. It declares peace—

CATHERINE [*outraged*] Peace!

PETKOFF [*appeasing her*]—but not friendly relations: remember that. They wanted to put that in; but I insisted on its being struck out. What more could I do?

CATHERINE. You could have annexed Serbia and made Prince Alexander Emperor of the Balkans. Thats what I would have done.

PETKOFF. I dont doubt it in the least, my dear. But I should have had to subdue the whole Austrian Empire first; and that would have kept me too long away from you. I missed you greatly.

CATHERINE [*relenting*] Ah! [*She stretches her hand affectionately across the table to squeeze his*].

PETKOFF. And how have you been, my dear?

CATHERINE. Oh, my usual sore throats: thats all.

PETKOFF [*with conviction*] That comes from washing your neck every day. Ive often told you so.

CATHERINE. Nonsense, Paul!

PETKOFF [*over his coffee and cigaret*] I dont believe in going too far with these modern customs. All this washing cant be good for the health: it's not natural. There was an Englishman at Philippopolis who used to wet himself all over with cold water every morning when he got up. Disgusting! It all comes from the English: their climate makes them so dirty that they have to be perpetually washing themselves. Look at my father! he never had a bath in his life; and he lived to be ninety-eight, the healthiest man in Bulgaria. I dont mind a good wash once a week to keep up my position; but once a day is carrying the thing to a ridiculous extreme.

CATHERINE. You are a barbarian at heart still, Paul.

I hope you behaved yourself before all those Russian officers.

PETKOFF. I did my best. I took care to let them know that we have a library.

CATHERINE. Ah; but you didnt tell them that we have an electric bell in it? I have had one put up.

PETKOFF. Whats an electric bell?

CATHERINE. You touch a button; something tinkles in the kitchen; and then Nicola comes up.

PETKOFF. Why not shout for him?

CATHERINE. Civilized people never shout for their servants. Ive learnt that while you were away.

PETKOFF. Well, I'll tell you something Ive learnt too. Civilized people dont hang out their washing to dry where visitors can see it; so youd better have all that [*indicating the clothes on the bushes*] put somewhere else.

CATHERINE. Oh, thats absurd, Paul: I dont believe really refined people notice such things.

SERGIUS [*knocking at the stable gates*] Gate, Nicola!

PETKOFF. Theres Sergius. [*Shouting*] Hollo, Nicola!

CATHERINE. Oh, dont shout, Paul: it really isnt nice.

PETKOFF. Bosh! [*He shouts louder than before*] Nicola!

NICOLA [*appearing at the house door*] Yes, sir.

PETKOFF. Are you deaf? Dont you hear Major Saranoff knocking? Bring him round this way. [*He pronounces the name with the stress on the second syllable: Sarahnoff*].

NICOLA. Yes, major. [*He goes into the stable yard*].

PETKOFF. You must talk to him, my dear, until Raina takes him off our hands. He bores my life out about our not promoting him. Over my head, if you please.

CATHERINE. He certainly ought to be promoted when he marries Raina. Besides, the country should insist on having at least one native general.

PETKOFF. Yes; so that he could throw away whole

brigades instead of regiments. It's no use, my dear: he hasnt the slightest chance of promotion until we're quite sure that the peace will be a lasting one.

NICOLA [*at the gate, announcing*] Major Sergius Saranoff! [*He goes into the house and returns presently with a third chair, which he places at the table. He then withdraws*].

Major Sergius Saranoff, the original of the portrait in Raina's room, is a tall romantically handsome man, with the physical hardihood, the high spirit, and the susceptible imagination of an untamed mountaineer chieftain. But his remarkable personal distinctions are of a characteristically civilized type. The ridges of his eyebrows, curving with an interrogative twist round the projections at the outer corners; his jealously observant eye; his nose, thin, keen, and apprehensive in spite of the pugnacious high bridge and large nostril; his assertive chin, would not be out of place in a Parisian salon, shewing that the clever imaginative barbarian has an acute critical faculty which has been thrown into intense activity by the arrival of western civilization in the Balkans. The result is precisely what the advent of nineteenth century thought first produced in England: to wit, Byronism. By his brooding on the perpetual failure, not only of others, but of himself, to live up to his ideals; by his consequent cynical scorn for humanity; by his jejune credulity as to the absolute validity of his concepts and the unworthiness of the world in disregarding them; by his wincings and mockeries under the sting of the petty disillusions which every hour spent among men brings to his sensitive observation, he has acquired the half tragic, half ironic air, the mysterious moodiness, the suggestion of a strange and terrible history that has left nothing but undying remorse, by which Childe Harold fascinated the grandmothers of his English contemporaries. It is clear that here or nowhere is Raina's ideal hero. Catherine is hardly less enthusiastic about him than her daughter, and much less reserved in shewing her enthusiasm. As he enters from the stable gate, she rises effusively to greet him. Petkoff is distinctly less disposed to make a fuss about him.

PETKOFF. Here already, Sergius! Glad to see you.

CATHERINE. My dear Sergius! [*She holds out both her hands*].

SERGIUS [*kissing them with scrupulous gallantry*] My dear mother, if I may call you so.

PETKOFF [*drily*] Mother-in-law, Sergius: mother-in-law! Sit down; and have some coffee.

SERGIUS. Thank you: none for me. [*He gets away from the table with a certain distaste for Petkoff's enjoyment of it, and posts himself with conscious dignity against the rail of the steps leading to the house*].

CATHERINE. You look superb. The campaign has improved you, Sergius. Everybody here is mad about you. We were all wild with enthusiasm about that magnificent cavalry charge.

SERGIUS [*with grave irony*] Madam: it was the cradle and the grave of my military reputation.

CATHERINE. How so?

SERGIUS. I won the battle the wrong way when our worthy Russian generals were losing it the right way. In short, I upset their plans, and wounded their self-esteem. Two Cossack colonels had their regiments routed on the most correct principles of scientific warfare. Two major-generals got killed strictly according to military etiquette. The two colonels are now major-generals; and I am still a simple major.

CATHERINE. You shall not remain so, Sergius. The women are on your side; and they will see that justice is done you.

SERGIUS. It is too late. I have only waited for the peace to send in my resignation.

PETKOFF [*dropping his cup in his amazement*] Your resignation!

CATHERINE. Oh, you must withdraw it!

SERGIUS [*with resolute measured emphasis, folding his arms*] I never withdraw.

PETKOFF [*vexed*] Now who could have supposed you were going to do such a thing?

SERGIUS [*with fire*] Everyone that knew me. But enough of myself and my affairs. How is Raina; and where is Raina?

RAINA [*suddenly coming round the corner of the house and standing at the top of the steps in the path*] Raina is here.

She makes a charming picture as they turn to look at her. She wears an underdress of pale green silk, draped with an overdress of thin ecru canvas embroidered with gold. She is crowned with a dainty eastern cap of gold tinsel. Sergius goes impulsively to meet her. Posing regally, she presents her hand: he drops chivalrously on one knee and kisses it.

PETKOFF [*aside to Catherine, beaming with parental pride*] Pretty, isnt it? She always appears at the right moment.

CATHERINE [*impatiently*] Yes: she listens for it. It is an abominable habit.

Sergius leads Raina forward with splendid gallantry. When they arrive at the table, she turns to him with a bend of the head: he bows; and thus they separate, he coming to his place, and she going behind her father's chair.

RAINA [*stooping and kissing her father*] Dear father! Welcome home!

PETKOFF [*patting her cheek*] My little pet girl. [*He kisses her. She goes to the chair left by Nicola for Sergius, and sits down*].

CATHERINE. And so youre no longer a soldier, Sergius.

SERGIUS. I am no longer a soldier. Soldiering, my dear madam, is the coward's art of attacking mercilessly when you are strong, and keeping out of harm's way when you are weak. That is the whole secret of successful fighting. Get your enemy at a disadvantage; and never, on any account, fight him on equal terms.

PETKOFF. They wouldnt let us make a fair stand-up fight of it. However, I suppose soldiering has to be a trade like any other trade.

SERGIUS. Precisely. But I have no ambition to shine as a tradesman; so I have taken the advice of that bagman of a captain that settled the exchange of prisoners with us at Pirot, and given it up.

PETKOFF. What! that Swiss fellow? Sergius: Ive often thought of that exchange since. He over-reached us about those horses.

SERGIUS. Of course he over-reached us. His father was a hotel and livery stable keeper; and he owed his first step to his knowledge of horse-dealing. [*With mock enthusiasm*] Ah, he was a soldier: every inch a soldier! If only I had bought the horses for my regiment instead of foolishly leading it into danger, I should have been a field-marshal now!

CATHERINE. A Swiss? What was he doing in the Serbian army?

PETKOFF. A volunteer, of course: keen on picking up his profession. [*Chuckling*] We shouldnt have been able to begin fighting if these foreigners hadnt shewn us how to do it: we knew nothing about it; and neither did the Serbs. Egad, there'd have been no war without them!

RAINA. Are there many Swiss officers in the Serbian army?

PETKOFF. No. All Austrians, just as our officers were all Russians. This was the only Swiss I came across. I'll never trust a Swiss again. He humbugged us into giving him fifty ablebodied men for two hundred worn out chargers. They werent even eatable!

SERGIUS. We were two children in the hands of that consummate soldier, Major: simply two innocent little children.

RAINA. What was he like?

CATHERINE. Oh, Raina, what a silly question!

SERGIUS. He was like a commercial traveller in uniform. Bourgeois to his boots!

PETKOFF [*grinning*] Sergius: tell Catherine that queer story his friend told us about how he escaped after Slivnitza. You remember. About his being hid by two women.

SERGIUS [*with bitter irony*] Oh yes: quite a romance! He was serving in the very battery I so unprofessionally charged. Being a thorough soldier, he ran away like the rest of them, with our cavalry at his heels. To escape their sabres he climbed a waterpipe and made his way into the bedroom of a young Bulgarian lady. The young lady was enchanted by his persuasive commercial traveller's manners. She very modestly entertained him for an hour or so, and then called in her mother lest her conduct should appear unmaidenly. The old lady was equally fascinated; and the fugitive was sent on his way in the morning, disguised in an old coat belonging to the master of the house, who was away at the war.

RAINA [*rising with marked stateliness*] Your life in the camp has made you coarse, Sergius. I did not think you would have repeated such a story before me. [*She turns away coldly*].

CATHERINE [*also rising*] She is right, Sergius. If such women exist, we should be spared the knowledge of them.

PETKOFF. Pooh! nonsense! what does it matter?

SERGIUS [*ashamed*] No, Petkoff: I was wrong. [*To Raina, with earnest humility*] I beg your pardon. I have behaved abominably. Forgive me, Raina. [*She bows reservedly*]. And you too, madam. [*Catherine bows graciously and sits down. He proceeds solemnly, again addressing Raina*] The glimpses I have had of the seamy side of life during the last few months have made me cynical; but I should not have brought my cynicism here: least of all into your presence, Raina. I—[*Here, turning to the others, he is evidently going to begin a long speech when the Major interrupts him*].

PETKOFF. Stuff and nonsense, Sergius! Thats quite enough fuss about nothing: a soldier's daughter should be able to stand up without flinching to a little strong conversation. [*He rises*]. Come: it's time for us to get to business. We have to make up our minds how those three regiments are to get back to Philippopolis: theres no forage for them on the Sofia route. [*He goes towards the house*]. Come along. [*Sergius is about to follow him when Catherine rises and intervenes*].

CATHERINE. Oh, Paul, cant you spare Sergius for a few moments? Raina has hardly seen him yet. Perhaps I can help you to settle about the regiments.

SERGIUS [*protesting*] My dear madam, impossible: you—

CATHERINE [*stopping him playfully*] You stay here, my dear Sergius: theres no hurry. I have a word or two to say to Paul. [*Sergius instantly bows and steps back*]. Now, dear [*taking Petkoff's arm*]: come and see the electric bell.

PETKOFF. Oh, very well, very well.

They go into the house together affectionately. Sergius, left alone with Raina, looks anxiously at her, fearing that she is still offended. She smiles, and stretches out her arms to him.

SERGIUS [*hastening to her*] Am I forgiven?

RAINA [*placing her hands on his shoulders as she looks up at him with admiration and worship*] My hero! My king!

SERGIUS. My queen! [*He kisses her on the forehead*].

RAINA. How I have envied you, Sergius! You have been out in the world, on the field of battle, able to prove yourself there worthy of any woman in the world; whilst I have had to sit at home inactive—dreaming—useless—doing nothing that could give me the right to call myself worthy of any man.

SERGIUS. Dearest: all my deeds have been yours. You inspired me. I have gone through the war like a knight in a tournament with his lady looking down at him!

RAINA. And you have never been absent from my thoughts for a moment. [*Very solemnly*] Sergius: I think we two have found the higher love. When I think of you, I feel that I could never do a base deed or think an ignoble thought.

SERGIUS. My lady and my saint! [*He clasps her reverently*].

RAINA [*returning his embrace*] My lord and my—

SERGIUS. Sh—sh! Let me be the worshipper, dear. You little know how unworthy even the best man is of a girl's pure passion!

RAINA. I trust you. I love you. You will never disappoint me, Sergius. [*Louka is heard singing within the house. They quickly release each other*]. I cant pretend to talk indifferently before her: my heart is too full. [*Louka comes from the house with her tray. She goes to the table, and begins to clear it, with her back turned to them*]. I will get my hat; and then we can go out until lunch time. Wouldnt you like that?

SERGIUS. Be quick. If you are away five minutes, it will seem five hours. [*Raina runs to the top of the steps, and turns there to exchange looks with him and wave him a kiss with both hands. He looks after her with emotion for a moment; then turns slowly away, his face radiant with the loftiest exaltation. The movement shifts his field of vision, into the corner of which there now comes the tail of Louka's double apron. His attention is arrested at once. He takes a stealthy look at her, and begins to twirl his moustache mischievously, with his left hand akimbo on his hip. Finally, striking the ground with his heels in something of a cavalry swagger, he strolls over to the other side of the table, opposite her, and says*] Louka: do you know what the higher love is?

LOUKA [*astonished*] No, sir.

SERGIUS. Very fatiguing thing to keep up for any length of time, Louka. One feels the need of some relief after it.

LOUKA [*innocently*] Perhaps you would like some coffee, sir? [*She stretches her hand across the table for the coffee pot*].

SERGIUS [*taking her hand*] Thank you, Louka.

LOUKA [*pretending to pull*] Oh, sir, you know I didnt mean that. I'm surprised at you!

SERGIUS [*coming clear of the table and drawing her with him*] I am surprised at myself, Louka. What would Sergius, the hero of Slivnitza, say if he saw me now? What would Sergius, the apostle of the higher love, say if he saw me now? What would the half dozen Sergiuses who keep popping in and out of this handsome figure of mine say if they caught us here? [*Letting go her hand and slipping his arm dexterously round her waist*] Do you consider my figure handsome, Louka?

LOUKA. Let me go, sir. I shall be disgraced. [*She struggles: he holds her inexorably*]. Oh, will you let go?

SERGIUS [*looking straight into her eyes*] No.

LOUKA. Then stand back where we cant be seen. Have you no common sense?

SERGIUS. Ah! thats reasonable. [*He takes her into the stableyard gateway, where they are hidden from the house*].

LOUKA [*plaintively*] I may have been seen from the windows: Miss Raina is sure to be spying about after you.

SERGIUS [*stung: letting her go*] Take care, Louka. I may be worthless enough to betray the higher love; but do not you insult it.

LOUKA [*demurely*] Not for the world, sir, I'm sure. May I go on with my work, please, now?

SERGIUS [*again putting his arm round her*] You are a provoking little witch, Louka. If you were in love with me, would you spy out of windows on me?

LOUKA. Well, you see, sir, since you say you are half a dozen different gentlemen all at once, I should have a great deal to look after.

SERGIUS [*charmed*] Witty as well as pretty. [*He tries to kiss her*].

LOUKA [*avoiding him*] No: I dont want your kisses. Gentlefolk are all alike: you making love to me behind Miss Raina's back; and she doing the same behind yours.

SERGIUS [*recoiling a step*] Louka!

LOUKA. It shews how little you really care.

SERGIUS [*dropping his familiarity, and speaking with freezing politeness*] If our conversation is to continue, Louka, you will please remember that a gentleman does not discuss the conduct of the lady he is engaged to with her maid.

LOUKA. It's so hard to know what a gentleman considers right. I thought from your trying to kiss me that you had given up being so particular.

SERGIUS [*turning from her and striking his forehead as he comes back into the garden from the gateway*] Devil! devil!

LOUKA. Ha! ha! I expect one of the six of you is very like me, sir; though I am only Miss Raina's maid. [*She goes back to her work at the table, taking no further notice of him*].

SERGIUS [*speaking to himself*] Which of the six is the real man? thats the question that torments me. One of them is a hero, another a buffoon, another a humbug, another perhaps a bit of a blackguard. [*He pauses, and looks furtively at Louka as he adds, with deep bitterness*] And one, at least, is a coward: jealous, like all cowards. [*He goes to the table*]. Louka.

LOUKA. Yes?

SERGIUS. Who is my rival?

LOUKA. You shall never get that out of me, for love or money.

SERGIUS. Why?

LOUKA. Never mind why. Besides, you would tell that I told you; and I should lose my place.

SERGIUS [*holding out his right hand in affirmation*] No! on the honor of a—[*He checks himself; and his hand drops, nerveless, as he concludes sardonically*]—of a man capable of behaving as I have been behaving for the last five minutes. Who is he?

LOUKA. I dont know. I never saw him. I only heard his voice through the door of her room.

SERGIUS. Damnation! How dare you?

LOUKA [*retreating*] Oh, I mean no harm: youve no right to take up my words like that. The mistress knows all about it. And I tell you that if that gentleman ever comes here again, Miss Raina will marry him, whether he likes it or not. I know the difference between the sort of manner you and she put on before one another and the real manner.

Sergius shivers as if she had stabbed him. Then, setting his face like iron, he strides grimly to her, and grips her above the elbows with both hands.

SERGIUS. Now listen you to me.

LOUKA [*wincing*] Not so tight: youre hurting me.

SERGIUS. That doesnt matter. You have stained my honor by making me a party to your eavesdropping. And you have betrayed your mistress.

LOUKA [*writhing*] Please—

SERGIUS. That shews that you are an abominable little clod of common clay, with the soul of a servant. [*He lets her go as if she were an unclean thing, and turns away, dusting his hands of her, to the bench by the wall, where he sits down with averted head, meditating gloomily*].

LOUKA [*whimpering angrily with her hands up her sleeves, feeling her bruised arms*] You know how to hurt with your tongue as well as with your hands. But I dont care, now Ive found out that whatever clay I'm made of, youre made of the same. As for her, she's a liar; and her fine airs are a cheat; and I'm worth six of her. [*She shakes the pain off hardily; tosses her head; and sets to work to put the things on the tray*].

He looks doubtfully at her. She finishes packing the tray, and laps the cloth over the edges, so as to carry all out together. As she stoops to lift it, he rises.

SERGIUS. Louka! [*She stops and looks defiantly at him*]. A gentleman has no right to hurt a woman under any circumstances. [*With profound humility, uncovering his head*] I beg your pardon.

LOUKA. That sort of apology may satisfy a lady. Of what use is it to a servant?

SERGIUS [*rudely crossed in his chivalry, throws it off with a bitter laugh, and says slightingly*] Oh! you wish to be paid for the hurt? [*He puts on his shako, and takes some money from his pocket*].

LOUKA [*her eyes filling with tears in spite of herself*] No: I want my hurt made well.

SERGIUS [*sobered by her tone*] How?

She rolls up her left sleeve; clasps her arm with the thumb and fingers of her right hand; and looks down at the bruise. Then she raises her head and looks straight at him. Finally, with a superb gesture, she presents her arm to be kissed. Amazed, he looks at her; at the arm; at her again; hesitates; and then, with shuddering intensity, exclaims Never! *and gets away as far as possible from her.*

Her arm drops. Without a word, and with unaffected dignity, she takes her tray, and is approaching the house when Raina returns, wearing a hat and jacket in the height of the Vienna fashion of the previous year, 1885. Louka makes way proudly for her, and then goes into the house.

RAINA. I'm ready. Whats the matter? [*Gaily*] Have you been flirting with Louka?

SERGIUS [*hastily*] No, no. How can you think such a thing?

RAINA [*ashamed of herself*] Forgive me, dear: it was only a jest. I am so happy to-day.

He goes quickly to her, and kisses her hand remorsefully. Catherine comes out and calls to them from the top of the steps.

CATHERINE [*coming down to them*] I am sorry to disturb you, children; but Paul is distracted over those three regiments. He doesnt know how to send them to Philippopolis; and he objects to every suggestion of mine. You must go and help him, Sergius. He is in the library.

RAINA [*disappointed*] But we are just going out for a walk.

SERGIUS. I shall not be long. Wait for me just five minutes. [*He runs up the steps to the door*].

RAINA [*following him to the foot of the steps and looking up at him with timid coquetry*] I shall go round and wait in full view of the library windows. Be sure you draw father's attention to me. If you are a moment longer than five minutes, I shall go in and fetch you, regiments or no regiments.

SERGIUS [*laughing*] Very well. [*He goes in*].

Raina watches him until he is out of her sight. Then, with a perceptible relaxation of manner, she begins to pace up and down the garden in a brown study.

CATHERINE. Imagine their meeting that Swiss and hearing the whole story! The very first thing your father asked for was the old coat we sent him off in. A nice mess you have got us into!

RAINA [*gazing thoughtfully at the gravel as she walks*] The little beast!

CATHERINE. Little beast! What little beast?

RAINA. To go and tell! Oh, if I had him here, I'd cram him with chocolate creams til he couldnt ever speak again!

CATHERINE. Dont talk such stuff. Tell me the truth, Raina. How long was he in your room before you came to me?

RAINA [*whisking round and recommencing her march in the opposite direction*] Oh, I forget.

CATHERINE. You cannot forget! Did he really climb up after the soldiers were gone; or was he there when that officer searched the room?

RAINA. No. Yes: I think he must have been there then.

CATHERINE. You think! Oh, Raina! Raina! Will anything ever make you straightforward? If Sergius finds out, it will be all over between you.

RAINA [*With cool impertinence*] Oh, I know Sergius is your pet. I sometimes wish you could marry him instead of me. You would just suit him. You would pet him, and spoil him, and mother him to perfection.

CATHERINE [*opening her eyes very widely indeed*] Well, upon my word!

RAINA [*capriciously: half to herself*] I always feel a longing to do or say something dreadful to him—to shock his propriety—to scandalize the five senses out of him. [*To Catherine, perversely*] I dont care whether he finds out about the chocolate cream soldier or not. I half hope he may. [*She again turns and strolls flippantly away up the path to the corner of the house*].

CATHERINE. And what should I be able to say to your father, pray?

RAINA [*over her shoulder, from the top of the two steps*] Oh, poor father! As if he could help himself! [*She turns the corner and passes out of sight*].

CATHERINE [*looking after her, her fingers itching*] Oh, if you were only ten years younger! [*Louka comes from the house with a salver, which she carries hanging down by her side*]. Well?

LOUKA. Theres a gentleman just called, madam. A Serbian officer.

CATHERINE [*flaming*] A Serb! And how dare he—[*checking herself bitterly*] Oh, I forgot. We are at peace now. I suppose we shall have them calling every day to pay their compliments. Well: if he is an officer why dont you tell your master? He is in the library with Major Saranoff. Why do you come to me?

LOUKA. But he asks for you, madam. And I dont think he knows who you are: he said the lady of the house. He gave me this little ticket for you. [*She takes a card out of her bosom; puts it on the salver; and offers it to Catherine*].

CATHERINE [*reading*] "Captain Bluntschli"? Thats a German name.

LOUKA. Swiss, madam, I think.

CATHERINE [*with a bound that makes Louka jump back*] Swiss! What is he like?

LOUKA [*timidly*] He has a big carpet bag, madam.

CATHERINE. Oh Heavens! he's come to return the coat. Send him away: say we're not at home: ask him to leave his address and I'll write to him. Oh stop: that will never do. Wait! [*She throws herself into a chair to think it out. Louka waits*]. The master and Major Saranoff are busy in the library, arnt they?

LOUKA. Yes, madam.

CATHERINE [*decisively*] Bring the gentleman out here at once. [*Peremptorily*] And be very polite to him. Dont delay. Here [*impatiently snatching the salver from her*]: leave that here; and go straight back to him.

LOUKA. Yes, madam [*going*].

CATHERINE. Louka!

LOUKA [*stopping*] Yes, madam.

CATHERINE. Is the library door shut?

LOUKA. I think so, madam.

CATHERINE. If not, shut it as you pass through.

LOUKA. Yes, madam [*going*].

CATHERINE. Stop! [*Louka stops*]. He will have to go that way [*indicating the gate of the stableyard*]. Tell Nicola to bring his bag here after him. Dont forget.

LOUKA [*surprised*] His bag?

CATHERINE. Yes: here: as soon as possible. [*Vehemently*] Be quick! [*Louka runs into the house. Catherine snatches her apron off and throws it behind a bush. She then takes up the salver and uses it as a mirror, with the result that the handkerchief tied round her head follows the apron. A touch to her hair and a shake to her dressing gown make her presentable*]. Oh, how? how? how can a man be such a fool! Such a moment to select! [*Louka appears at the door of the house, announcing* Captain Bluntschli. *She stands aside at the top of the steps to let him pass before she goes in again. He is the man of the midnight adventure in Raina's room, clean, well brushed, smartly uniformed, and out of trouble, but still unmistakably the same man. The moment Louka's back is turned, Catherine swoops on him with impetuous, urgent, coaxing appeal*]. Captain Bluntschli: I am very glad to see you; but you must leave this house at once. [*He raises his eyebrows*]. My husband has just returned with my future son-in-law; and they know nothing. If they did, the consequences would be terrible. You are a foreigner: you do not feel our national animosities as we do. We still hate the Serbs: the effect of the peace on my husband has been to make him feel like a lion baulked of his prey. If he discovers our secret, he will never forgive me; and my daughter's life will hardly be safe. Will you, like the chivalrous gentleman and soldier you are, leave at once before he finds you here?

BLUNTSCHLI [*disappointed, but philosophical*] At once, gracious lady. I only came to thank you and return the coat you lent me. If you will allow me to take it out of my bag and leave it with your servant as I pass out, I need detain you no further. [*He turns to go into the house*].

CATHERINE [*catching him by the sleeve*] Oh, you must not think of going back that way. [*Coaxing him across to the stable gates*] This is the shortest way out. Many thanks. So glad to have been of service to you. Good-bye.

BLUNTSCHLI. But my bag?

CATHERINE. It shall be sent on. You will leave me your address.

BLUNTSCHLI. True. Allow me. [*He takes out his card-*

case, and stops to write his address, keeping Catherine in an agony of impatience. As he hands her the card, Petkoff, hatless, rushes from the house in a fluster of hospitality, followed by Sergius].

PETKOFF [*as he hurries down the steps*] My dear Captain Bluntschli—

CATHERINE. Oh Heavens! [*She sinks on the seat against the wall*].

PETKOFF [*too preoccupied to notice her as he shakes Bluntschli's hand heartily*] Those stupid people of mine thought I was out here, instead of in the—haw!—library [*he cannot mention the library without betraying how proud he is of it*]. I saw you through the window. I was wondering why you didnt come in. Saranoff is with me: you remember him, dont you?

SERGIUS [*saluting humorously, and then offering his hand with great charm of manner*] Welcome, our friend the enemy!

PETKOFF. No longer the enemy, happily. [*Rather anxiously*] I hope youve called as a friend, and not about horses or prisoners.

CATHERINE. Oh, quite as a friend, Paul. I was just asking Captain Bluntschli to stay to lunch; but he declares he must go at once.

SERGIUS [*sardonically*] Impossible, Bluntschli. We want you here badly. We have to send on three cavalry regiments to Philippopolis; and we dont in the least know how to do it.

BLUNTSCHLI [*suddenly attentive and businesslike*] Philippopolis? The forage is the trouble, I suppose.

PETKOFF [*eagerly*] Yes: thats it. [*To Sergius*] He sees the whole thing at once.

BLUNTSCHLI. I think I can shew you how to manage that.

SERGIUS. Invaluable man! Come along! [*Towering

over Bluntschli, he puts his hand on his shoulder and takes him to the steps, Petkoff following].

Raina comes from the house as Bluntschli puts his foot on the first step.

RAINA. Oh! The chocolate cream soldier!

Bluntschli stands rigid. Sergius, amazed, looks at Raina, then at Petkoff, who looks back at him and then at his wife.

CATHERINE [*with commanding presence of mind*] My dear Raina, dont you see that we have a guest here? Captain Bluntschli: one of our new Serbian friends.

Raina bows: Bluntschli bows.

RAINA. How silly of me! [*She comes down into the center of the group, between Bluntschli and Petkoff*]. I made a beautiful ornament this morning for the ice pudding; and that stupid Nicola has just put down a pile of plates on it and spoilt it. [*To Bluntschli, winningly*] I hope you didnt think that you were the chocolate cream soldier, Captain Bluntschli.

BLUNTSCHLI [*laughing*] I assure you I did. [*Stealing a whimsical glance at her*] Your explanation was a relief.

PETKOFF [*suspiciously, to Raina*] And since when, pray, have you taken to cooking?

CATHERINE. Oh, whilst you were away. It is her latest fancy.

PETKOFF [*testily*] And has Nicola taken to drinking? He used to be careful enough. First he shews Captain Bluntschli out here when he knew quite well I was in the library; and then he goes downstairs and breaks Raina's chocolate soldier. He must—[*Nicola appears at the top of the steps with the bag. He descends; places it respectfully before Bluntschli; and waits for further orders. General amazement. Nicola, unconscious of the effect he is producing, looks perfectly satisfied with himself. When Petkoff recovers his power of speech, he breaks out at him with*] Are you mad, Nicola?

NICOLA [*taken aback*] Sir?

PETKOFF. What have you brought that for?

NICOLA. My lady's orders, major. Louka told me that—

CATHERINE [*interrupting him*] My orders! Why should I order you to bring Captain Bluntschli's luggage out here? What are you thinking of, Nicola?

NICOLA [*after a moment's bewilderment, picking up the bag as he addresses Bluntschli with the very perfection of servile discretion*] I beg your pardon, captain, I am sure. [*To Catherine*] My fault, madam: I hope youll overlook it. [*He bows, and is going to the steps with the bag, when Petkoff addresses him angrily*].

PETKOFF. Youd better go and slam that bag, too, down on Miss Raina's ice pudding! [*This is too much for Nicola. The bag drops from his hand almost on his master's toes, eliciting a roar of*] Begone, you butter-fingered donkey.

NICOLA [*snatching up the bag, and escaping into the house*] Yes, major.

CATHERINE. Oh, never mind, Paul: dont be angry.

PETKOFF [*blustering*] Scoundrel! He's got out of hand while I was away. I'll teach him. Infernal blackguard! The sack next Saturday! I'll clear out the whole establishment—[*He is stifled by the caresses of his wife and daughter, who hang round his neck, petting him*].

CATHERINE / RAINA [*together*]

CATHERINE	RAINA
Now, now, now, it mustnt be angry. He meant no harm. Be good to please me, dear. Sh-sh-sh-sh!	Wow, wow, wow: not on your first day at home. I'll make another ice pudding. Tch-ch-ch!

PETKOFF [*yielding*] Oh well, never mind. Come, Bluntschli: let's have no more nonsense about going away. You know very well youre not going back to Switzerland yet. Until you do go back youll stay with us.

RAINA. Oh, do, Captain Bluntschli.

PETKOFF [*to Catherine*] Now, Catherine: it's of you he's afraid. Press him; and he'll stay.

CATHERINE. Of course I shall be only too delighted if [*appealingly*] Captain Bluntschli really wishes to stay. He knows my wishes.

BLUNTSCHLI [*in his driest military manner*] I am at madam's orders.

SERGIUS [*cordially*] That settles it.

PETKOFF [*heartily*] Of course!

RAINA. You see you must stay.

BLUNTSCHLI [*smiling*] Well, if I must, I must.

Gesture of despair from Catherine.

Act Three

In the library after lunch. It is not much of a library. Its literary equipment consists of a single fixed shelf stocked with old paper covered novels, broken backed, coffee stained, torn and thumbed; and a couple of little hanging shelves with a few gift books on them: the rest of the wall space being occupied by trophies of war and the chase. But it is a most comfortable sitting room. A row of three large windows shews a mountain panorama, just now seen in one of its friendliest aspects in the mellowing afternoon light. In the corner next the right hand window a square earthenware stove, a perfect tower of glistening pottery, rises nearly to the ceiling and guarantees plenty of warmth. The ottoman is like that in Raina's room, and similarly placed; and the window seats are luxurious with decorated cushions. There is one object, however, hopelessly out of keeping with its surroundings. This is a small kitchen table, much the worse for wear, fitted as a writing table with an old canister full of pens, an eggcup filled with ink, and a deplorable scrap of heavily used pink blotting paper.

At the side of this table, which stands to the left of anyone facing the window, Bluntschli is hard at work with a couple of maps before him, writing orders. At the head of it sits Sergius, who is supposed to be also at work, but is actually gnawing the feather of a pen, and contemplating Bluntschli's quick, sure, businesslike progress with a mixture of envious irritation at his own incapacity and awestruck wonder at an ability which seems to him almost miraculous, though its prosaic character forbids him to esteem it. The Major is comfortably established on the ottoman, with a newspaper in his hand and the tube of his hookah within easy reach. Catherine sits at the stove, with her back to them, embroidering. Raina, reclining on the divan, is gazing in a daydream out at the Balkan landscape, with a neglected novel in her lap.

The door is on the same side as the stove, farther from the window. The button of the electric bell is at the opposite side, behind Bluntschli.

PETKOFF [*looking up from his paper to watch how they are getting on at the table*] Are you sure I cant help you in any way, Bluntschli?

BLUNTSCHLI [*without interrupting his writing or looking up*] Quite sure, thank you. Saranoff and I will manage it.

SERGIUS [*grimly*] Yes: we'll manage it. He finds out what to do; draws up the orders; and I sign em. Division of labor! [*Bluntschli passes him a paper*]. Another one? Thank you. [*He plants the paper squarely before him; sets his chair carefully parallel to it; and signs with his cheek on his elbow and his protruded tongue following the movements of his pen*]. This hand is more accustomed to the sword than to the pen.

PETKOFF. It's very good of you, Bluntschli: it is indeed, to let yourself be put upon in this way. Now are you quite sure I can do nothing?

CATHERINE [*in a low warning tone*] You can stop interrupting, Paul.

PETKOFF [*starting and looking round at her*] Eh? Oh! Quite right, my love: quite right. [*He takes his newspaper up again, but presently lets it drop*]. Ah, you havnt been campaigning, Catherine: you dont know how pleasant it is for us to sit here, after a good lunch, with nothing to do but enjoy ourselves. Theres only one thing I want to make me thoroughly comfortable.

CATHERINE. What is that?

PETKOFF. My old coat. I'm not at home in this one: I feel as if I were on parade.

CATHERINE. My dear Paul, how absurd you are

about that old coat! It must be hanging in the blue closet where you left it.

PETKOFF. My dear Catherine, I tell you Ive looked there. Am I to believe my own eyes or not? [*Catherine rises and crosses the room to press the button of the electric bell*]. What are you shewing off that bell for? [*She looks at him majestically and silently resumes her chair and her needlework*]. My dear: if you think the obstinacy of your sex can make a coat out of two old dressing gowns of Raina's, your waterproof, and my mackintosh, youre mistaken. Thats exactly what the blue closet contains at present.

Nicola presents himself.

CATHERINE. Nicola: go to the blue closet and bring your master's old coat here: the braided one he wears in the house.

NICOLA. Yes, madame. [*He goes out*].

PETKOFF. Catherine.

CATHERINE. Yes, Paul?

PETKOFF. I bet you any piece of jewellery you like to order from Sofia against a week's housekeeping money that the coat isnt there.

CATHERINE. Done, Paul!

PETKOFF [*excited by the prospect of a gamble*] Come: here's an opportunity for some sport. Wholl bet on it? Bluntschli: I'll give you six to one.

BLUNTSCHLI [*imperturbably*] It would be robbing you, major. Madame is sure to be right. [*Without looking up, he passes another batch of papers to Sergius*].

SERGIUS [*also excited*] Bravo, Switzerland! Major: I bet my best charger against an Arab mare for Raina that Nicola finds the coat in the blue closet.

PETKOFF [*eagerly*] Your best char—

CATHERINE [*hastily interrupting him*] Dont be foolish, Paul. An Arabian mare will cost you 50,000 levas.

RAINA [*suddenly coming out of her picturesque revery*] Really, mother, if you are going to take the jewellery, I dont see why you should grudge me my Arab.

Nicola comes back with the coat, and brings it to Petkoff, who can hardly believe his eyes.

CATHERINE. Where was it, Nicola?

NICOLA. Hanging in the blue closet, madame.

PETKOFF. Well, I am d—

CATHERINE [*stopping him*] Paul!

PETKOFF. I could have sworn it wasnt there. Age is beginning to tell on me. I'm getting hallucinations. [*To Nicola*] Here: help me to change. Excuse me, Bluntschli. [*He begins changing coats, Nicola acting as valet*]. Remember: I didnt take that bet of yours, Sergius. Youd better give Raina that Arab steed yourself, since youve roused her expectations. Eh, Raina? [*He looks round at her; but she is again rapt in the landscape. With a little gush of parental affection and pride, he points her out to them, and says*] She's dreaming, as usual.

SERGIUS. Assuredly she shall not be the loser.

PETKOFF. So much the better for her. *I* shant come off so cheaply, I expect. [*The change is now complete. Nicola goes out with the discarded coat*]. Ah, now I feel at home at last. [*He sits down and takes his newspaper with a grunt of relief*].

BLUNTSCHLI [*to Sergius, handing a paper*] Thats the last order.

PETKOFF [*jumping up*] What! Finished?

BLUNTSCHLI. Finished.

PETKOFF [*with childlike envy*] Havnt you anything for me to sign?

BLUNTSCHLI. Not necessary. His signature will do.

PETKOFF [*inflating his chest and thumping it*] Ah well, I think weve done a thundering good day's work. Can I do anything more?

BLUNTSCHLI. You had better both see the fellows that are to take these. [*Sergius rises*] Pack them off at once; and shew them that Ive marked on the orders the time they should hand them in by. Tell them that if they stop to drink or tell stories—if theyre five minutes late, theyll have the skin taken off their backs.

SERGIUS [*stiffening indignantly*] I'll say so. [*He strides to the door*]. And if one of them is man enough to spit in my face for insulting him, I'll buy his discharge and give him a pension. [*He goes out*].

BLUNTSCHLI [*confidentially*] Just see that he talks to them properly, major, will you?

PETKOFF [*officiously*] Quite right, Bluntschli, quite right. I'll see to it. [*He goes to the door importantly, but hesitates on the threshold*]. By the bye, Catherine, you may as well come too. Theyll be far more frightened of you than of me.

CATHERINE [*putting down her embroidery*] I daresay I had better. You would only splutter at them. [*She goes out, Petkoff holding the door for her and following her*].

BLUNTSCHLI. What an army! They make cannons out of cherry trees; and the officers send for their wives to keep discipline! [*He begins to fold and docket the papers*].

Raina, who has risen from the divan, marches slowly down the room with her hands clasped behind her, and looks mischievously at him.

RAINA. You look ever so much nicer than when we last met. [*He looks up, surprised*]. What have you done to yourself?

BLUNTSCHLI. Washed; brushed; good night's sleep and breakfast. Thats all.

RAINA. Did you get back safely that morning?

BLUNTSCHLI. Quite, thanks.

RAINA. Were they angry with you for running away from Sergius's charge?

BLUNTSCHLI [*grinning*] No: they were glad; because theyd all just run away themselves.

RAINA [*going to the table, and leaning over it towards him*] It must have made a lovely story for them: all that about me and my room.

BLUNTSCHLI. Capital story. But I only told it to one of them: a particular friend.

RAINA. On whose discretion you could absolutely rely?

BLUNTSCHLI. Absolutely.

RAINA. Hm! He told it all to my father and Sergius the day you exchanged the prisoners. [*She turns away and strolls carelessly across to the other side of the room*].

BLUNTSCHLI [*deeply concerned, and half incredulous*] No! You dont mean that, do you?

RAINA [*turning, with sudden earnestness*] I do indeed. But they dont know that it was in this house you took refuge. If Sergius knew, he would challenge you and kill you in a duel.

BLUNTSCHLI. Bless me! then dont tell him.

RAINA. Please be serious, Captain Bluntschli. Can you not realize what it is to me to deceive him? I want to be quite perfect with Sergius: no meanness, no smallness, no deceit. My relation to him is the one really beautiful and noble part of my life. I hope you can understand that.

BLUNTSCHLI [*sceptically*] You mean that you wouldnt like him to find out that the story about the ice pudding was a—a—a—You know.

RAINA [*wincing*] Ah, dont talk of it in that flippant way. I lied: I know it. But I did it to save your life. He would have killed you. That was the second time I ever uttered a falsehood. [*Bluntschli rises quickly and looks doubtfully and somewhat severely at her*]. Do you remember the first time?

BLUNTSCHLI. I! No. Was I present?

RAINA. Yes; and I told the officer who was searching for you that you were not present.

BLUNTSCHLI. True. I should have remembered it.

RAINA [*greatly encouraged*] Ah, it is natural that you should forget it first. It cost you nothing: it cost me a lie! A lie!!

She sits down on the ottoman, looking straight before her with her hands clasped round her knee. Bluntschli, quite touched, goes to the ottoman with a particularly reassuring and considerate air, and sits down beside her.

BLUNTSCHLI. My dear young lady, dont let this worry you. Remember: I'm a soldier. Now what are the two things that happen to a soldier so often that he comes to think nothing of them? One is hearing people tell lies [*Raina recoils*]: the other is getting his life saved in all sorts of ways by all sorts of people.

RAINA [*rising in indignant protest*] And so he becomes a creature incapable of faith and of gratitude.

BLUNTSCHLI [*making a wry face*] Do you like gratitude? I dont. If pity is akin to love, gratitude is akin to the other thing.

RAINA. Gratitude! [*Turning on him*] If you are incapable of gratitude you are incapable of any noble sentiment. Even animals are grateful. Oh, I see now exactly what you think of me! You were not surprised to hear me lie. To you it was something I probably did every day! every hour!! That is how men think of women. [*She paces the room tragically*].

BLUNTSCHLI [*dubiously*] Theres reason in everything. You said youd told only two lies in your whole life. Dear young lady: isnt that rather a short allowance? I'm quite a straightforward man myself; but it wouldnt last me a whole morning.

RAINA [*staring haughtily at him*] Do you know, sir, that you are insulting me?

BLUNTSCHLI. I cant help it. When you strike that noble attitude and speak in that thrilling voice, I admire you; but I find it impossible to believe a single word you say.

RAINA [*superbly*] Captain Bluntschli!

BLUNTSCHLI [*unmoved*] Yes?

RAINA [*standing over him, as if she could not believe her senses*] Do you mean what you said just now? Do you know what you said just now?

BLUNTSCHLI. I do.

RAINA [*gasping*] I! I!!! [*She points to herself incredulously, meaning "I, Raina Petkoff, tell lies!" He meets her gaze unflinchingly. She suddenly sits down beside him, and adds, with a complete change of manner from the heroic to a babyish familiarity*] How did you find me out?

BLUNTSCHLI [*promptly*] Instinct, dear young lady. Instinct, and experience of the world.

RAINA [*wonderingly*] Do you know, you are the first man I ever met who did not take me seriously?

BLUNTSCHLI. You mean, dont you, that I am the first man that has ever taken you quite seriously?

RAINA. Yes: I suppose I do mean that. [*Cosily, quite at her ease with him*] How strange it is to be talked to in such a way! You know, Ive always gone on like that.

BLUNTSCHLI. You mean the—?

RAINA. I mean the noble attitude and the thrilling voice. [*They laugh together*]. I did it when I was a tiny child to my nurse. She believed in it. I do it before my parents. They believe in it. I do it before Sergius. He believes in it.

BLUNTSCHLI. Yes: he's a little in that line himself, isnt he?

RAINA [*startled*] Oh! Do you think so?

BLUNTSCHLI. You know him better than I do.

RAINA. I wonder—I wonder is he? If I thought that—! [*Discouraged*] Ah, well: what does it matter? I suppose, now youve found me out, you despise me.

BLUNTSCHLI [*warmly, rising*] No, my dear young lady, no, no, no a thousand times. It's part of your youth: part of your charm. I'm like all the rest of them: the nurse, your parents, Sergius: I'm your infatuated admirer.

RAINA [*pleased*] Really?

BLUNTSCHLI [*slapping his breast smartly with his hand, German fashion*] Hand aufs Herz! Really and truly.

RAINA [*very happy*] But what did you think of me for giving you my portrait?

BLUNTSCHLI [*astonished*] Your portrait! You never gave me your portrait.

RAINA [*quickly*] Do you mean to say you never got it?

BLUNTSCHLI. No. [*He sits down beside her, with renewed interest, and says, with some complacency*] When did you send it to me?

RAINA [*indignantly*] I did not send it to you. [*She turns her head away, and adds, reluctantly*] It was in the pocket of that coat.

BLUNTSCHLI [*pursing his lips and rounding his eyes*] Oh-o-oh! I never found it. It must be there still.

RAINA [*springing up*] There still! for my father to find the first time he puts his hand in his pocket! Oh, how could you be so stupid?

BLUNTSCHLI [*rising also*] It doesnt matter: I suppose it's only a photograph: how can he tell who it was intended for? Tell him he put it there himself.

RAINA [*bitterly*] Yes: that is so clever! isnt it? [*Distractedly*] Oh! what shall I do?

BLUNTSCHLI. Ah, I see. You wrote something on it. That was rash.

RAINA [*vexed almost to tears*] Oh, to have done such a thing for you, who care no more—except to laugh at me—oh! Are you sure nobody has touched it?

BLUNTSCHLI. Well, I cant be quite sure. You see, I couldnt carry it about with me all the time: one cant take much luggage on active service.

RAINA. What did you do with it?

BLUNTSCHLI. When I got through to Pirot I had to put it in safe keeping somehow. I thought of the railway cloakroom; but thats the surest place to get looted in modern warfare. So I pawned it.

RAINA. Pawned it!!!

BLUNTSCHLI. I know it doesnt sound nice; but it was much the safest plan. I redeemed it the day before yesterday. Heaven only knows whether the pawnbroker cleared out the pockets or not.

RAINA [*furious: throwing the words right into his face*] You have a low shopkeeping mind. You think of things that would never come into a gentleman's head.

BLUNTSCHLI [*phlegmatically*] Thats the Swiss national character, dear lady. [*He returns to the table*].

RAINA. Oh, I wish I had never met you. [*She flounces away, and sits at the window fuming*].

Louka comes in with a heap of letters and telegrams on her salver, and crosses, with her bold free gait, to the table. Her left sleeve is looped up to the shoulder with a brooch, shewing her naked arm, with a broad gilt bracelet covering the bruise.

LOUKA [*to Bluntschli*] For you. [*She empties the salver with a fling on to the table*]. The messenger is waiting. [*She is determined not to be civil to an enemy, even if she must bring him his letters*].

BLUNTSCHLI [*to Raina*] Will you excuse me: the last

postal delivery that reached me was three weeks ago. These are the subsequent accumulations. Four telegrams: a week old. [*He opens one*]. Oho! Bad news!

RAINA [*rising and advancing a little remorsefully*] Bad news?

BLUNTSCHLI. My father's dead. [*He looks at the telegram with his lips pursed, musing on the unexpected change in his arrangements. Louka crosses herself hastily*].

RAINA. Oh, how very sad!

BLUNTSCHLI. Yes: I shall have to start for home in an hour. He has left a lot of big hotels behind him to be looked after. [*He takes up a fat letter in a long blue envelope*]. Here's a whacking letter from the family solicitor. [*He pulls out the enclosures and glances over them*]. Great Heavens! Seventy! Two hundred! [*In a crescendo of dismay*] Four hundred! Four thousand!! Nine thousand six hundred!!! What on earth am I to do with them all?

RAINA [*timidly*] Nine thousand hotels?

BLUNTSCHLI. Hotels! nonsense. If you only knew! Oh, it's too ridiculous! Excuse me: I must give my fellow orders about starting. [*He leaves the room hastily, with the documents in his hand*].

LOUKA [*knowing instinctively that she can annoy Raina by disparaging Bluntschli*] He has not much heart, that Swiss. He has not a word of grief for his poor father.

RAINA [*bitterly*] Grief! A man who has been doing nothing but killing people for years! What does he care? What does any soldier care? [*She goes to the door, restraining her tears with difficulty*].

LOUKA. Major Saranoff has been fighting too; and he has plenty of heart left. [*Raina, at the door, draws herself up haughtily and goes out*]. Aha! I thought you wouldnt get much feeling out of your soldier. [*She is following Raina when Nicola enters with an armful of logs for the stove*].

NICOLA [*grinning amorously at her*] Ive been trying all the afternoon to get a minute alone with you, my girl. [*His countenance changes as he notices her arm*]. Why, what fashion is that of wearing your sleeve, child?

LOUKA [*proudly*] My own fashion.

NICOLA. Indeed! If the mistress catches you, she'll talk to you. [*He puts the logs down, and seats himself comfortably on the ottoman*].

LOUKA. Is that any reason why you should take it on yourself to talk to me?

NICOLA. Come! dont be so contrairy with me. Ive some good news for you. [*She sits down beside him. He takes out some paper money. Louka, with an eager gleam in her eyes, tries to snatch it; but he shifts it quickly to his left hand, out of her reach*]. See! a twenty leva bill! Sergius gave me that, out of pure swagger. A fool and his money are soon parted. Theres ten levas more. The Swiss gave me that for backing up the mistress's and Raina's lies about him. He's no fool, he isnt. You should have heard old Catherine downstairs as polite as you please to me, telling me not to mind the Major being a little impatient; for they knew what a good servant I was—after making a fool and a liar of me before them all! The twenty will go to our savings; and you shall have the ten to spend if youll only talk to me so as to remind me I'm a human being. I get tired of being a servant occasionally.

LOUKA. Yes: sell your manhood for 30 levas, and buy me for 10! [*Rising scornfully*] Keep your money. You were born to be a servant. I was not. When you set up your shop you will only be everybody's servant instead of somebody's servant. [*She goes moodily to the table and seats herself regally in Sergius's chair*].

NICOLA [*picking up his logs, and going to the stove*] Ah, wait til you see. We shall have our evenings to ourselves; and I shall be master in my own house, I promise you. [*He throws the logs down and kneels at the stove*].

LOUKA. You shall never be master in mine.

NICOLA [*turning, still on his knees, and squatting down rather forlornly on his calves, daunted by her implacable disdain*] You have a great ambition in you, Louka. Remember: if any luck comes to you, it was I that made a woman of you.

LOUKA. You!

NICOLA [*scrambling up and going at her*] Yes, me. Who was it made you give up wearing a couple of pounds of false black hair on your head and reddening your lips and cheeks like any other Bulgarian girl? I did. Who taught you to trim your nails, and keep your hands clean, and be dainty about yourself, like a fine Russian lady? Me: do you hear that? me! [*She tosses her head defiantly; and he turns away, adding, more coolly*] Ive often thought that if Raina were out of the way, and you just a little less of a fool and Sergius just a little more of one, you might come to be one of my grandest customers, instead of only being my wife and costing me money.

LOUKA. I believe you would rather be my servant than my husband. You would make more out of me. Oh, I know that soul of yours.

NICOLA [*going closer to her for greater emphasis*] Never you mind my soul; but just listen to my advice. If you want to be a lady, your present behavior to me wont do at all, unless when we're alone. It's too sharp and impudent; and impudence is a sort of familiarity: it shews affection for me. And dont you try being high and mighty with me, either. Youre like all country girls: you think it's genteel to treat a servant the way I treat a stableboy. Thats only your ignorance; and dont you forget it. And dont be so ready to defy everybody.

Act as if you expected to have your own way, not as if you expected to be ordered about. The way to get on as a lady is the same as the way to get on as a servant: youve got to know your place: thats the secret of it. And you may depend on me to know my place if you get promoted. Think over it, my girl. I'll stand by you: one servant should always stand by another.

LOUKA [*rising impatiently*] Oh, I must behave in my own way. You take all the courage out of me with your cold-blooded wisdom. Go and put those logs on the fire: thats the sort of thing you understand.

Before Nicola can retort, Sergius comes in. He checks himself a moment on seeing Louka; then goes to the stove.

SERGIUS [*to Nicola*] I am not in the way of your work, I hope.

NICOLA [*in a smooth, elderly manner*] Oh no, sir: thank you kindly. I was only speaking to this foolish girl about her habit of running up here to the library whenever she gets a chance, to look at the books. Thats the worst of her education, sir: it gives her habits above her station. [*To Louka*] Make that table tidy, Louka, for the Major. [*He goes out sedately*].

Louka, without looking at Sergius, pretends to arrange the papers on the table. He crosses slowly to her, and studies the arrangement of her sleeve reflectively.

SERGIUS. Let me see: is there a mark there? [*He turns up the bracelet and sees the bruise made by his grasp. She stands motionless, not looking at him: fascinated, but on her guard*]. Ffff! Does it hurt?

LOUKA. Yes.

SERGIUS. Shall I cure it?

LOUKA [*instantly withdrawing herself proudly, but still not looking at him*] No. You cannot cure it now.

SERGIUS [*masterfully*] Quite sure? [*He makes a movement as if to take her in his arms*].

LOUKA. Dont trifle with me, please. An officer should not trifle with a servant.

SERGIUS [*indicating the bruise with a merciless stroke of his forefinger*] That was no trifle, Louka.

LOUKA [*flinching; then looking at him for the first time*] Are you sorry?

SERGIUS [*with measured emphasis, folding his arms*] I am never sorry.

LOUKA [*wistfully*] I wish I could believe a man could be as unlike a woman as that. I wonder are you really a brave man?

SERGIUS [*unaffectedly, relaxing his attitude*] Yes: I am a brave man. My heart jumped like a woman's at the first shot; but in the charge I found that I was brave. Yes: that at least is real about me.

LOUKA. Did you find in the charge that the men whose fathers are poor like mine were any less brave than the men who are rich like you.

SERGIUS [*with bitter levity*] Not a bit. They all slashed and cursed and yelled like heroes. Psha! the courage to rage and kill is cheap. I have an English bull terrier who has as much of that sort of courage as the whole Bulgarian nation, and the whole Russian nation at its back. But he lets my groom thrash him, all the same. Thats your soldier all over! No, Louka: your poor men can cut throats; but they are afraid of their officers; they put up with insults and blows; they stand by and see one another punished like children: aye, and help to do it when they are ordered. And the officers!!! Well [*with a short harsh laugh*] *I* am an officer. Oh, [*fervently*] give me the man who will defy to the death any power on earth or in heaven that sets itself up against his own will and conscience: he alone is the brave man.

LOUKA. How easy it is to talk! Men never seem to

me to grow up: they all have schoolboy's ideas. You dont know what true courage is.

SERGIUS [*ironically*] Indeed! I am willing to be instructed. [*He sits on the ottoman, sprawling magnificently*].

LOUKA. Look at me! how much am I allowed to have my own will? I have to get your room ready for you: to sweep and dust, to fetch and carry. How could that degrade me if it did not degrade you to have it done for you? But [*with subdued passion*] if I were Empress of Russia, above everyone in the world, then!! Ah then, though according to you I could shew no courage at all, you should see, you should see.

SERGIUS. What would you do, most noble Empress?

LOUKA. I would marry the man I loved, which no other queen in Europe has the courage to do. If I loved you, though you would be as far beneath me as I am beneath you, I would dare to be the equal of my inferior. Would you dare as much if you loved me? No: if you felt the beginnings of love for me you would not let it grow. You would not dare: you would marry a rich man's daughter because you would be afraid of what other people would say of you.

SERGIUS [*bounding up*] You lie: it is not so, by all the stars! If I loved you, and I were the Czar himself, I would set you on the throne by my side. You know that I love another woman, a woman as high above you as heaven is above earth. And you are jealous of her.

LOUKA. I have no reason to be. She will never marry you now. The man I told you of has come back. She will marry the Swiss.

SERGIUS [*recoiling*] The Swiss!

LOUKA. A man worth ten of you. Then you can come

to me; and I will refuse you. You are not good enough for me. [*She turns to the door*].

SERGIUS [*springing after her and catching her fiercely in his arms*] I will kill the Swiss; and afterwards I will do as I please with you.

LOUKA [*in his arms, passive and steadfast*] The Swiss will kill you, perhaps. He has beaten you in love. He may beat you in war.

SERGIUS [*tormentedly*] Do you think I believe that she—she! whose worst thoughts are higher than your best ones, is capable of trifling with another man behind my back?

LOUKA. Do you think she would believe the Swiss if he told her now that I am in your arms?

SERGIUS [*releasing her in despair*] Damnation! Oh, damnation! Mockery! mockery everywhere! everything I think is mocked by everything I do. [*He strikes himself frantically on the breast*]. Coward! liar! fool! Shall I kill myself like a man, or live and pretend to laugh at myself? [*She again turns to go*]. Louka! [*She stops near the door*]. Remember: you belong to me.

LOUKA [*turning*] What does that mean? An insult?

SERGIUS [*commandingly*] It means that you love me, and that I have had you here in my arms, and will perhaps have you there again. Whether that is an insult I neither know nor care: take it as you please. But [*vehemently*] I will not be a coward and a trifler. If I choose to love you, I dare marry you, in spite of all Bulgaria. If these hands ever touch you again, they shall touch my affianced bride.

LOUKA. We shall see whether you dare keep your word. And take care. I will not wait long.

SERGIUS [*again folding his arms and standing motionless in the middle of the room*] Yes: we shall see. And you shall wait my pleasure.

Bluntschli, much preoccupied, with his papers still in his hand, enters, leaving the door open for Louka to go out. He goes across to the table, glancing at her as he passes. Sergius, without altering his resolute attitude, watches him steadily. Louka goes out, leaving the door open.

BLUNTSCHLI [*absently, sitting at the table as before, and putting down his papers*] Thats a remarkable looking young woman.

SERGIUS [*gravely, without moving*] Captain Bluntschli.

BLUNTSCHLI. Eh?

SERGIUS. You have deceived me. You are my rival. I brook no rivals. At six o'clock I shall be in the drilling-ground on the Klissoura road, alone, on horseback, with my sabre. Do you understand?

BLUNTSCHLI [*staring, but sitting quite at his ease*] Oh, thank you: thats a cavalry man's proposal. I'm in the artillery; and I have the choice of weapons. If I go, I shall take a machine gun. And there shall be no mistake about the cartridges this time.

SERGIUS [*flushing, but with deadly coldness*] Take care, sir. It is not our custom in Bulgaria to allow invitations of that kind to be trifled with.

BLUNTSCHLI [*warmly*] Pooh! dont talk to me about Bulgaria. You dont know what fighting is. But have it your own way. Bring your sabre along. I'll meet you.

SERGIUS [*fiercely delighted to find his opponent a man of spirit*] Well said, Switzer. Shall I lend you my best horse?

BLUNTSCHLI. No: damn your horse! thank you all the same, my dear fellow. [*Raina comes in, and hears the next sentence*]. I shall fight you on foot. Horseback's too dangerous: I dont want to kill you if I can help it.

RAINA [*hurrying forward anxiously*] I have heard what Captain Bluntschli said, Sergius. You are going to fight. Why? [*Sergius turns away in silence, and goes to the stove, where he stands watching her as she continues, to Bluntschli*] What about?

BLUNTSCHLI. I dont know: he hasnt told me. Better not interfere, dear young lady. No harm will be done: Ive often acted as sword instructor. He wont be able to touch me; and I'll not hurt him. It will save explanations. In the morning I shall be off home; and youll never see me or hear of me again. You and he will then make it up and live happily ever after.

RAINA [*turning away deeply hurt, almost with a sob in her voice*] I never said I wanted to see you again.

SERGIUS [*striding forward*] Ha! That is a confession.

RAINA [*haughtily*] What do you mean?

SERGIUS. You love that man!

RAINA [*scandalized*] Sergius!

SERGIUS. You allow him to make love to you behind my back, just as you treat me as your affianced husband behind his. Bluntschli: you knew our relations; and you deceived me. It is for that that I call you to account, not for having received favors *I* never enjoyed.

BLUNTSCHLI [*jumping up indignantly*] Stuff! Rubbish! I have received no favors. Why, the young lady doesnt even know whether I'm married or not.

RAINA [*forgetting herself*] Oh! [*Collapsing on the ottoman*] Are you?

SERGIUS. You see the young lady's concern, Captain Bluntschli. Denial is useless. You have enjoyed the privilege of being received in her own room, late at night—

BLUNTSCHLI [*interrupting him pepperily*] Yes, you blockhead! she received me with a pistol at her head. Your cavalry were at my heels. I'd have blown out her brains if she'd uttered a cry.

SERGIUS [*taken aback*] Bluntschli! Raina: is this true?

RAINA [*rising in wrathful majesty*] Oh, how dare you, how dare you?

BLUNTSCHLI. Apologize, man: apologize. [*He resumes his seat at the table*].

SERGIUS [*with the old measured emphasis, folding his arms*] I never apologize!

RAINA [*passionately*] This is the doing of that friend of yours, Captain Bluntschli. It is he who is spreading this horrible story about me. [*She walks about excitedly*].

BLUNTSCHLI. No: he's dead. Burnt alive.

RAINA [*stopping, shocked*] Burnt alive!

BLUNTSCHLI. Shot in the hip in a woodyard. Couldnt drag himself out. Your fellows' shells set the timber on fire and burnt him, with half a dozen other poor devils in the same predicament.

RAINA. How horrible!

SERGIUS. And how ridiculous! Oh, war! war! the dream of patriots and heroes! A fraud, Bluntschli. A hollow sham, like love.

RAINA [*outraged*] Like love! You say that before me!

BLUNTSCHLI. Come, Saranoff: that matter is explained.

SERGIUS. A hollow sham, I say. Would you have come back here if nothing had passed between you except at the muzzle of your pistol? Raina is mistaken about your friend who was burnt. He was not my informant.

RAINA. Who then? [*Suddenly guessing the truth*] Ah, Louka! my maid! my servant! You were with her this morning all that time after—after—Oh, what sort of god is this I have been worshipping! [*He meets her gaze with sardonic enjoyment of her disenchantment. Angered all the more, she goes closer to him, and says, in a lower, intenser tone*] Do you know that I looked out of the window as I went upstairs, to have another sight of my hero;

and I saw something I did not understand then. I know now that you were making love to her.

SERGIUS [*with grim humor*] You saw that?

RAINA. Only too well. [*She turns away, and throws herself on the divan under the centre window, quite overcome*].

SERGIUS [*cynically*] Raina: our romance is shattered. Life's a farce.

BLUNTSCHLI [*to Raina, whimsically*] You see: he's found himself out now.

SERGIUS [*going to him*] Bluntschli: I have allowed you to call me a blockhead. You may now call me a coward as well. I refuse to fight you. Do you know why?

BLUNTSCHLI. No; but it doesnt matter. I didnt ask the reason when you cried on; and I dont ask the reason now that you cry off. I'm a professional soldier: I fight when I have to, and am very glad to get out of it when I havnt to. Youre only an amateur: you think fighting's an amusement.

SERGIUS [*sitting down at the table, nose to nose with him*] You shall hear the reason all the same, my professional. The reason is that it takes two men—real men—men of heart, blood and honor—to make a genuine combat. I could no more fight with you than I could make love to an ugly woman. Youve no magnetism: youre not a man: youre a machine.

BLUNTSCHLI [*apologetically*] Quite true, quite true. I always was that sort of chap. I'm very sorry.

SERGIUS. Psha!

BLUNTSCHLI. But now that youve found that life isnt a farce, but something quite sensible and serious, what further obstacle is there to your happiness?

RAINA [*rising*] You are very solicitous about my happiness and his. Do you forget his new love—Louka? It is not you that he must fight now, but his rival, Nicola.

SERGIUS. Rival!! [*bounding half across the room*].

RAINA. Dont you know that theyre engaged?

SERGIUS. Nicola! Are fresh abysses opening? Nicola!!

RAINA [*sarcastically*] A shocking sacrifice, isnt it? Such beauty! such intellect! such modesty! wasted on a middle-aged servant man. Really, Sergius, you cannot stand by and allow such a thing. It would be unworthy of your chivalry.

SERGIUS [*losing all self-control*] Viper! Viper! [*He rushes to and fro, raging*].

BLUNTSCHLI. Look here, Saranoff: youre getting the worst of this.

RAINA [*getting angrier*] Do you realize what he has done, Captain Bluntschli? He has set this girl as a spy on us; and her reward is that he makes love to her.

SERGIUS. False! Monstrous!

RAINA. Monstrous! [*Confronting him*] Do you deny that she told you about Captain Bluntschli being in my room?

SERGIUS. No; but—

RAINA [*interrupting*] Do you deny that you were making love to her when she told you?

SERGIUS. No; but I tell you—

RAINA [*cutting him short contemptuously*] It is unnecessary to tell us anything more. That is quite enough for us. [*She turns away from him and sweeps majestically back to the window*].

BLUNTSCHLI [*quietly, as Sergius, in an agony of mortification, sinks on the ottoman, clutching his averted head between his fists*] I told you you were getting the worst of it, Saranoff.

SERGIUS. Tiger cat!

RAINA [*running excitedly to Bluntschli*] You hear this man calling me names, Captain Bluntschli?

BLUNTSCHLI. What else can he do, dear lady? He

must defend himself somehow. Come [*very persuasively*]: dont quarrel. What good does it do?

Raina, with a gasp, sits down on the ottoman, and after a vain effort to look vexedly at Bluntschli, falls a victim to her sense of humor, and actually leans back babyishly against the writhing shoulder of Sergius.

SERGIUS. Engaged to Nicola! Ha! ha! Ah well, Bluntschli, you are right to take this huge imposture of a world coolly.

RAINA [*quaintly to Bluntschli, with an intuitive guess at his state of mind*] I daresay you think us a couple of grown-up babies, dont you?

SERGIUS [*grinning savagely*] He does: he does. Swiss civilization nursetending Bulgarian barbarism, eh?

BLUNTSCHLI [*blushing*] Not at all, I assure you. I'm only very glad to get you two quieted. There! there! let's be pleasant and talk it over in a friendly way. Where is this other young lady?

RAINA. Listening at the door, probably.

SERGIUS [*shivering as if a bullet had struck him, and speaking with quiet but deep indignation*] I will prove that that, at least, is a calumny. [*He goes with dignity to the door and opens it. A yell of fury bursts from him as he looks out. He darts into the passage, and returns dragging in Louka, whom he flings violently against the table, exclaiming*] Judge her, Bluntschli. You, the cool impartial man: judge the eavesdropper.

Louka stands her ground, proud and silent.

BLUNTSCHLI [*shaking his head*] I mustnt judge her. I once listened myself outside a tent when there was a mutiny brewing. It's all a question of the degree of provocation. My life was at stake.

LOUKA. My love was at stake. I am not ashamed.

RAINA [*contemptuously*] Your love! Your curiosity, you mean.

LOUKA [*facing her and retorting her contempt with interest*] My love, stronger than anything you can feel, even for your chocolate cream soldier.

SERGIUS [*with quick suspicion, to Louka*] What does that mean?

LOUKA [*fiercely*] It means—

SERGIUS [*interrupting her slightingly*] Oh, I remember: the ice pudding. A paltry taunt, girl!

Major Petkoff enters, in his shirtsleeves.

PETKOFF. Excuse my shirtsleeves, gentlemen. Raina: somebody has been wearing that coat of mine: I'll swear it. Somebody with a differently shaped back. It's all burst open at the sleeve. Your mother is mending it. I wish she'd make haste: I shall catch cold. [*He looks more attentively at them*]. Is anything the matter?

RAINA. No. [*She sits down at the stove, with a tranquil air*].

SERGIUS. Oh no. [*He sits down at the end of the table, as at first*].

BLUNTSCHLI [*who is already seated*] Nothing. Nothing.

PETKOFF [*sitting down on the ottoman in his old place*] Thats all right. [*He notices Louka*]. Anything the matter, Louka?

LOUKA. No, sir

PETKOFF. [*genially*] Thats all right. [*He sneezes*]. Go and ask your mistress for my coat, like a good girl, will you?

Nicola enters with the coat. Louka makes a pretence of having business in the room by taking the little table with the hookah away to the wall near the windows.

RAINA [*rising quickly as she sees the coat on Nicola's arm*] Here it is, papa. Give it to me, Nicola; and do you put some more wood on the fire. [*She takes the coat, and brings it to the Major, who stands up to put it on. Nicola attends to the fire*].

PETKOFF [*to Raina, teasing her affectionately*] Aha! Going to be very good to poor old papa just for one day after his return from the wars, eh?

RAINA [*with solemn reproach*] Ah, how can you say that to me, father?

PETKOFF. Well, well, only a joke, little one. Come: give me a kiss. [*She kisses him*]. Now give me the coat.

RAINA. No: I am going to put it on for you. Turn your back. [*He turns his back and feels behind him with his arms for the sleeves. She dexterously takes the photograph from the pocket and throws it on the table before Bluntschli, who covers it with a sheet of paper under the very nose of Sergius, who looks on amazed, with his suspicions roused in the highest degree. She then helps Petkoff on with his coat*]. There, dear! Now are you comfortable?

PETKOFF. Quite, little love. Thanks. [*He sits down; and Raina returns to her seat near the stove*]. Oh, by the bye, Ive found something funny. Whats the meaning of this? [*He puts his hand into the picked pocket*]. Eh? Hallo! [*He tries the other pocket*]. Well, I could have sworn—! [*Much puzzled, he tries the breast pocket*]. I wonder—[*trying the original pocket*] Where can it—? [*He rises, exclaiming*] Your mother's taken it!

RAINA [*very red*] Taken what?

PETKOFF. Your photograph, with the inscription: "Raina, to her Chocolate Cream Soldier: a Souvenir." Now you know theres something more in this than meets the eye; and I'm going to find it out. [*Shouting*] Nicola!

NICOLA [*coming to him*] Sir!

PETKOFF. Did you spoil any pastry of Miss Raina's this morning?

NICOLA. You heard Miss Raina say that I did, sir.

PETKOFF. I know that, you idiot. Was it true?

NICOLA. I am sure Miss Raina is incapable of saying anything that is not true, sir.

PETKOFF. Are you? Then I'm not. [*Turning to the others*] Come: do you think I dont see it all? [*He goes to Sergius, and slaps him on the shoulder*]. Sergius: youre the chocolate cream soldier, arnt you?

SERGIUS [*starting up*] I! A chocolate cream soldier! Certainly not.

PETKOFF. Not! [*He looks at them. They are all very serious and very conscious*]. Do you mean to tell me that Raina sends things like that to other men?

SERGIUS [*enigmatically*] The world is not such an innocent place as we used to think, Petkoff.

BLUNTSCHLI [*rising*] It's all right, Major. I'm the chocolate cream soldier. [*Petkoff and Sergius are equally astonished*]. The gracious young lady saved my life by giving me chocolate creams when I was starving: shall I ever forget their flavour! My late friend Stolz told you the story at Pirot. I was the fugitive.

PETKOFF. You! [*He gasps*]. Sergius: do you remember how those two women went on this morning when we mentioned it? [*Sergius smiles cynically. Petkoff confronts Raina severely*]. Youre a nice young woman, arnt you?

RAINA [*bitterly*] Major Saranoff has changed his mind. And when I wrote that on the photograph, I did not know that Captain Bluntschli was married.

BLUNTSCHLI [*startled into vehement protest*] I'm not married.

RAINA [*with deep reproach*] You said you were.

BLUNTSCHLI. I did not. I positively did not. I never was married in my life.

PETKOFF [*exasperated*] Raina: will you kindly inform me, if I am not asking too much, which of these gentlemen you are engaged to?

RAINA. To neither of them. This young lady [*intro-*

ducing Louka, who faces them all proudly] is the object of Major Saranoff's affections at present.

PETKOFF. Louka! Are you mad, Sergius? Why, this girl's engaged to Nicola.

NICOLA. I beg your pardon, sir. There is a mistake. Louka is not engaged to me.

PETKOFF. Not engaged to you, you scoundrel! Why, you had twenty-five levas from me on the day of your betrothal; and she had that gilt bracelet from Miss Raina.

NICOLA [*with cool unction*] We gave it out so, sir. But it was only to give Louka protection. She had a soul above her station; and I have been no more than her confidential servant. I intend, as you know, sir, to set up a shop later on in Sofia; and I look forward to her custom and recommendation should she marry into the nobility. [*He goes out with impressive discretion, leaving them all staring after him*].

PETKOFF [*breaking the silence*] Well, I am—hm!

SERGIUS. This is either the finest heroism or the most crawling baseness. Which is it, Bluntschli?

BLUNTSCHLI. Never mind whether it's heroism or baseness. Nicola's the ablest man Ive met in Bulgaria. I'll make him manager of a hotel if he can speak French and German.

LOUKA [*suddenly breaking out at Sergius*] I have been insulted by everyone here. You set them the example. You owe me an apology.

Sergius, like a repeating clock of which the spring has been touched, immediately begins to fold his arms.

BLUNTSCHLI [*before he can speak*] It's no use. He never apologizes.

LOUKA. Not to you, his equal and his enemy. To me, his poor servant, he will not refuse to apologize.

SERGIUS [*approvingly*] You are right. [*He bends his knee in his grandest manner*] Forgive me.

LOUKA. I forgive you. [*She timidly gives him her hand, which he kisses*]. That touch makes me your affianced wife.

SERGIUS [*springing up*] Ah! I forgot that.

LOUKA [*coldly*] You can withdraw if you like.

SERGIUS. Withdraw! Never! You belong to me. [*He puts his arm about her*].

Catherine comes in and finds Louka in Sergius's arms, with all the rest gazing at them in bewildered astonishment.

CATHERINE. What does this mean?

Sergius releases Louka.

PETKOFF. Well, my dear, it appears that Sergius is going to marry Louka instead of Raina. [*She is about to break out indignantly at him: he stops her by exclaiming testily*] Dont blame me: Ive nothing to do with it. [*He retreats to the stove*].

CATHERINE. Marry Louka! Sergius: you are bound by your word to us!

SERGIUS [*folding his arms*] Nothing binds me.

BLUNTSCHLI [*much pleased by this piece of common sense*] Saranoff: your hand. My congratulations. These heroics of yours have their practical side after all. [*To Louka*] Gracious young lady: the best wishes of a good Republican! [*He kisses her hand, to Raina's great disgust, and returns to his seat*].

CATHERINE. Louka: you have been telling stories.

LOUKA. I have done Raina no harm.

CATHERINE [*haughtily*] Raina!

Raina, equally indignant, almost snorts at the liberty.

LOUKA. I have a right to call her Raina: she calls me Louka. I told Major Saranoff she would never marry him if the Swiss gentleman came back.

BLUNTSCHLI [*rising, much surprised*] Hallo!

LOUKA [*turning to Raina*] I thought you were fonder of him than of Sergius. You know best whether I was right.

BLUNTSCHLI. What nonsense! I assure you, my dear Major, my dear Madame, the gracious young lady simply saved my life, nothing else. She never cared two straws for me. Why, bless my heart and soul, look at the young lady and look at me. She, rich, young, beautiful, with her imagination full of fairy princes and noble natures and cavalry charges and goodness knows what! And I, a commonplace Swiss soldier who hardly knows what a decent life is after fifteen years of barracks and battles: a vagabond, a man who has spoiled all his chances in life through an incurably romantic disposition, a man—

SERGIUS [*starting as if a needle had pricked him and interrupting Bluntschli in incredulous amazement*] Excuse me, Bluntschli: what did you say had spoiled your chances in life?

BLUNTSCHLI [*promptly*] An incurably romantic disposition. I ran away from home twice when I was a boy. I went into the army instead of into my father's business. I climbed the balcony of this house when a man of sense would have dived into the nearest cellar. I came sneaking back here to have another look at the young lady when any other man of my age would have sent the coat back—

PETKOFF. My coat!

BLUNTSCHLI.—yes: thats the coat I mean—would have sent it back and gone quietly home. Do you suppose I am the sort of fellow a young girl falls in love with? Why, look at our ages! I'm thirty-four: I dont suppose the young lady is much over seventeen. [*This estimate produces a marked sensation, all the rest turning and staring at one another. He proceeds innocently*] All that adventure which was life or death to me, was only a schoolgirl's game to her—chocolate creams and hide and seek. Heres the proof! [*He takes the photograph from the table*]. Now, I ask you, would a woman who took the affair seriously have sent me this and written on it "Raina, to her Chocolate Cream Soldier: a Souvenir"? [*He exhibits the photograph triumphantly, as if it settled the matter beyond all possibility of refutation*].

PETKOFF. Thats what I was looking for. How the deuce did it get there? [*He comes from the stove to look at it, and sits down on the ottoman*].

BLUNTSCHLI [*to Raina, complacently*] I have put everything right, I hope, gracious young lady.

RAINA [*going to the table to face him*] I quite agree with your account of yourself. You are a romantic idiot. [*Bluntschli is unspeakably taken aback*]. Next time, I hope you will know the difference between a schoolgirl of seventeen and a woman of twenty-three.

BLUNTSCHLI [*stupefied*] Twenty-three!

Raina snaps the photograph contemptuously from his hand; tears it up; throws the pieces in his face; and sweeps back to her former place.

SERGIUS [*with grim enjoyment of his rival's discomfiture*] Bluntschli: my one last belief is gone. Your sagacity is a fraud, like everything else. You have less sense than even I!

BLUNTSCHLI [*overwhelmed*] Twenty-three! Twenty-three!! [*He considers*]. Hm! [*Swiftly making up his mind and coming to his host*] In that case, Major Petkoff, I beg to propose formally to become a suitor for your daughter's hand, in place of Major Saranoff retired.

RAINA. You dare!

BLUNTSCHLI. If you were twenty-three when you said those things to me this afternoon, I shall take them seriously.

CATHERINE [*loftily polite*] I doubt, sir, whether you quite realize either my daughter's position or that of Major Sergius Saranoff, whose place you propose to take. The Petkoffs and the Saranoffs are known as the richest and most important families in the country. Our position is almost historical: we can go back for twenty years.

PETKOFF. Oh, never mind that, Catherine. [*To Bluntschli*] We should be most happy, Bluntschli, if it were only a question of your position; but hang it, you know, Raina is accustomed to a very comfortable establishment. Sergius keeps twenty horses.

BLUNTSCHLI. But who wants twenty horses? We're not going to keep a circus.

CATHERINE [*severely*] My daughter, sir, is accustomed to a first-rate stable.

RAINA. Hush, mother: youre making me ridiculous.

BLUNTSCHLI. Oh well, if it comes to a question of an establishment, here goes! [*He darts impetuously to the table; seizes the papers in the blue envelope; and turns to Sergius*]. How many horses did you say?

SERGIUS. Twenty, noble Switzer.

BLUNTSCHLI. I have two hundred horses. [*They are amazed*]. How many carriages?

SERGIUS. Three.

BLUNTSCHLI. I have seventy. Twenty-four of them will hold twelve inside, besides two on the box, without counting the driver and conductor. How many tablecloths have you?

SERGIUS. How the deuce do I know?

BLUNTSCHLI. Have you four thousand?

SERGIUS. No.

BLUNTSCHLI. I have. I have nine thousand six hundred pairs of sheets and blankets, with two thousand four hundred eider-down quilts. I have ten thousand knives and forks, and the same quantity of dessert spoons. I have three hundred servants. I have six palatial establishments, besides two livery stables, a tea gardens, and a private house. I have four medals for distinguished services; I have the rank of an officer and the standing of a gentleman; and I have three native languages. Shew me any man in Bulgaria that can offer as much!

PETKOFF [*with childish awe*] Are you Emperor of Switzerland?

BLUNTSCHLI. My rank is the highest known in Switzerland: I am a free citizen.

CATHERINE. Then, Captain Bluntschli, since you are my daughter's choice—

RAINA [*mutinously*] He's not.

CATHERINE [*ignoring her*]—I shall not stand in the way of her happiness. [*Petkoff is about to speak*] That is Major Petkoff's feeling also.

PETKOFF. Oh, I shall be only too glad. Two hundred horses! Whew!

SERGIUS. What says the lady?

RAINA [*pretending to sulk*] The lady says that he can keep his tablecloths and his omnibuses. I am not here to be sold to the highest bidder. [*She turns her back on him*].

BLUNTSCHLI. I wont take that answer. I appealed to you as a fugitive, a beggar, and a starving man. You accepted me. You gave me your hand to kiss, your bed to sleep in, and your roof to shelter me.

RAINA. I did not give them to the Emperor of Switzerland.

BLUNTSCHLI. Thats just what I say. [*He catches her by the shoulders and turns her face-to-face with him*]. Now tell us whom you did give them to.

RAINA [*succumbing with a shy smile*] To my chocolate cream soldier.

BLUNTSCHLI [*with a boyish laugh of delight*] Thatll do. Thank you. [*He looks at his watch and suddenly becomes businesslike*]. Time's up, Major. Youve managed those regiments so well that youre sure to be asked to get rid of some of the infantry of the Timok division. Send them home by way of Lom Palanka. Saranoff: dont get married until I come back: I shall be here punctually at five in the evening on Tuesday fortnight. Gracious ladies [*his heels click*] good evening. [*He makes them a military bow, and goes*].

SERGIUS. What a man! Is he a man?

A Dramatic Realist to His Critics

(*The New Review*, London, July 1894, and, unauthorized, in *Eclectic Magazine*, New York, September 1894. Reprinted in *Shaw on Theatre*, ed. E. J. West, 1958)

I think very few people know how troublesome dramatic critics are. It is not that they are morally worse than other people; but they know nothing. Or, rather, it is a good deal worse than that: they know everything wrong. Put a thing on the stage for them as it is in real life, and instead of receiving it with the blank wonder of plain ignorance, they reject it with scorn as an imposture, on the ground that the real thing is known to the whole world to be quite different. Offer them Mr Crummles's real pump and tubs, and they will denounce both as spurious on the ground that tubs have no handles, and the pump no bung-hole.

I am, among other things, a dramatist; but I am

not an original one, and so have to take all my dramatic material either from real life at first hand, or from authentic documents. The more usual course is to take it out of other dramas, in which case, on tracing it back from one drama to another, you finally come to its origin in the inventive imagination of some original dramatist. Now a fact as invented by a dramatist differs widely from the fact of the same name as it exists or occurs objectively in real life. Not only stage pumps and tubs, but (much more) stage morality and stage human nature differ from the realities of these things. Consequently to a man who derives all his knowledge of life from witnessing plays, nothing appears more unreal than objective life. A dramatic critic is generally such a man; and the more exactly I reproduce objective life for him on the stage, the more certain he is to call my play an extravaganza.

It may be asked here whether it is possible for one who every day contemplates the real world for fourteen of his waking hours, and the stage for only two, to know more of the stage world than the real world. As well might it be argued that a farmer's wife, churning for only two hours a week, and contemplating nature almost constantly, must know more about geology, forestry, and botany than about butter. A man knows what he works at, not what he idly stares at. A dramatic critic works at the stage, writes about the stage, thinks about the stage, and understands nothing of the real life he idly stares at until he has translated it into stage terms. For the rest, seeing men daily building houses, driving engines, marching to the band, making political speeches, and what not, he is stimulated by these spectacles to *imagine* what it is to be a builder, an engine driver, a soldier, or a statesman. Of course, he imagines a stage builder, engine driver, soldier, and so on, not a real one. Simple as this is, few dramatic critics are intelligent enough to discover it for themselves. No class is more idiotically confident of the reality of its own unreal knowledge than the literary class in general and dramatic critics in particular.

We have, then, two sorts of life to deal with: one subjective or stagey, the other objective or real. What are the comparative advantages of the two for the purposes of the dramatist? Stage life is artificially simple and well understood by the masses; but it is very stale; its feeling is conventional; it is totally unsuggestive of thought because all its conclusions are foregone; and it is constantly in conflict with the real knowledge which the separate members of the audience derive from their own daily occupations. For instance, a naval or military melodrama only goes down with civilians. Real life, on the other hand, is so ill understood, even by its clearest observers, that no sort of consistency is discoverable in it; there is no "natural justice" corresponding to that simple and pleasant concept, "poetic justice"; and, as a whole, it is unthinkable. But, on the other hand, it is credible, stimulating, suggestive, various, free from creeds and systems—in short, it is real.

This rough contrast will suffice to show that the two sorts of life, each presenting dramatic potentialities to the author, will, when reproduced on the stage, affect different men differently. The stage world is for the people who cannot bear to look facts in the face, because they dare not be pessimists, and yet cannot see real life otherwise than as the pessimist sees it. It might be supposed that those who conceive all the operations of our bodies as repulsive, and of our minds as sinful, would take refuge in the sects which abstain from playgoing on principle. But this is by no means what happens. If such a man has an artistic or romantic turn, he takes refuge, not in the conventicle, but in the theatre, where, in the contemplation of the idealised, or stage life, he finds some relief from his haunting conviction of omnipresent foulness and baseness. Confront him with anything like reality, and his chronic pain is aggravated instead of relieved: he raises a terrible outcry against the spectacle of cowardice, selfishness, faithlessness, sensuality—in short, everything that he went to the theatre to escape from. This is not the effect on those pessimists who dare face facts and profess their own faith. They are great admirers of the realist playwright, whom they embarrass greatly by their applause. Their cry is "Quite right: strip off the whitewash from the sepulchre; expose human nature in all its tragi-comic baseness; tear the mask of respectability from the smug bourgeois, and show the liar, the thief, the coward, the libertine beneath."

Now to me, as a realist playwright, the applause of the conscious, hardy pessimist is more exasperating than the abuse of the unconscious, fearful one. I am not a pessimist at all. It does not concern me that, according to certain ethical systems, all human beings fall into classes labelled liar, coward, thief, and so on. I am myself, according to these systems, a liar, a coward, a thief, and a sensualist; and it is my deliberate, cheerful, and entirely self-respecting intention to continue to the end of my life deceiving people, avoiding danger, making my bargains with publishers and managers on principles of supply and demand instead of abstract justice, and indulging all my appetites, whenever circumstances commend such actions to my judgment. If any creed or system deduces from this that I am a rascal incapable on occasion of telling the truth, facing a risk, foregoing a commercial advantage, or resisting an intemperate impulse of any sort, then so much the worse for the creed or system, since I have done all these things, and will probably do them again. The saying "All have sinned," is, in the sense in which it was written, certainly true of all the people I have ever known. But the sinfulness of my friends is not unmixed with saintliness: some of their actions are sinful, others saintly. And here, again, if the ethical system to which the classifications of saint and sinner belong, involves the conclusion that a line of cleavage drawn between my friends' sinful actions and their saintly ones will coincide exactly with one drawn between their mistakes and their successes (I include the highest and widest sense of the two terms), then so much the worse for the system; for the facts contradict it. Persons obsessed by systems may retort: "No; so much the worse for your friends"—implying that I must move in a circle of rare blackguards; but I am quite prepared not only to publish a list of friends of mine whose names would put such a retort to open shame, but to take any human being, alive or dead, of whose actions a genuinely miscellaneous unselected dozen can be brought to light, to show that none of the ethical systems habitually applied by dramatic critics (not to mention other people) can verify their inferences. As a realist dramatist, therefore, it is my business to get outside these systems. For instance, in the play of mine which is most in evidence in London just now, the heroine has been classified by critics as a minx, a liar, and a *poseuse*. I have nothing to do with that: the only moral question for me is, does she do good or harm? If you admit that she does good, that she generously saves a man's life and wisely extricates herself from a false position with another man, then you may classify her as you please—brave, generous, and affectionate; or artful, dangerous, faithless—it is all one to me: you can no more prejudice me for or against her by such artificial categorising than you could have made Molière dislike Monsieur Jourdain by a lecture on the vanity and pretentiousness of that amiable "bourgeois gentilhomme." The fact is, though I am willing and anxious to see the human race improved, if possible, still I find that, with reasonably sound specimens, the more intimately I know people the better I like them; and when a man concludes from this that I am a cynic, and that he, who prefers stage monsters—walking catalogues of the systematised virtues—to his own species, is a person of wholesome philanthropic tastes, why, how can I feel towards him except as an Englishwoman feels towards the Arab who, faithful to *his* system, denounces her indecency in appearing in public with her mouth uncovered.

The production of "Arms and the Man" at the Avenue Theatre, about nine weeks ago, brought the misunderstanding between my real world and the stage world of the critics to a climax, because the misunderstanding was itself, in a sense, the subject of the play. I need not describe the action of the piece in any detail: suffice it to say that the scene is laid in Bulgaria in 1885–6, at a moment when the need for repelling the onslaught of the Servians made the Bulgarians for six months a nation of heroes. But as they had only just been redeemed from centuries of miserable bondage to the Turks, and were, therefore, but beginning to work out their own redemption from barbarism—or, if you prefer it, beginning to contract the disease of civilisation—they were very ignorant heroes, with boundless courage and patriotic enthusiasm, but with so little military skill that they had to place themselves under the command of Russian officers. And their attempts at Western civilisation were much the same as their attempts at war—instructive, romantic, ignorant. They were a nation of plucky beginners in every department. Into their country comes, in the play, a professional officer from the high democratic civilisation of Switzerland—a man completely acquainted by long, practical experience with the realities of war. The comedy arises, of course, from the collision of the knowledge of the Swiss with the illusions of the Bulgarians. In this dramatic scheme Bulgaria may be taken as symbolic of the stalls on the first night of a play. The Bulgarians are dramatic critics; the Swiss is the realist playwright invading their realm; and the comedy is the comedy of the collision of the realities represented by the realist playwright with the preconceptions of stageland. Let us follow this comedy a little into particulars.

War, as we all know, appeals very strongly to the romantic imagination. We owe the greatest realistic novel in the world, "Don Quixote," to the awakening lesson which a romantically imaginative man received from some practical experience of real soldiering. Nobody is now foolish enough to call Cervantes a cynic because he laughed at Amadis de Gaul, or Don Quixote a worthless creature because he charged windmills and flocks of sheep. But I have been plentifully denounced as a cynic, my Swiss soldier as a coward, and my Bulgarian Don Quixote as a humbug, because I have acted on the same impulse and pursued the same method as Cervantes. Not being myself a soldier like Cervantes, I had to take my facts at second hand; but the difficulties were not very great, as such wars as the Franco-Prussian and Russo-Turkish have left a considerable number of experienced soldiers who may occasionally be met and consulted even in England; whilst the publication of such long-delayed works as

Marbot's Memoirs, and the success with which magazine editors have drawn some of our generals, both here and in America, on the enthralling subject of military courage, has placed a mass of documentary evidence at the disposal of the realist. Even realistic fiction has become valuable in this way: for instance, it is clear that Zola, in his "Débâcle," has gone into the evidence carefully enough to give high authority to his description of what a battle is really like.

The extent to which this method brought me into conflict with the martial imaginings of the critics is hardly to be conveyed by language. The notion that there could be any limit to a soldier's courage, or any preference on his part for life and a whole skin over a glorious death in the service of his country, was inexpressibly revolting to them. Their view was simple, manly, and straightforward, like most impracticable views. A man is either a coward or he is not. If a brave man, then he is afraid of nothing. If a coward, then he is no true soldier; and to represent him as such is to libel a noble profession.

The tone of men who know what they are talking about is remarkably different. Compare, for instance, this significant little passage from no less an authority than Lord Wolseley, who far from being a cynic, writes about war with an almost schoolboyish enthusiasm, considering that he has seen so much of it:—

> "One of the most trying things for the captain or subaltern is to make their men who have found some temporary haven of refuge from the enemy's fire, leave it and spring forward in a body to advance over the open upon a position to be attacked. It is even difficult to make a line of men who have lain down, perhaps to take breath after

a long advance at a running pace, rise up together."—*Fortnightly Review*, Aug., 1888.

This, you will observe, is your British soldier, who is quite as brave as any soldier in the world. It may be objected, however, by believers in the gameness of blue blood, that it is the British officer who wins our battles, on the playing fields of Eton and elsewhere. Let me, therefore, quote another passage from our veteran commander:—

"I have seen a whole division literally crazy with terror when suddenly aroused in the dark by some senseless alarm. I have known even officers to tackle and wound their own comrades upon such occasions. Reasoning men are for the time reduced to the condition of unreasoning animals who, stricken with terror, will charge walls or houses, unconscious of what they do. . . . [Here Lord Wolseley describes a scare which took place on a certain occasion.] In that night's panic several lost their lives; and many still bear the marks of wounds then received." *Ib.*, pp. 284–5.

Now let us hear General Horace Porter, a veteran of the American War, which had the advantage of being a civil war, the most respectable sort of war, since there is generally a valuable idea of some kind at stake in it. General Porter, a cooler writer than our General, having evidently been trained in the world, and not in the army, delivers himself as follows:—

"The question most frequently asked of soldiers is 'How does a man feel in battle?' There is a belief, among some who have never indulged in the pastime of setting themselves up as targets to be shot at, that there is a delicious sort of exhilaration experienced in battle, which arouses a romantic enthusiasm; surfeits the mind with delightful sensations; makes one yearn for a lifetime of fighting, and feel that peace is a pusillanimous sort of thing at best. Others suppose, on the contrary, that one's knees rattle like a Spanish ballerina's castanets, and that one's mind dwells on little else than the most approved means of running away.

"A happy mean between these two extremes would doubtless define the condition of the average man when he finds that, as a soldier, he is compelled to devote himself to stopping bullets as well as directing them. He stands his ground and faces the dangers into which his profession leads him, under a sense of duty and a regard for his self-respect, but often feels that the sooner the firing ceases, the better it would accord with his notion of the general fitness of things, and that if the enemy is going to fall back, the present moment would be as good a time as any at which to begin such a highly judicious and commendable movement. Braving danger, of course, has its compensations. 'The blood more stirs to rouse a lion than to start a hare.' In the excitement of a charge, or in the enthusiasm of approaching victory, there is a sense of pleasure which no one should attempt to underrate. It is the gratification which is always born of success, and, coming to one at the supreme moment of a favourable crisis in battle, rewards the soldier for many severe trials and perilous tasks."—(Article in *The Century*, June, 1888, p. 251.)

Probably nothing could convey a more sickening sense of abandoned pusillanimity to the dramatic critic than the ignoble spectacle of a soldier dodging a bullet. [Alfred] Bunn's sublime conception of Don Cæsar de Bazan, with his breast "expanding to the ball," has fixed for ever the stage ideal of the soldier under fire. General Porter falls far beneath Bunn in this passage:—

> "I can recall only two persons who, throughout a rattling musketry fire, always sat in their saddles without moving a muscle or even winking an eye. One was a bugler in the regular cavalry, and the other was General Grant."

It may be urged against me here that in my play I have represented a soldier as shying like a nervous horse, not at bullets, but at such trifles as a young lady snatching a box of sweets from him and throwing it away. But my soldier explains that he has been three days under fire; and though that would, of course, make no difference to the ideal soldier, it makes a considerable difference to the real one, according to General Porter.

> "Courage, like everything else, wears out. Troops used to go into action during our late war, displaying a coolness and steadiness the first day that made them seem as if the screeching of shot and shell was the music on which they had been brought up. After fighting a couple of days their nerves gradually lost their tension; their buoyancy of spirits gave way; and dangers they would have laughed at the first day, often sent them panic-stricken to the rear on the third. It was al-

ways a curious sight in camp after a three days' fight to watch the effect of the sensitiveness of the nerves: men would start at the slightest sound, and dodge the flight of a bird or a pebble tossed at them. One of the chief amusements on such occasions used to be to throw stones and chips past one another's heads to see the active dodging that would follow."

A simple dramatic paraphrase of that matter-of-fact statement in the first act of "Arms and the Man" has been received as a wild topsy-turvyist invention; and when Captain Bluntschli said to the young lady, "If I were in camp now they'd play all sorts of tricks on me," he was supposed to be confessing himself the champion coward of the Servian army. But the truth is that he was rather showing off, in the style characteristic of the old military hand. When an officer gets over the youthful vanity of cutting a figure as a hero, and comes to understand that courage is a quality for use and not for display, and that the soldier who wins with the least risk is the best soldier, his vanity takes another turn; and, if he is a bit of a humorist, he begins to appreciate the comedy latent in the incongruity between himself and the stage soldier which civilians suppose him. General Porter puts this characteristic of the veteran before us with perfect clearness:—

"At the beginning of the war officers felt that, as untested men, they ought to do many things for the sake of appearance that were wholly unnecessary. This at times led to a great deal of posing for effect and useless exposure of life. Officers used to accompany assaulting columns over causeways on horseback, and occupy the most exposed positions that could be found. They were not playing the bravo: they were confirming their own belief in their courage, and acting under the impression that bravery ought not only to be undoubted, but conspicuous. They were simply putting their courage beyond suspicion.

"At a later period of the war, *when men began to plume themselves as veterans*, they could afford to be more conservative: they had won their spurs; their reputations were established; they were beyond reproach. Officers then dismounted to lead close assaults, dodged shots to their hearts' content, did not hesitate to avail themselves of the cover of earthworks when it was wise to seek such shelter, and resorted to many acts which conserved human life and in no wise detracted from their efficiency as soldiers. There was no longer anything done for buncombe: they had settled down to practical business."—*Ib.*, p. 249.

In "Arms and the Man," this very simple and intelligible picture is dramatized by the contrast between the experienced Swiss officer, with a high record for distinguished services, and the Bulgarian hero who wins the battle by an insanely courageous charge for which the Swiss thinks he ought to be court-martialled. Result: the dramatic critics pronounce the Swiss "a poltroon." I again appeal to General Porter for a precedent both for the Swiss's opinion of the heroic Bulgarian, and the possibility of a novice, in "sheer ignorance of the art of war" (as the Swiss puts it), achieving just such a success as I have attributed to Sergius Saranoff:—

"Recruits sometimes rush into dangers from which veterans would shrink. When Thomas was holding on to his position at Chickamauga on the afternoon of the second day, and resisting charge after charge of an enemy flushed with success, General Granger came up with a division of troops, many of whom had never before been under fire. As soon as they were deployed in front of the enemy, they set up a yell, sprang over the earthworks, charged into the ranks, and created such consternation that the Confederate veterans were paralysed by the very audacity of such conduct. Granger said, as he watched their movements, 'Just look at them: they don't know any better; they think that's the way it ought to be done. I'll bet they'll never do it again.' "

According to the critics, Granger was a cynic and a worldling, incapable of appreciating true courage.

I shall perhaps here be reminded by some of my critics that the charge in "Arms and the Man" was a cavalry charge; and that I am suppressing the damning sneer at military courage implied in Captain Bluntschli's reply to Raïna Petkoff's demand to have a cavalry charge described to her:—

"Bluntschli—You never saw a cavalry charge, did you?

"Raïna—No: how could I?

"Bluntschli—Of course not. Well, it's a funny sight. It's like slinging a handful of peas against a window-pane—first one comes, then two or three close behind them, and then all the rest in a lump.

"Raïna (*thinking of her lover, who has just covered*

himself with glory in a cavalry charge)—Yes; first one, the bravest of the brave!

"Bluntschli—Hm! you should see the poor devil pulling at his horse.

"Raïna—Why should he pull at his horse?

"Bluntschli—It's running away with him, of course: do you suppose the fellow wants to get there before the others and be killed?"

Imagine the feelings of the critics—countrymen of the heroes of Balaclava, and trained in warfare by repeated contemplation of the reproduction of Miss Elizabeth Thompson's pictures in the Regent Street shop windows, not to mention the recitations of Tennyson's "Charge of the Light Brigade," which they have criticised—on hearing this speech from a mere Swiss! I ask them now to put aside these authorities for a moment and tell me whether they have ever seen a horse bolt in Piccadilly or the Row. If so, I would then ask them to consider whether it is not rather likely that in a battlefield, which is, on the whole, rather a startling place, it is not conceivable and even likely that at least one horse out of a squadron may bolt in a charge. Having gently led them to this point, I further ask them how they think they would feel if they happened to be on the back of that horse, with the danger that has so often ended in death in Rotten Row complicated with the glory of charging a regiment practically single-handed. If we are to believe their criticisms, they would be delighted at the distinction. The Swiss captain in my play takes it for granted that they would pull the horse's head off. Leaving the difference of opinion unsettled, there can be no doubt as to what their duty would be if they were soldiers. A cavalry charge attains its maximum effect only when it strikes the enemy solid. This fact ought to be particularly well known to Balaclava amateurs; for Kinglake, the popular authority on the subject, gives us specimens of the orders that were heard during the frightful advance down "the valley of death." The dramatic-critical formula on that occasion would undoubtedly have been, "Charge, Chester, charge! on, Stanley, on!" Here is the reality:—

> "The crash of dragoons overthrown by round shot, by grape and by rifle-ball, was alternate with dry technical precepts: 'Back, right flank!' 'Keep back, private This,' 'Keep back private That!' 'Close in to your centre!' 'Do look to your dressing!' 'Right squadron, right squadron, keep back!' "

There is cynicism for you! Nothing but "keep back!" Then consider the conduct of Lord Cardigan, who rode at the head of the Light Brigade. Though he, too, said "Keep back," when Captain White tried to force the pace, he charged the centre gun of the battery just like a dramatic critic, and was the first man to sweep through the Russian gunners. In fact, he got clean out at the other side of the battery, happening to hit on a narrow opening by chance. The result was that he found himself presently riding down, quite alone, upon a mass of Russian cavalry. Here was a chance to cut them all down single-handed and plant the British flag on a mountain of Muscovite corpses. By refusing it, he flinched from the first-nighter's ideal. Realising the situation when he was twenty yards from the foe, he pulled up and converted that twenty yards into 200 as quickly as was consistent with his dignity as an officer. The stage hero finds in death the supreme consolation of being able to get up and go home when the curtain falls; but the real soldier, even when he leads Balaclava charges under conditions of appalling and prolonged danger, does not commit suicide for nothing. The fact is, Captain Bluntschli's description of the cavalry charge is taken almost verbatim from an account given privately to a friend of mine by an officer who served in the Franco-Prussian war. I am well aware that if I choose to be guided by men grossly ignorant of dramatic criticism, whose sole qualification is that they have seen cavalry charges on stricken fields, I must take the consequences. Happily, as between myself and the public, the consequences have not been unpleasant; and I recommend the experiment to my fellow dramatists with every confidence.

But great as has been the offence taken at my treating a soldier as a man with no stomach for unnecessary danger, I have given still greater by treating him as a man with a stomach for necessary food. Nature provides the defenders of our country with regular and efficient appetites. The taxpayer provides, at considerable cost to himself, rations for the soldier which are insufficient in time of peace and occasionally irregular in time of war. The result is that our young, growing soldiers sometimes go for months without once experiencing the sensation of having had enough to eat, and will often, under stress of famine, condescend to borrow florins and other trifles in silver from the young ladies who walk out with them, in order to eke out "the living wage." Let me quote a passage from Cobbett's description of his soldiering days in his "Advice to Young Men," which nobody who has read the book ever forgets:—

"I remember, and well I may! that, upon occasion, I, after all absolutely necessary expenses, had, on Friday, made shift to have a halfpenny in reserve, which I had destined for the purchase of a *red herring* in the morning; but, when I pulled off my clothes at night, so hungry then as to be hardly able to endure life, I found that I had *lost my halfpenny*. I buried my head under the miserable sheet and rug and cried like a child."

I am by no means convinced that the hidden tears still shed by young soldiers (who would rather die than confess to them) on similar provocation would not fill a larger cask than those shed over lost comrades or wounds to the national honour of England. In the field the matter is more serious. It is a mistake to suppose that in a battle the waiters come round regularly with soup, fish, an entrée, a snack of game, a cut from the joint, ice pudding, coffee and cigarettes, with drinks at discretion. When battles last for several days, as modern battles often do, the service of food and ammunition may get disorganised or cut off at any point; and the soldier may suffer exceedingly from hunger in consequence. To guard against this the veteran would add a picnic hamper to his equipment if it were portable enough and he could afford it, or if Fortnum and Mason would open a shop on the field. As it is, he falls back on the cheapest, most portable and most easily purchased sort of stomach-stayer, which, as every cyclist knows, is chocolate. This chocolate, which so shocks Raïna in the play—for she, poor innocent, classes it as "sweets"—and which seems to so many of my critics to be the climax of my audacious extravagances, is a commonplace of modern warfare. I know of a man who lived on it for two days in the Shipka Pass.

By the way, I have been laughed at in this connection for making my officer carry an empty pistol, preferring chocolate to cartridges. But I might have gone further and represented him as going without any pistol at all. Lord Wolseley mentions two officers who seldom carried any weapons. One of them had to defend himself by shying stones when the Russians broke into his battery at Sebastopol. The other was Gordon.

The report that my military realism is a huge joke has once or twice led audiences at the Avenue Theatre to laugh at certain grim touches which form no part of the comedy of disillusionment elsewhere so constant between the young lady and the Swiss. Readers of General Marbot's Memoirs will remember his description of how, at the battle of Wagram, the standing corn was set on fire by the shells and many of the wounded were roasted alive. "This often happens," says Marbot, coolly, "in battles fought in summer." The Servo-Bulgarian war was fought in winter; but Marbot will be readily recognised as the source of the incident of Bluntschli's friend Stolz, who is shot in the hip in a wood-yard and burnt in the conflagration of the timber caused by the Servian shells. There is, no doubt, a certain barbarous humour in the situation—enough to explain why the Bulgarian, on hearing Raïna exclaim, "How horrible!" adds bitterly, "And how ridiculous!" but I can assure those who are anxious to fully appreciate the fun of the travesty of war discovered in my work by the critics, and whose rule is, "When in doubt, laugh," that I should not laugh at that passage myself were I looking at my own play. Marbot's picture of the fire-eaters fire-eaten is one which I recommend to our music-hall tableauists when they are in need of a change. Who that has read that Wagram chapter does not remember Marbot forcing his wretched horse to gallop through the red-hot straw embers on his way to Massena; finding that general with no *aide-de-camp* left to send on a probably fatal errand except his only son; being sent in the son's place as soon as he had changed the roasted horse for a fresh one; being followed into the danger by the indignant son; and, finally—Nature seldom fails with her touch of farce—discovering that the son could not handle his sabre, and having to defend him against the pursuing cavalry of the enemy, who, as Bluntschli would have prophesied, no sooner found that they had to choose between two men who stood to fight and hundreds who were running away and allowing themselves to be slaughtered like sheep, [than they] devoted themselves entirely to the sheep, and left Marbot to come out of the battle of Wagram with a whole skin?

I might considerably multiply my citations of documents; but the above will, I hope, suffice to show that what struck my critics as topsy-turvy extravaganza, having no more relation to real soldiering than Mr. Gilbert's "Pinafore" has to real sailoring, is the plainest matter-of-fact. There is no burlesque: I have stuck to the routine of war, as described by real warriors, and avoided such farcical incidents as Sir William Gordon defending his battery by throwing stones, or General Porter's story of the two generals who, though brave and capable men, always got sick under fire, to their own great mortification. I claim that the dramatic effect produced by the shock which these realities give to the notions of romantic young ladies and fierce civilians is not burlesque, but legitimate comedy, none the less pungent because, on the first night at least, the romantic young lady was on the stage and the fierce civilians in the stalls. And since my authorities, who record many acts almost too brave to make pleasant reading, are beyond suspicion of that cynical disbelief in courage which has been freely attributed to me, I would ask whether it is not plain that the difference between my authenticated conception of real warfare and the stage conception lies in the fact that in real warfare there is real personal danger, the sense of which is constantly present to the mind of the soldier, whereas in stage warfare there is nothing but glory? Hence Captain Bluntschli, who thinks of a battlefield as a very busy and very dangerous place, is incredible to the critic who thinks of it only as a theatre in which to enjoy the luxurious excitements of patriotism, victory, and bloodshed without risk or retribution.

There are one or two general points in the play on which I may as well say a word whilst I have the opportunity. It is a common practice in England to speak of the courage of the common soldier as "bulldog pluck." I grant that it is an insulting practice—who would dream of comparing the spirit in which an ancient Greek went to battle with the ferocity of an animal?—though it is not so intended, as it generally comes from people who are thoughtless enough to suppose that they are paying the army a compliment. A passage in the play which drove home the true significance of the comparison greatly startled these same thoughtless ones. Can we reasonably apply such a word as valour to the quality exhibited in the field by, for instance, the armies of Frederick the Great, consisting of kidnapped men, drilled, caned, and flogged to the verge of suicide, and sometimes over it? Flogging, sickeningly common in English barracks all through the most "glorious" periods of our military history, was not abolished here by any revolt of the English soldier against it: our warriors would be flogging one another to-day as abjectly as ever but for the interference of humanitarians who hated the whole conception of military glory. We still hear of soldiers severely punished for posting up in the barrack stables a newspaper paragraph on the subject of an army grievance. Such absurd tyranny would, in a dockyard or a factory full of matchgirls, produce a strike; but it cows a whole regiment of soldiers. The fact is, armies as we know them are made possible, not by valour in the rank and file, but by the lack of it; not by physical courage (we test the eyes and lungs of our recruits, never their courage), but by civic impotence and moral cowardice. I am afraid of a soldier, not because he is a brave man, but because he is so utterly unmanned by discipline that he will kill me if he is told, even when he knows that the order is given because I am trying to overthrow the oppression which he fears and hates. I respect a regiment for a mutiny more than for a hundred victories; and I confess to the heartiest contempt for the warlike civilian who pays poor men a pittance to induce them to submit to be used as pawns on a battlefield in time of war, he himself, meanwhile, sitting at home talking impudent nonsense about patriotism, heroism, devotion to duty, the inspiring sound of the British cheer, and so on. "Bulldog pluck" is much more sensible and candid. And so the idealist in my play continues to admit nightly that his bull terrier, which will fight as fiercely as a soldier, will let himself be thrashed as helplessly by the man in authority over him. One critic seems to think that it requires so much courage to say such things that he describes me as "protecting" myself by "ostensibly throwing the burden of my attack upon a couple of small and unimportant nationalities," since "there would have been a certain danger in bringing my malevolent mockery too near home." I can assure the gentleman that I meant no mockery at all. The observation is made in the play in a manner dramatically appropriate to the character of an idealist who is made a pessimist by the shattering of his illusions. His conclusion is that "life is a farce." My conclusion is that a soldier ought to be made a citizen and treated like any other citizen. And I am not conscious of running any risk in making that proposal, except the risk of being foolishly criticised.

I have been much lectured for my vulgarity in introducing certain references to soap and water in Bulgaria. I did so as the shortest and most effective way of bringing home to the audience the stage of civilisation in which the Bulgarians were in 1885, when, having clean air and clean clothes, which made them much cleaner than any frequency of ablution can make us in the dirty air of London, they were adopting the washing habits of big western cities as pure ceremonies of culture and civilisation, and not on hygienic grounds. I had not the slightest intention of suggesting that my Bulgarian major, who submits to a good wash for the sake of his social position, or his father, who never had a bath in his life, are uncleanly people, though a cockney, who by simple exposure to the atmosphere becomes more unpresentable in three hours than a Balkan mountaineer in three years, may feel bound to pretend to be shocked at them, and to shrink with disgust from even a single omission of the daily bath which, as he knows very well, the majority of English, Irish, and Scotch people do not take, and which the majority of the inhabitants of the world do not even tell lies about.

Major Petkoff is quite right in his intuitive perception that soap, instead of being the radical remedy for dirt, is really one of its worst consequences. And his remark that the cultus of soap comes from the English because their climate makes them exceptionally dirty, is one of the most grimly and literally accurate passages in the play, as we who dwell in smoky towns know to our cost. However, I am sorry that my piece of realism should have been construed as an insult to the Bulgarian nation; and perhaps I should have hesitated to introduce it had I known that a passionate belief in the scrupulous cleanliness of the inhabitants of the Balkan peninsula is a vital part of Liberal views on foreign policy. But what is done is done. I close the incident by quoting from the daily papers of the 5th May last the following item of Parliamentary intelligence, which gives a basis for a rough calculation of the value of English cleanliness as measured by the pecuniary sacrifices we are willing to make for it:—

> "ARMY BEDDING
>
> "The SECRETARY for WAR, replying to Mr. Hanbury's question as to the provision made in the Army for the washing of soldiers' bedding, stated that soldiers are now allowed to have their sheets washed once a month, and their blankets once a year and the right hon. gentleman stated that the cost of allowing clean sheets fortnightly instead of monthly would amount to something like £10,000 a year, money which might be spent more advantageously in other directions, he thought. (Hear, hear.)"

I am afraid most of my critics will receive the above explanations with an indignant sense of personal ingratitude on my part. The burden of their mostly very kind notices has been that I am a monstrously clever fellow, who has snatched a brilliant success by amusingly whimsical perversions of patent facts and piquantly cynical ridicule of human nature. I hardly have the heart to turn upon such friendly help with a cold-blooded confession that all my audacious originalities are simple liftings from stores of evidence which lie ready to everybody's hand. Even that triumph of eccentric invention which nightly brings down the house, Captain Bluntschli's proposal for the hand of Raïna, is a paraphrase of an actual proposal made by an Austrian hotel proprietor for the hand of a member of my own family. To that gentleman, and to him alone, is due the merit of the irresistible joke of the four thousand tablecloths and the seventy equipages of which twenty-four will hold twelve inside. I have plundered him as I have plundered Lord Wolseley and General Porter and everyone else who had anything that was good to steal. I created nothing; I invented nothing; I imagined nothing; I perverted nothing; I simply discovered drama in real life.

I now plead strongly for a theatre to supply the want of this sort of drama. I declare that I am tired to utter disgust of imaginary life; imaginary law, imaginary ethics, science, peace, war, love, virtue, villainy, and imaginary everything else, both on the stage and off it. I demand respect, interest, affection for human nature as it is, and life as we must still live it even when we have bettered it and ourselves to the utmost. If the critics really believe all their futile sermonising about "poor humanity" and the "seamy side of life" and meanness, cowardice, selfishness, and all the other names they give to qualities which are as much and as obviously a necessary part of themselves as their arms and legs, why do they not shoot themselves like men instead of coming whimpering to the dramatist to pretend that they are something else? I, being a man like to themselves, know what they are perfectly well; and as I do not find that I dislike them for what they persist in calling their vanity, and sensuality, and mendacity, and dishonesty, and hypocrisy, and venality, and so forth; as, furthermore, they would not interest me in the least if they were otherwise, I shall continue to put them on the stage as they are to the best of my ability, in the hope that some day it may strike them that if they were to try a little self-respect, and stop calling themselves offensive names, they would discover that the affection of their friends, wives, and sweethearts for them is not a reasoned tribute to their virtues, but a human impulse towards their very selves. When Raïna says in the play, "Now that you have found me out, I suppose you despise me," she discovers that that result does not follow in the least, Captain Bluntschli not being quite dramatic critic enough to feel bound to repudiate the woman who has saved his life as "a false and lying minx," because, at twenty-three, she has some generous illusions which lead her into a good deal of pretty nonsense.

I demand, moreover, that when I deal with facts into which the critic has never inquired, and of which he has had no personal experience, he shall not make his vain imaginings the criterion of my accuracy. I really cannot undertake, every time I write a play, to follow it up by a text-book on mortgages, or soldiering, or whatever else it may be about, for the instruction of gentlemen who will neither accept the result of my study of the subject (lest it should destroy their cherished ideals), nor undertake any study on their own account. When I have written a play the whole novelty of which lies in the fact that it is void of malice to my fellow creatures, and laboriously exact as to all essential facts, I object to be complimented on my "brilliancy" as a fabricator of cynical extravaganzas. Nor do I consider it decent for critics to call their own ignorance "the British public," as they almost invariably do.

It must not be supposed that the whole Press has gone wrong over "Arms and the Man" to the same extent and in the same direction. Several of the London correspondents of the provincial papers, accustomed to deal with the objective world outside the theatre, came off with greater credit than the hopelessly specialised critics. Some of the latter saved themselves by a strong liking for the play, highly agreeable to me; but most of them hopelessly misunderstood me. I should have lain open to the retort that I had failed to make myself comprehensible had it not been for the masterly critical exploit achieved by Mr. A. B. Walkley, whose article in the *Speaker* was a completely successful analysis of my position. Mr. Walkley here saved the critics from the reproach of having failed where the actors had succeeded. Nobody who has seen Mr. Yorke Stephens's impersonation of the Swiss captain will suspect him for a moment of mistaking his man, as most of the critics did, for "a poltroon who prefers chocolate to fighting." It was Mr. Walkley who recognised that Bluntschli, "dogged, hopelessly unromantic, incurably frank, always *terre à terre*, yet a man every inch of him, is one of the most artistic things Mr. Yorke Stephens has done."

Here we have the actor making Bluntschli appear to a fine critic, as he undoubtedly did to the gallery, a brave, sincere, unaffected soldier; and yet some of the other critics, unable to rise to the actor's level, moralised in a positively dastardly way about a "cowardly and cynical mercenary." Imagine English dramatic critics, who, like myself, criticise for the paper that pays them best, without regard to its politics, and whose country's regular army is exclusively a paid professional one, waxing virtuous over a "mercenary" soldier! After that, one hardly noticed their paying tribute to the ideal woman (a sort of female George Washington) by calling Raïna a minx, and feebly remonstrating with Miss Alma Murray for charming them in such a character; whilst as to the heroic Sergius, obsessed with their own ideals, and desperately resolved to live up to them in spite of his real nature, which he is foolish enough to despise, I half expected them to stone him; and I leave Mr. Bernard Gould and Mr. Walkley to divide the credit, as actor and critic, the one of having realised the man, and the other of having analysed him—the nicety of the second operation proving the success of the first.

Here I must break off, lest I should appear to talk too much about my own play. I should have broken off sooner but for the temptation of asserting the right of the authors to decide who is the best critic, since the critics take it upon themselves to decide who is the best author.

John Bull's Other Island

Preface for Politicians

John Bull's Other Island was written in 1904 at the request of Mr William Butler Yeats, as a patriotic contribution to the repertory of the Irish Literary Theatre. Like most people who have asked me to write plays, Mr Yeats got rather more than he bargained for. The play was at that time beyond the resources of the new Abbey Theatre, which the Irish enterprise owed to the public spirit of Miss A. E. F. Horniman (an Englishwoman, of course), who, twelve years ago, played an important part in the history of the modern English stage as well as in my own personal destiny by providing the necessary capital for that memorable season at the Avenue Theatre which forced my Arms and The Man and Mr Yeats's Land of Heart's Desire on the recalcitrant London playgoer, and gave a third Irish playwright, Dr John Todhunter, an opportunity which the commercial theatres could not have afforded him.

There was another reason for changing the destination of John Bull's Other Island. It was uncongenial to the whole spirit of the neo-Gaelic movement, which is bent on creating a new Ireland after its own ideal, whereas my play is a very uncompromising presentment of the real old Ireland. The next thing that happened was the production of the play in London at the Court Theatre by Messrs Vedrenne and Barker, and its immediate and enormous popularity with delighted and flattered English audiences. This constituted it a successful commercial play, and made it unnecessary to resort to the special machinery or tax the special resources of the Irish Literary Theatre for its production.

HOW TOM BROADBENT TOOK IT

Now I have a good deal more to say about the relations between the Irish and the English than will be found in my play. Writing the play for an Irish audience, I thought it would be good for them to be shewn very clearly that the loudest laugh they could raise at the expense of the absurdest Englishman was not really a laugh on their side; that he would succeed where they would fail; that he could inspire strong affection and loyalty in an Irishman who knew the world and was moved only to dislike, mistrust, impatience and even exasperation by his own countrymen; that his power of taking himself seriously, and his insensibility to anything funny in danger and destruction, was the first condition of economy and concentration of force, sustained purpose, and rational conduct. But the need for this lesson in Ireland is the measure of its demoralizing superfluousness in England. English audiences very naturally swallowed it eagerly and smacked their lips over it, laughing all the more heartily because they felt that they were taking a caricature of themselves with the most tolerant and large-minded goodhumor. They were perfectly willing to allow me to represent Tom Broadbent as infatuated in politics, hypnotized by his newspaper leader-writers and parliamentary orators into an utter paralysis of his common sense, without moral delicacy or social tact, provided I made him cheerful, robust, goodnatured, free from envy, and above all, a successful muddler-through in business and love. Not only did no English critic allow that the success in business of Messrs English Broadbent and Irish Doyle might possibly have been due to some extent to Doyle, but one writer actually dwelt with much feeling on the pathos of Doyle's failure as an engineer (a circumstance not mentioned nor suggested in my play) in contrast with Broadbent's solid success. No doubt, when the play is performed in Ireland, the Dublin critics will regard it as self-evident that without Doyle Broadbent would have become bankrupt in six months. I should say, myself, that the combination was probably much more effective than either of the partners would have been alone. I am persuaded further—without pretending to know more about it than anyone else—that Broadbent's special contribution was simply the strength, self-satisfaction, social confidence and cheerful bumptiousness that money, comfort, and good feeding bring to all healthy people; and that Doyle's special contribution was the freedom from illusion, the power of facing facts, the nervous industry, the sharpened wits, the sensitive pride of the imaginative man who has fought his way up through social persecution and poverty. I do not say that the confidence of the Englishman in Broadbent is not for the moment justified. The virtues of the English soil are not less real because they consist of coal and iron, not of metaphysical sources of character. The virtues of Broadbent are not less real because they are the virtues of the money that coal and iron have produced. But as the mineral virtues are being discovered and developed in other soils, their derivative virtues are appearing so rapidly in other nations that Broadbent's relative advantage is vanishing. In truth I am afraid (the misgiving is natural to a by-this-time slightly elderly playwright) that Broadbent is out of date. The successful Englishman of today, when he is not a transplanted Scotchman or Irishman, often turns out on investigation to be, if not an American, an Italian, or a Jew, at least to be depending on the brains, the nervous energy, and the freedom from romantic illusions (often called cynicism) of such foreigners for the management of his sources of income. At all events I am persuaded that a modern nation that is satisfied with Broadbent is in a dream. Much as I like him, I object to be governed by him, or entangled in his political destiny. I therefore propose to give him a piece of my mind here, as an Irishman, full of an instinctive pity for those of my fellow-creatures who are only English.

WHAT IS AN IRISHMAN?

When I say that I am an Irishman I mean that I was born in Ireland, and that my native language is the English of Swift and not the unspeakable jargon of the mid-XIX century London newspapers. My extraction is the extraction of most Englishmen: that is, I have no trace in me of the commercially imported North Spanish strain which passes for aboriginal Irish: I am a genuine typical Irishman of the Danish, Norman, Cromwellian, and (of course) Scotch invasions. I am violently and arrogantly Protestant by family tradition; but let no English Government therefore count on my allegiance: I am English enough to be an inveterate Republican and Home Ruler. It is true that one of my grandfathers was an Orangeman; but then his sister was an abbess; and his uncle, I am proud to say, was hanged as a rebel. When I look round me on the hybrid cosmopolitans, slum poisoned or square pampered, who call themselves Englishmen today, and see them bullied by the Irish Protestant garrison as no Bengalee now lets himself be bullied by an Englishman; when I see the Irishman everywhere standing clearheaded, sane, hardily callous to the boyish sentimentalities, susceptibilities, and credulities that make the Englishman the dupe of every charlatan and the idolater of every numskull, I perceive that Ireland is the only spot on earth which still produces the ideal Englishman of history. Blackguard, bully, drunkard, liar, foulmouth, flatterer, beggar, backbiter, venal functionary, corrupt judge, envious friend, vindictive opponent, unparalleled political traitor: all these your Irishman may easily be, just as he may be a gentleman (a species extinct in England, and nobody a penny the worse); but he is never quite the hysterical, nonsense-crammed, factproof, truth-terrified, unballasted sport of all the bogey panics and all the silly enthusiasms that now calls itself "God's Englishman." England cannot do without its Irish and its Scots today, because it cannot do without at least a little sanity.

THE PROTESTANT GARRISON

The more Protestant an Irishman is—the more English he is, if it flatters you to have it put that way, the more intolerable he finds it to be ruled by English instead of Irish folly. A "loyal" Irishman is an abhorrent phenomenon, because it is an unnatural one. No doubt English rule is vigorously exploited in the interests of the property, power, and promotion of the Irish classes as against the Irish masses. Our delicacy is part of a keen sense of reality which makes us a very practical, and even, on occasion, a very coarse people. The Irish soldier takes the King's shilling and drinks the King's health; and the Irish squire takes the title deeds of the English settlement and rises uncovered to the strains of the English national anthem. But do not mistake this cupboard loyalty for anything deeper. It gains a broad base from the normal attachment of every reasonable man to the established government as long as it is bearable; for we all, after a certain age, prefer peace to revolution and order to chaos, other things being equal. Such considerations produce loyal Irishmen as they produce loyal Poles and Fins, loyal Hindoos, loyal Filipinos, and faithful slaves. But there is nothing more in it than that. If there is an entire lack of gall in the feeling of the Irish gentry towards the English, it is because the Englishman is always gaping admiringly at the Irishman as at some clever child prodigy. He overrates him with a generosity born of a traditional conviction of his own superiority in the deeper aspects of human character. As the Irish gentleman, tracing his pedigree to the conquest or one of the invasions, is equally convinced that if this superiority really exists, he is the genuine true blue heir to it, and as he is easily able to hold his own in all the superficial social accomplishments, he finds English society agreeable, and English houses very comfortable, Irish establishments being generally straitened by an attempt to keep a park and a stable on an income which would not justify an Englishman in venturing upon a wholly detached villa.

OUR TEMPERAMENTS CONTRASTED

But however pleasant the relations between the Protestant garrison and the English gentry may be, they are always essentially of the nature of an *entente cordiale* between foreigners. Personally I like Englishmen much better than Irishmen (no doubt because they make more of me) just as many Englishmen like Frenchmen better than Englishmen, and never go on board a Peninsular and Oriental steamer when one of the ships of the Messageries Maritimes is available. But I never think of an Englishman as my countryman. I should as soon think of applying that term to a German. And the Englishman has the same feeling. When a Frenchman fails to make the distinction, we both feel a certain disparagement involved in the misapprehension. Macaulay, seeing that the Irish had in Swift an author worth stealing, tried to annex him by contending that he must be classed as an Englishman because he was not an aboriginal Celt. He might as well have refused the name of Briton to Addison because he did not stain himself blue and attach scythes to the poles of his sedan chair. In spite of all such trifling with facts, the actual distinction between the idolatrous Englishman and the fact-facing Irishman, of the same extraction though they be, remains to explode those two hollowest of fictions, the Irish and English "races." There is no Irish race any more than there is an English race or a Yankee race. There *is* an Irish climate, which will stamp an immigrant more deeply and durably in two years, apparently, than the English climate will in two hundred. It is reinforced by an artificial economic climate which does some of the work attributed to the natural geographic one; but the geographic climate is eternal and irresistible, making a mankind and a womankind that Kent, Middlesex, and East Anglia cannot produce and do not want to imitate.

How can I sketch the broad lines of the contrast as they strike me? Roughly I should say that the Englishman is wholly at the mercy of his imagination, having no sense of reality to check it. The Irishman, with a far subtler and more fastidious imagination, has one eye always on things as they are. If you compare Moore's visionary Minstrel Boy with Mr Rudyard Kipling's quasi-realistic Soldiers Three, you may yawn over Moore or gush over him, but you will not suspect him of having had any illusions about the contemporary British private; whilst as to Mr Kipling, you will see that he has not, and unless he settles in Ireland for a few years will always remain constitutionally and congenitally incapable of having, the faintest inkling of the reality which he idolizes as Tommy Atkins. Perhaps you have never thought of illustrating the contrast between English and Irish by Moore and Mr Kipling, or even by Parnell and Gladstone. Sir Boyle Roche and Shakespear may seem more to your point. Let me find you a more dramatic instance. Think of the famous meeting between the Duke of Wellington, that intensely Irish Irishman, and Nelson, that intensely English Englishman. Wellington's contemptuous disgust at Nelson's theatricality as a professed hero, patriot, and rhapsode, a theatricality which in an Irishman would have been an insufferably vulgar affectation, was quite natural and inevitable. Wellington's formula for that kind of thing was a well-known Irish one: "Sir: dont be a damned fool." It is the formula of all Irishmen for all Englishmen to this day. It is the formula of Larry Doyle for Tom Broadbent in my play, in spite of Doyle's affection for Tom.

John Bull's Other Island

Act One

Great George Street, Westminster, is the address of Doyle and Broadbent, civil engineers. On the threshold one reads that the firm consists of Mr Laurence Doyle and Mr Thomas Broadbent, and that their rooms are on the first floor. Most of these rooms are private; for the partners, being bachelors and bosom friends, live there; and the door marked Private, next the clerks' office, is their domestic sitting room as well as their reception room for clients. Let me describe it briefly from the point of view of a sparrow on the window sill. The outer door is in the opposite wall, close to the right hand corner. Between this door and the left hand corner is a hat-stand and a table consisting of large drawing boards on trestles, with plans, rolls of tracing paper, mathematical instruments, and other draughtsman's accessories on it. In the left hand wall is the fireplace, and the door of an inner room between the fireplace and our observant sparrow. Against the right hand wall is a filing cabinet, with a cupboard on it, and, nearer, a tall office desk and stool for one person. In the middle of the room a large double writing table is set across, with a chair at each end for the two partners. It is a room which no woman would tolerate, smelling of tobacco, and much in need of repapering, repainting, and recarpeting; but this is the effect of bachelor untidiness and indifference, not want of means; for nothing that Doyle and Broadbent themselves have purchased is cheap; nor is anything they want lacking. On the walls hang a large map of South America, a pictorial advertisement of a steamship company, an impressive portrait of Gladstone, and several caricatures of Mr Balfour as a rabbit and Mr Chamberlain as a fox by Francis Carruthers Gould.

At twenty minutes to five o'clock on a summer afternoon in 1904, the room is empty. Presently the outer door is opened, and a valet comes in laden with a large Gladstone bag and a strap of rugs. He carries them into the inner room. He is a respectable valet, old enough to have lost all alacrity and acquired an air of putting up patiently with a great deal of trouble and indifferent health. The luggage belongs to Broadbent, who enters after the valet. He pulls off his overcoat and hangs it with his hat on the stand. Then he comes to the writing table and looks through the letters waiting there for him. He is a robust, full-blooded, energetic man in the prime of life, sometimes eager and credulous, sometimes shrewd and roguish, sometimes portentously solemn, sometimes jolly and impetuous, always buoyant and irresistible, mostly likeable, and enormously absurd in his most earnest moments. He bursts open his letters with his thumb, and glances through them, flinging the envelopes about the floor with reckless untidiness whilst he talks to the valet.

BROADBENT [*calling*] Hodson.

HODSON [*in the bedroom*] Yes sir.

BROADBENT. Dont unpack. Just take out the things Ive worn; and put in clean things.

HODSON [*appearing at the bedroom door*] Yes sir. [*He turns to go back into the bedroom*].

BROADBENT. And look here! [*Hodson turns again*]. Do you remember where I put my revolver?

HODSON. Revolver, sir! Yes sir. Mr Doyle uses it as a paper-weight, sir, when he's drawing.

BROADBENT. Well, I want it packed. Theres a packet of cartridges somewhere, I think. Find it and pack it as well.

HODSON. Yes sir.

BROADBENT. By the way, pack your own traps too. I shall take you with me this time.

HODSON [*hesitant*] Is it a dangerous part youre going to, sir? Should I be expected to carry a revolver, sir?

BROADBENT. Perhaps it might be as well. I'm going to Ireland.

HODSON [*reassured*] Yes sir.

BROADBENT. You dont feel nervous about it, I suppose?

HODSON. Not at all, sir. I'll risk it, sir.

BROADBENT. Ever been in Ireland?

HODSON. No sir. I understand it's a very wet climate, sir. I'd better pack your india-rubber overalls.

BROADBENT. Do. Wheres Mr Doyle?

HODSON. I'm expecting him at five, sir. He went out after lunch.

BROADBENT. Anybody been looking for me?

HODSON. A person giving the name of Haffigan has called twice today, sir.

BROADBENT. Oh, I'm sorry. Why didnt he wait? I told him to wait if I wasnt in.

HODSON. Well sir, I didnt know you expected him; so I thought it best to—to—not to encourage him, sir.

BROADBENT. Oh, he's all right. He's an Irishman, and not very particular about his appearance.

HODSON. Yes sir: I noticed that he was rather Irish.

BROADBENT. If he calls again let him come up.

HODSON. I think I saw him waiting about, sir, when you drove up. Shall I fetch him, sir?

BROADBENT. Do, Hodson.

HODSON. Yes sir. [*He makes for the outer door*].

BROADBENT. He'll want tea. Let us have some.

HODSON. [*stopping*] I shouldnt think he drank tea, sir.

BROADBENT. Well, bring whatever you think he'd like.

HODSON. Yes sir. [*An electric bell rings*]. Here he is, sir. Saw you arrive, sir.

BROADBENT. Right. Shew him in. [*Hodson goes out. Broadbent gets through the rest of his letters before Hodson returns with the visitor*].

HODSON. Mr Affigan.

Haffigan is a stunted, shortnecked, smallheaded man of about 30, with a small bullet head, a red nose, and furtive eyes. He is dressed in seedy black, almost clerically, and might be a tenth-rate schoolmaster ruined by drink. He hastens to shake Broadbent's hand with a show of reckless geniality and high spirits, helped out by a rollicking stage brogue. This is perhaps a comfort to himself, as he is secretly pursued by the horrors of incipient delirium tremens.

HAFFIGAN. Tim Haffigan, sir, at your service. The top o the mornin to you, Misther Broadbent.

BROADBENT [*delighted with his Irish visitor*] Good afternoon, Mr Haffigan.

TIM. An is it the afthernoon it is already? Begorra,

what I call the mornin is all the time a man fasts afther breakfast.

BROADBENT. Havnt you lunched?

TIM. Divil a lunch!

BROADBENT. I'm sorry I couldnt get back from Brighton in time to offer you some; but—

TIM. Not a word, sir, not a word. Sure itll do tomorrow. Besides, I'm Irish, sir: a poor aither, but a powerful dhrinker.

BROADBENT. I was just about to ring for tea when you came. Sit down, Mr Haffigan.

TIM. Tay is a good dhrink if your nerves can stand it. Mine cant.

Haffigan sits down at the writing table, with his back to the filing cabinet. Broadbent sits opposite him. Hodson enters emptyhanded; takes two glasses, a siphon, and a tantalus from the cupboard; places them before Broadbent on the writing table; looks ruthlessly at Haffigan, who cannot meet his eye; and retires.

BROADBENT. Try a whisky and soda.

TIM [*sobered*] There you touch the national wakeness, sir. [*Piously*] Not that I share it meself. Ive seen too much of the mischief of it.

BROADBENT [*pouring the whisky*] Say when.

TIM. Not too sthrong. [*Broadbent stops and looks inquiringly at him*]. Say half-an-half. [*Broadbent, somewhat startled by this demand, pours a little more, and again stops and looks*]. Just a dhrain more: the lower half o the tumbler doesnt hold a fair half. Thankya.

BROADBENT [*laughing*] You Irishmen certainly do know how to drink. [*Pouring some whisky for himself*] Now thats my poor English idea of a whisky and soda.

TIM. An a very good idea it is too. Dhrink is the curse o me unhappy counthry. I take it meself because Ive a wake heart and a poor digestion; but in principle I'm a teetoatler.

BROADBENT [*suddenly solemn and strenuous*] So am I, of course. I'm a Local Optionist to the backbone. You have no idea, Mr Haffigan, of the ruin that is wrought in this country by the unholy alliance of the publicans, the bishops, the Tories, and The Times. We must close the public-houses at all costs [*he drinks*].

TIM. Sure I know. It's awful [*he drinks*]. I see youre a good Liberal like meself, sir.

BROADBENT. I am a lover of liberty, like every true Englishman, Mr Haffigan. My name is Broadbent. If my name were Breitstein, and I had a hooked nose and a house in Park Lane, I should carry a Union Jack handkerchief and a penny trumpet, and tax the food of the people to support the Navy League, and clamor for the destruction of the last remnants of national liberty—

TIM. Not another word. Shake hands.

BROADBENT. But I should like to explain—

TIM. Sure I know every word youre goin to say before ye said it. *I* know the sort o man yar. An so youre thinkin o comin to Ireland for a bit?

BROADBENT. Where else can I go? I am an Englishman and a Liberal; and now that South Africa has been enslaved and destroyed, there is no country left to me to take an interest in but Ireland. Mind: I dont say that an Englishman has not other duties. He has a duty to Finland and a duty to Macedonia. But what sane man can deny that an Englishman's first duty is his duty to Ireland? Unfortunately, we have politicians here more unscrupulous than Bobrikoff, more bloodthirsty than Abdul the Damned; and it is under their heel that Ireland is now writhing.

TIM. Faith, theyve reckoned up with poor oul Bobrikoff anyhow.

BROADBENT. Not that I defend assassination: God forbid! However strongly we may feel that the unfortunate and patriotic young man who avenged the wrongs of Finland on the Russian tyrant was perfectly right from his own point of view, yet every civilized man must regard murder with abhorrence. Not even in defence of Free Trade would I lift my hand against a political opponent, however richly he might deserve it.

TIM. I'm sure you wouldnt; and I honor you for it. Youre goin to Ireland, then, out o sympithy: is it?

BROADBENT. I'm going to develop an estate there for the Land Development Syndicate, in which I am interested. I am convinced that all it needs to make it pay is to handle it properly, as estates are handled in England. You know the English plan, Mr Haffigan, dont you?

TIM. Bedad I do, sir. Take all you can out of Ireland and spend it in England: thats it.

BROADBENT [*not quite liking this*] My plan, sir, will be to take a little money out of England and spend it in Ireland.

TIM. More power to your elbow! an may your shadda never be less! for youre the broth of a boy intirely. An how can I help you? Command me to the last dhrop o me blood.

BROADBENT. Have you ever heard of Garden City?

TIM [*doubtfully*] D'ye mane Heavn?

BROADBENT. Heaven! No: it's near Hitchin. If you can spare half an hour I'll go into it with you.

TIM. I tell you hwat. Gimme a prospectus. Lemmy take it home and reflect on it.

BROADBENT. Youre quite right: I will. [*He gives him a*

copy of Ebenezer Howard's book, and several pamphlets]. You understand that the map of the city—the circular construction—is only a suggestion.

TIM. I'll make a careful note o that [*looking dazedly at the map*].

BROADBENT. What I say is, why not start a Garden City in Ireland?

TIM [*with enthusiasm*] Thats just what was on the tip o me tongue to ask you. Why not? [*Defiantly*] Tell me why not.

BROADBENT. There are difficulties. I shall overcome them; but there are difficulties. When I first arrive in Ireland I shall be hated as an Englishman. As a Protestant, I shall be denounced from every altar. My life may be in danger. Well, I am prepared to face that.

TIM. Never fear, sir. We know how to respict a brave innimy.

BROADBENT. What I really dread is misunderstanding. I think you could help me to avoid that. When I heard you speak the other evening in Bermondsey at the meeting of the National League, I saw at once that you were—You wont mind my speaking frankly?

TIM. Tell me all me faults as man to man. I can stand anything but flatthery.

BROADBENT. May I put it in this way? that I saw at once that you are a thorough Irishman, with all the faults and all the qualities of your race; rash and improvident but brave and goodnatured; not likely to succeed in business on your own account perhaps, but eloquent, humorous, a lover of freedom, and a true follower of that great Englishman Gladstone.

TIM. Spare me blushes. I mustnt sit here to be praised to me face. But I confess to the goodnature: it's an Irish wakeness. I'd share me last shillin with a friend.

BROADBENT. I feel sure you would, Mr Haffigan.

TIM [*impulsively*] Damn it! call me Tim. A man that talks about Ireland as you do may call me anything. Gimmy a howlt o that whisky bottle [*he replenishes*].

BROADBENT [*smiling indulgently*] Well, Tim, will you come with me and help to break the ice between me and your warmhearted, impulsive countrymen?

TIM. Will I come to Madagascar or Cochin China wid you? Bedad I'll come to the North Pole wid you if yll pay me fare; for the divil a shillin I have to buy a third class ticket.

BROADBENT. Ive not forgotten that, Tim. We must put that little matter on a solid English footing, though the rest can be as Irish as you please. You must come as my—my—well, I hardly know what to call it. If we call you my agent, theyll shoot you. If we call you a bailiff, theyll duck you in the horsepond. I have a secretary already; and—

TIM. Then we'll call him the Home Secretary and me the Irish Secretary. Eh?

BROADBENT [*laughing industriously*] Capital. Your Irish wit has settled the first difficulty. Now about your salary—

TIM. A salary, is it? Sure I'd do it for nothin, only me cloes ud disgrace you; and I'd be dhriven to borra money from your friends: a thing thats agin me nacher. But I wont take a penny more than a hundherd a year. [*He looks with restless cunning at Broadbent, trying to guess how far he may go*].

BROADBENT. If that will satisfy you—

TIM [*more than reassured*] Why shouldnt it satisfy me? A hundherd a year is twelve pound a month, isnt it?

BROADBENT. No. Eight pound six and eightpence.

TIM. Oh murdher! An I'll have to send five timmy poor oul mother in Ireland. But no matther: I said a hundherd; and what I said I'll stick to, if I have to starve for it.

BROADBENT [*with business caution*] Well, let us say twelve pounds for the first month. Afterwards, we shall see how we get on.

TIM. Youre a gentleman, sir. Whin me mother turns up her toes, you shall take the five pounds off; for your expinses must be kep down wid a sthrong hand; an— [*He is interrupted by the arrival of Broadbent's partner*].

Mr Laurence Doyle is a man of 36, with cold grey eyes, strained nose, fine fastidious lips, critical brows, clever head, rather refined and goodlooking on the whole, but with a suggestion of thinskinnedness and dissatisfaction that contrasts strongly with Broadbent's eupeptic jollity.

He comes in as a man at home there, but on seeing the stranger shrinks at once, and is about to withdraw when Broadbent reassures him. He then comes forward to the table, between the two others.

DOYLE [*retreating*] Youre engaged.

BROADBENT. Not at all, not at all. Come in. [*To Tim*] This gentleman is a friend who lives with me here: my partner, Mr Doyle. [*To Doyle*] This is a new Irish friend of mine, Mr Tim Haffigan.

TIM [*rising with effusion*] Sure it's meself thats proud to meet any friend o Misther Broadbent's. The top o the mornin to you, sir! Me heart goes out teeye both. It's not often I meet two such splendid speciments iv the Anglo-Saxon race.

BROADBENT [*chuckling*] Wrong for once, Tim. My friend Mr Doyle is a countryman of yours.

Tim is noticeably dashed by this announcement. He draws in his horns at once, and scowls suspiciously at Doyle under a vanishing mask of goodfellowship: cringing a little, too, in mere nerveless fear of him.

DOYLE [*with cool disgust*] Good evening. [*He retires to

the fireplace, and says to Broadbent in a tone which conveys the strongest possible hint to Haffigan that he is unwelcome] Will you soon be disengaged?

TIM [*his brogue decaying into a common would-be genteel accent with an unexpected strain of Glasgow in it*] I must be going. Avnmpoartnt engeegement in the west end.

BROADBENT [*rising*] It's settled then, that you come with me.

TIM. Ashll be verra pleased to accompany ye, sir.

BROADBENT. But how soon? Can you start tonight? from Paddington? We go by Milford Haven.

TIM [*hesitating*] Well—A'm afraid—A [*Doyle goes abruptly into the bedroom, slamming the door and shattering the last remnant of Tim's nerve. The poor wretch saves himself from bursting into tears by plunging again into his role of daredevil Irishman. He rushes to Broadbent; plucks his sleeve with trembling fingers; and pours forth his entreaty with all the brogue he can muster, subduing his voice lest Doyle should hear and return*]. Misther Broadbent: dont humiliate me before a fella counthryman. Look here: me cloes is up the spout. Gimmy a fypounnote—I'll pay ya nex Choosda whin me ship comes home—or you can stop it out o me month's sallery. I'll be on the platform at Paddnton punctial an ready. Gimmy it quick, before he comes back. You wont mind me axin, will ye?

BROADBENT. Not at all. I was about to offer you an advance for travelling expenses. [*He gives him a bank note*].

TIM [*pocketing it*] Thank you. I'll be there half an hour before the thrain starts. [*Larry is heard at the bedroom door, returning*]. Whisht: he's comin back. Goodbye an God bless ye. [*He hurries out almost crying, the £5 note and all the drink it means to him being too much for his empty stomach and over-strained nerves*].

DOYLE [*returning*] Where the devil did you pick up that seedy swindler? What was he doing here? [*He goes up to the table where the plans are, and makes a note on one of them, referring to his pocketbook as he does so*].

BROADBENT. There you go! Why are you so down on every Irishman you meet, especially if he's a bit shabby? poor devil! Surely a fellow-countryman may pass you the top of the morning without offence, even if his coat is a bit shiny at the seams.

DOYLE [*contemptuously*] The top of the morning! Did he call you the broth of a boy? [*He comes to the writing table*].

BROADBENT [*triumphantly*] Yes.

DOYLE. And wished you more power to your elbow?

BROADBENT. He did.

DOYLE. And that your shadow might never be less?

BROADBENT. Certainly.

DOYLE [*taking up the depleted whisky bottle and shaking his head at it*] And he got about half a pint of whisky out of you.

BROADBENT. It did him no harm. He never turned a hair.

DOYLE. How much money did he borrow?

BROADBENT. It was not borrowing exactly. He shewed a very honorable spirit about money. I believe he would share his last shilling with a friend.

DOYLE. No doubt he would share his friend's last shilling if his friend was fool enough to let him. How much did he touch you for?

BROADBENT. Oh, nothing. An advance on his salary—for travelling expenses.

DOYLE. Salary! In Heaven's name, what for?

BROADBENT. For being my Home Secretary, as he very wittily called it.

DOYLE. I dont see the joke.

BROADBENT. You can spoil any joke by being cold blooded about it. I saw it all right when he said it. It was something—something really very amusing—about the Home Secretary and the Irish Secretary. At all events, he's evidently the very man to take with me to Ireland to break the ice for me. He can gain the confidence of the people there, and make them friendly to me. Eh? [*He seats himself on the office stool, and tilts it back so that the edge of the standing desk supports his back and prevents his toppling over*].

DOYLE. A nice introduction, by George! Do you suppose the whole population of Ireland consists of drunken begging letter writers, or that even if it did, they would accept one another as references?

BROADBENT. Pooh! nonsense! he's only an Irishman. Besides, you dont seriously suppose that Haffigan can humbug me, do you?

DOYLE. No: he's too lazy to take the trouble. All he has to do is to sit there and drink your whisky while you humbug yourself. However, we neednt argue about Haffigan, for two reasons. First, with your money in his pocket he will never reach Paddington: there are too many public houses on the way. Second, he's not an Irishman at all.

BROADBENT. Not an Irishman! [*He is so amazed by the statement that he straightens himself and brings the stool bolt upright*].

DOYLE. Born in Glasgow. Never was in Ireland in his life. I know all about him.

BROADBENT. But he spoke—he behaved just like an Irishman.

DOYLE. Like an Irishman!! Man alive, dont you know that all this top-o-the-morning and broth-of-a-boy and more-power-to-your-elbow business is got up in England to fool you, like the Albert Hall concerts of Irish music? No Irishman ever talks like that in Ireland, or ever did, or ever will. But when a thoroughly worthless Irishman comes to England, and finds the whole place full of romantic duffers like you, who will let him loaf and drink and sponge and brag as long as he flatters your sense of moral superiority by playing the fool and degrading himself and his country, he soon learns the antics that take you in. He picks them up at the theatre or the music hall. Haffigan learnt the rudiments from his father, who came from my part of Ireland. I knew his uncles, Matt and Andy Haffigan of Rosscullen.

BROADBENT [*still incredulous*] But his brogue?

DOYLE. His brogue! A fat lot you know about brogues! Ive heard you call a Dublin accent that you could hang your hat on, a brogue. Heaven help you! you dont know the difference between Connemara and Rathmines. [*With violent irritation*] Oh, damn Tim Haffigan! lets drop the subject: he's not worth wrangling about.

BROADBENT. Whats wrong with you today, Larry? Why are you so bitter?

Doyle looks at him perplexedly; comes slowly to the writing table; and sits down at the end next the fireplace before replying.

DOYLE. Well: your letter completely upset me, for one thing.

BROADBENT. Why?

DOYLE. Your foreclosing this Rosscullen mortgage and turning poor Nick Lestrange out of house and home has rather taken me aback; for I liked the old rascal when I was a boy and had the run of his park to play in. I was brought up on the property.

BROADBENT. But he wouldnt pay the interest. I had to foreclose on behalf of the Syndicate. So now I'm off to Rosscullen to look after the property myself. [*He sits down at the writing table opposite Larry, and adds, casually, but with an anxious glance at his partner*] Youre coming with me, of course?

DOYLE [*rising nervously and recommencing his restless movements*] Thats it. Thats what I dread. Thats what has upset me.

BROADBENT. But dont you want to see your country again after 18 years absence? to see your people? to be in the old home again? to—

DOYLE [*interrupting him very impatiently*] Yes, yes: I know all that as well as you do.

BROADBENT. Oh well, of course [*with a shrug*] if you take it in that way, I'm sorry.

DOYLE. Never mind my temper: it's not meant for you, as you ought to know by this time. [*He sits down again, a little ashamed of his petulance; reflects a moment bitterly; then bursts out*] I have an instinct against going back to Ireland: an instinct so strong that I'd rather go with you to the South Pole than to Rosscullen.

BROADBENT. What! Here you are, belonging to a nation with the strongest patriotism! the most inveterate homing instinct in the world! and you pretend youd rather go anywhere than back to Ireland. You dont suppose I believe you, do you? In your heart—

DOYLE. Never mind my heart: an Irishman's heart is nothing but his imagination. How many of all those millions that have left Ireland have ever come back or wanted to come back? But whats the use of talking to you? Three verses of twaddle about the Irish emigrant "sitting on the stile, Mary," or three hours of Irish patriotism in Bermondsey or the Scotland Division of Liverpool, go further with you than all the facts that stare you in the face. Why, man alive, look at me! You know the way I nag, and worry, and carp, and cavil, and disparage, and am never satisfied and never quiet, and try the patience of my best friends.

BROADBENT. Oh, come, Larry! do yourself justice. Youre very amusing and agreeable to strangers.

DOYLE. Yes, to strangers. Perhaps if I was a bit stiffer to strangers, and a bit easier at home, like an Englishman, I'd be better company for you.

BROADBENT. We get on well enough. Of course you have the melancholy of the Keltic race—

DOYLE [*bounding out of his chair*] Good God!!!

BROADBENT [*slyly*]—and also its habit of using strong language when theres nothing the matter.

DOYLE. Nothing the matter! When people talk about the Celtic race, I feel as if I could burn down London. That sort of rot does more harm than ten Coercion Acts. Do you suppose a man need be a Celt to feel melancholy in Rosscullen? Why, man, Ireland was peopled just as England was; and its breed was crossed by just the same invaders.

BROADBENT. True. All the capable people in Ireland are of English extraction. It has often struck me as a most remarkable circumstance that the only party in parliament which shews the genuine old English character and spirit is the Irish party. Look at its independence, its determination, its defiance of bad Governments, its sympathy with oppressed nationalities all the world over! How English!

DOYLE. Not to mention the solemnity with which it talks old-fashioned nonsense which it knows perfectly well to be a century behind the times. Thats English, if you like.

BROADBENT. No, Larry, no. You are thinking of the modern hybrids that now monopolize England. Hypocrites, humbugs, Germans, Jews, Yankees, foreigners, Park Laners, cosmopolitan riffraff. Dont call them English. They dont belong to the dear old island, but to their confounded new empire; and by George! theyre worthy of it; and I wish them joy of it.

DOYLE [*unmoved by this outburst*] There! You feel better now, dont you?

BROADBENT [*defiantly*] I do. Much better.

DOYLE. My dear Tom, you only need a touch of the Irish climate to be as big a fool as I am myself. If all my Irish blood were poured into your veins, you wouldnt turn a hair of your constitution and character. Go and marry the most English Englishwoman you can find, and then bring up your son in Rosscullen; and that son's character will be so like mine and so unlike yours that everybody will accuse me of being his father. [*With sudden anguish*] Rosscullen! oh, good Lord, Rosscullen! The dullness! the hopelessness! the ignorance! the bigotry!

BROADBENT [*matter-of-factly*] The usual thing in the country, Larry. Just the same here.

DOYLE [*hastily*] No, no: the climate is different. Here, if the life is dull, you can be dull too, and no great harm done. [*Going off into a passionate dream*] But your wits cant thicken in that soft moist air, on those white springy roads, in those misty rushes and brown bogs, on those hillsides of granite rocks and magenta heather. Youve no such colors in the sky, no such lure in the distances, no such sadness in the evenings. Oh, the dreaming! the dreaming! the torturing, heart-scalding, never satisfying dreaming, dreaming, dreaming, dreaming! [*Savagely*] No debauchery that ever coarsened and brutalized an Englishman can take the worth and usefulness out of him like that dreaming. An Irishman's imagination never lets him alone, never convinces him, never satisfies him; but it makes him that he cant face reality nor deal with it nor handle it nor conquer it: he can only sneer at them that do, and [*bitterly, at Broadbent*] be "agreeable to strangers," like a good-for-nothing woman on the streets. [*Gabbling at Broadbent across the table*] It's all dreaming, all imagination. He cant be religious. The inspired Churchman that teaches him the sanctity of life and the importance of conduct is sent away empty; while the poor village priest that gives him a miracle or a sentimental story of a saint, has cathedrals built for him out of the pennies of the poor. He cant be intelligently political: he dreams of what the Shan Van Vocht said in ninety-eight. If you want to interest him in Ireland youve got to call the unfortunate island Kathleen ni Hollihan and pretend she's a little old woman. It saves thinking. It saves working. It saves everything except imagination, imagination, imagination; and imagination's such a torture that you cant bear it without whisky. [*With fierce shivering self-contempt*] At last you get that you can bear nothing real at all: youd rather starve than cook a meal; youd rather go shabby and dirty than set your mind to take care of your clothes and wash yourself; you nag and squabble at home because your wife isnt an angel, and she despises you because youre not a hero; and you hate the whole lot round you because theyre only poor slovenly useless devils like yourself. [*Dropping his voice like a man making some shameful confidence*] And all the while there goes on a horrible, senseless, mischievous laughter. When youre young, you exchange drinks with other young men; and you exchange vile stories with them; and as youre too futile to be able to help or cheer them, you chaff and sneer and taunt them for not doing the things you darent do yourself. And all the time you laugh! laugh! laugh! eternal derision, eternal envy, eternal folly, eternal fouling and staining and degrading, until, when you come at last to a country where men take a question seriously and give a serious answer to it, you deride them for having no sense of humor, and plume yourself on your own worthlessness as if it made you better than them.

BROADBENT [*roused to intense earnestness by Doyle's eloquence*] Never despair, Larry. There are great possibilities for Ireland. Home Rule will work wonders under English guidance.

DOYLE [*pulled up short, his face twitching with a reluctant smile*] Tom: why do you select my most tragic moments for your most irresistible strokes of humor?

BROADBENT. Humor! I was perfectly serious. What do you mean? Do you doubt my seriousness about Home Rule?

DOYLE. I am sure you are serious, Tom, about the English guidance.

BROADBENT [*quite reassured*] Of course I am. Our guidance is the important thing. We English must place our capacity for government without stint at the service of nations who are less fortunately endowed in that respect; so as to allow them to develop in perfect freedom to the English level of self-government, you know. You understand me?

DOYLE. Perfectly. And Rosscullen will understand you too.

BROADBENT [*cheerfully*] Of course it will. So thats all right. [*He pulls up his chair and settles himself comfortably to lecture Doyle*]. Now, Larry, Ive listened carefully to all youve said about Ireland; and I can see nothing whatever to prevent your coming with me. What does it all come to? Simply that you were only a young fellow when you were in Ireland. Youll find all that chaffing and drinking and not knowing what to be at in Peckham just the same as in Donnybrook. You looked at Ireland with a boy's eyes and saw only boyish things. Come back with me and look at it with a man's; and get a better opinion of your country.

DOYLE. I daresay youre partly right in that; at all events I know very well that if I had been the son of a laborer instead of the son of a country landagent, I should have struck more grit than I did. Unfortunately I'm not going back to visit the Irish nation, but to visit my father and Aunt Judy and Nora Reilly and Father Dempsey and the rest of them.

BROADBENT. Well, why not? Theyll be delighted to see you, now that England has made a man of you.

DOYLE [*struck by this*] Ah! you hit the mark there, Tom, with true British inspiration.

BROADBENT. Common sense, you mean.

DOYLE [*quickly*] No I dont: youve no more common sense than a gander. No Englishman has any common sense, or ever had, or ever will have. Youre going on a sentimental expedition for perfectly ridiculous reasons, with your head full of political nonsense that would not take in any ordinarily intelligent donkey; but you can hit me in the eye with the simple truth about myself and my father.

BROADBENT [*amazed*] I never mentioned your father.

DOYLE [*not heeding the interruption*] There he is in Rosscullen, a landagent who's always been in a small way because he's a Catholic, and the landlords are mostly Protestants. What with land courts reducing rents and Land Purchase Acts turning big estates into little holdings, he'd be a beggar if he hadnt taken to collecting the new purchase instalments instead of the old rents. I doubt if he's been further from home than Athenmullet for twenty years. And here am I, made a man of, as you say, by England.

BROADBENT [*apologetically*] I assure you I never meant—

DOYLE. Oh, dont apologize: it's quite true. I daresay Ive learnt something in America and a few other remote and inferior spots; but in the main it is by living with you and working in double harness with you that I have learnt to live in a real world and not in an imaginary one. I owe more to you than to any Irishman.

BROADBENT [*shaking his head with a twinkle in his eye*] Very friendly of you, Larry, old man, but all blarney. I like blarney; but it's rot, all the same.

DOYLE. No it's not. I should never have done anything without you; though I never stop wondering at that blessed old head of yours with all its ideas in watertight compartments, and all the compartments warranted impervious to anything it doesnt suit you to understand.

BROADBENT [*invincible*] Unmitigated rot, Larry, I assure you.

DOYLE. Well, at any rate you will admit that all my friends are either Englishmen or men of the big world that belongs to the big Powers. All the serious part of my life has been lived in that atmosphere: all the serious part of my work has been done with men of that sort. Just think of me as I am now going back to Rosscullen! to that hell of littleness and monotony! How am I to get on with a little country landagent that ekes out his 5 per cent with a little farming and a scrap of house property in the nearest country town? What am I to say to him? What is he to say to me?

BROADBENT [*scandalized*] But youre father and son, man!

DOYLE. What difference does that make? What would you say if I proposed a visit to your father?

BROADBENT [*with filial rectitude*] I always made a

point of going to see my father regularly until his mind gave way.

DOYLE [*concerned*] Has he gone mad? You never told me.

BROADBENT. He has joined the Tariff Reform League. He would never have done that if his mind had not been weakened. [*Beginning to declaim*] He has fallen a victim to the arts of a political charlatan who—

DOYLE [*interrupting him*] You mean that you keep clear of your father because he differs from you about Free Trade, and you dont want to quarrel with him. Well, think of me and my father! He's a Nationalist and a Separatist. I'm a metallurgical chemist turned civil engineer. Now whatever else metallurgical chemistry may be, it's not national. It's international. And my business and yours as civil engineers is to join countries, not to separate them. The one real political conviction that our business has rubbed into us is that frontiers are hindrances and flags confounded nuisances.

BROADBENT [*still smarting under Mr Chamberlain's economic heresy*] Only when there is a protective tariff—

DOYLE [*firmly*] Now look here, Tom: you want to get in a speech on Free Trade; and youre not going to do it: I wont stand it. My father wants to make St George's Channel a frontier and hoist a green flag on College Green; and I want to bring Galway within 3 hours of Colchester and 24 of New York. I want Ireland to be the brains and imagination of a big Commonwealth, not a Robinson Crusoe island. Then theres the religious difficulty. My Catholicism is the Catholicism of Charlemagne or Dante, qualified by a great deal of modern science and folklore which Father Dempsey would call the ravings of an Atheist. Well, my father's Catholicism is the Catholicism of Father Dempsey.

BROADBENT [*shrewdly*] I dont want to interrupt you, Larry; but you know this is all gammon. These differences exist in all families; but the members rub on together all right. [*Suddenly relapsing into portentousness*] Of course there are some questions which touch the very foundations of morals; and on these I grant you even the closest relationships cannot excuse any compromise or laxity. For instance—

DOYLE [*impatiently springing up and walking about*] For instance, Home Rule, South Africa, Free Trade, and putting the Church schools on the Education Rate. Well, I should differ from my father on every one of them, probably, just as I differ from you about them.

BROADBENT. Yes; but you are an Irishman; and these things are not serious to you as they are to an Englishman.

DOYLE. What! not even Home Rule!

BROADBENT [*steadfastly*] Not even Home Rule. We owe Home Rule not to the Irish, but to our English Gladstone. No, Larry: I cant help thinking that theres something behind all this.

DOYLE [*hotly*] What is there behind it? Do you think I'm humbugging you?

BROADBENT. Dont fly out, old chap. I only thought—

DOYLE. What did you think?

BROADBENT. Well, a moment ago I caught a name which is new to me: a Miss Nora Reilly, I think. [*Doyle stops dead and stares at him with something like awe*]. I dont wish to be impertinent, as you know, Larry; but are you sure she has nothing to do with your reluctance to come to Ireland with me?

DOYLE [*sitting down again, vanquished*] Thomas Broadbent: I surrender. The poor silly-clever Irishman takes off his hat to God's Englishman. The man who could in all seriousness make that recent remark of yours about Home Rule and Gladstone must be simply the champion idiot of all the world. Yet the man who could in the very next sentence sweep away all my special pleading and go straight to the heart of my motives must be a man of genius. But that the idiot and the genius should be the same man! how is that possible? [*Springing to his feet*] By Jove, I see it all now. I'll write an article about it, and send it to Nature.

BROADBENT [*staring at him*] What on earth—

DOYLE. It's quite simple. You know that a caterpillar—

BROADBENT. A caterpillar!!!

DOYLE. Yes, a caterpillar. Now give your mind to what I am going to say; for it's a new and important scientific theory of the English national character. A caterpillar—

BROADBENT. Look here, Larry: dont be an ass.

DOYLE [*insisting*] I say a caterpillar and I mean a caterpillar. Youll understand presently. A caterpillar [*Broadbent mutters a slight protest, but does not press it*] when it gets into a tree, instinctively makes itself look exactly like a leaf; so that both its enemies and its prey may mistake it for one and think it not worth bothering about.

BROADBENT. Whats that got to do with our English national character?

DOYLE. I'll tell you. The world is as full of fools as a tree is full of leaves. Well, the Englishman does what the caterpillar does. He instinctively makes himself look like a fool, and eats up all the real fools at his ease while his enemies let him alone and laugh at him for being a fool like the rest. Oh, nature is cunning! cunning! [*He sits down, lost in contemplation of his word-picture*].

BROADBENT [*with hearty admiration*] Now you know, Larry, that would never have occurred to me. You Irish people are amazingly clever. Of course it's all tommy rot; but it's so brilliant, you know! How the dickens do you think of such things! You really must write an article about it: theyll pay you something for it. If Nature wont have it, I can get it into Engineering for you: I know the editor.

DOYLE. Lets get back to business. I'd better tell you about Nora Reilly.

BROADBENT. No: never mind. I shouldnt have alluded to her.

DOYLE. I'd rather. Nora has a fortune.

BROADBENT [*keenly interested*] Eh? How much?

DOYLE. Forty per annum.

BROADBENT. Forty thousand?

DOYLE. No, forty. Forty pounds.

BROADBENT [*much dashed*] Thats what you call a fortune in Rosscullen, is it?

DOYLE. A girl with a dowry of five pounds calls it a fortune in Rosscullen. Whats more, £40 a year is a fortune there; and Nora Reilly enjoys a good deal of social consideration as an heiress on the strength of it. It has helped my father's household through many a tight place. My father was her father's agent. She came on a visit to us when he died, and has lived with us ever since.

BROADBENT [*attentively, beginning to suspect Larry of misconduct with Nora, and resolving to get to the bottom of it*] Since when? I mean how old were you when she came?

DOYLE. I was seventeen. So was she: if she'd been older she'd have had more sense than to stay with us. We were together for 18 months before I went up to Dublin to study. When I went home for Christmas and

Easter, she was there. I suppose it used to be something of an event for her; though of course I never thought of that then.

BROADBENT. Were you at all hard hit?

DOYLE. Not really. I had only two ideas at that time: first, to learn to do something; and then to get out of Ireland and have a chance of doing it. She didnt count. I was romantic about her, just as I was romantic about Byron's heroines or the old Round Tower of Rosscullen; but she didnt count any more than they did. Ive never crossed St George's Channel since for her sake—never even landed at Queenstown and come back to London through Ireland.

BROADBENT. But did you ever say anything that would justify her in waiting for you?

DOYLE. No, never. But she is waiting for me.

BROADBENT. How do you know?

DOYLE. She writes to me—on her birthday. She used to write on mine, and send me little things as presents; but I stopped that by pretending that it was no use when I was travelling, as they got lost in the foreign post-offices. [*He pronounces post-offices with the stress on offices, instead of on post*].

BROADBENT. You answer the letters?

DOYLE. Not very punctually. But they get acknowledged at one time or another.

BROADBENT. How do you feel when you see her handwriting?

DOYLE. Uneasy. I'd give £50 to escape a letter.

BROADBENT [*looking grave, and throwing himself back in his chair to intimate that the cross-examination is over, and the result very damaging to the witness*] Hm!

DOYLE. What d'ye mean by Hm!

BROADBENT. Of course I know that the moral code

is different in Ireland. But in England it's not considered fair to trifle with a woman's affections.

DOYLE. You mean that an Englishman would get engaged to another woman and return Nora her letters and presents with a letter to say he was unworthy of her and wished her every happiness?

BROADBENT. Well, even that would set the poor girl's mind at rest.

DOYLE. Would it? I wonder! One thing I can tell you; and that is that Nora would wait until she died of old age sooner than ask my intentions or condescend to hint at the possibility of my having any. You dont know what Irish pride is. England may have knocked a good deal of it out of me; but she's never been in England; and if I had to choose between wounding that delicacy in her and hitting her in the face, I'd hit her in the face without a moment's hesitation.

BROADBENT [*who has been nursing his knee and reflecting, apparently rather agreeably*] You know, all this sounds rather interesting. Theres the Irish charm about it. Thats the worst of you: the Irish charm doesnt exist for you.

DOYLE. Oh yes it does. But it's the charm of a dream. Live in contact with dreams and you will get something of their charm: live in contact with facts and you will get something of their brutality. I wish I could find a country to live in where the facts were not brutal and the dreams not unreal.

BROADBENT [*changing his attitude and responding to Doyle's earnestness with deep conviction: his elbows on the table and his hands clenched*] Dont despair, Larry, old boy: things may look black; but there will be a great change after the next election.

DOYLE [*jumping up*] Oh, get out, you idiot!

BROADBENT [*rising also, not a bit snubbed*] Ha! ha! you

may laugh; but we shall see. However, dont let us argue about that. Come now! you ask my advice about Miss Reilly?

DOYLE [*reddening*] No I dont. Damn your advice! [*Softening*] Lets have it, all the same.

BROADBENT. Well, everything you tell me about her impresses me favorably. She seems to have the feelings of a lady; and though we must face the fact that in England her income would hardly maintain her in the lower middle class—

DOYLE [*interrupting*] Now look here, Tom. That reminds me. When you go to Ireland, just drop talking about the middle class and bragging of belonging to it. In Ireland youre either a gentleman or youre not. If you want to be particularly offensive to Nora, you can call her a Papist; but if you call her a middle-class woman, Heaven help you!

BROADBENT [*irrepressible*] Never fear. Youre all descended from the ancient kings: I know that. [*Complacently*] I'm not so tactless as you think, my boy. [*Earnest again*] I expect to find Miss Reilly a perfect lady; and I strongly advise you to come and have another look at her before you make up your mind about her. By the way, have you a photograph of her?

DOYLE. Her photographs stopped at twenty-five.

BROADBENT [*saddened*] Ah yes, I suppose so. [*With feeling, severely*] Larry: youve treated that poor girl disgracefully.

DOYLE. By George, if she only knew that two men were talking about her like this—!

BROADBENT. She wouldnt like it, would she? Of course not. We ought to be ashamed of ourselves, Larry. [*More and more carried away by his new fancy*]. You know, I have a sort of presentiment that Miss Reilly is a very superior woman.

DOYLE [*staring hard at him*] Oh! you have, have you?

BROADBENT. Yes I have. There is something very touching about the history of this beautiful girl.

DOYLE. Beau—! Oho! Heres a chance for Nora! and for me! [*Calling*] Hodson.

HODSON [*appearing at the bedroom door*] Did you call, sir?

DOYLE. Pack for me too. I'm going to Ireland with Mr Broadbent.

HODSON. Right, sir. [*He retires into the bedroom*].

BROADBENT [*clapping Doyle on the shoulder*] Thank you, old chap. Thank you.

Act Two

Rosscullen. Westward a hillside of granite rock and heather slopes upward across the prospect from south to north. A huge stone stands on it in a naturally impossible place, as if it had been tossed up there by a giant. Over the brow, in the desolate valley beyond, is a round tower. A lonely white high road trending away westward past the tower loses itself at the foot of the far mountains. It is evening; and there are great breadths of silken green in the Irish sky. The sun is setting.

A man with the face of a young saint, yet with white hair and perhaps 50 years on his back, is standing near the stone in a trance of intense melancholy, looking over the hills as if by mere intensity of gaze he could pierce the glories of the sunset and see into the streets of heaven. He is dressed in black, and is rather more clerical in appearance than most English curates are nowadays; but he does not wear the collar and waistcoat of a parish priest. He is roused from his trance by the chirp of an insect from a tuft of grass in a crevice of the stone. His face relaxes: he turns quietly, and gravely takes off his hat to the tuft, addressing the insect in a brogue which is the jocular assumption of a gentleman and not the natural speech of a peasant.

THE MAN. An is that yourself, Misther Grasshopper? I hope I see you well this fine evenin.

THE GRASSHOPPER [*prompt and shrill in answer*] X.X.

THE MAN [*encouragingly*] Thats right. I suppose now youve come out to make yourself miserable be admyerin the sunset?

THE GRASSHOPPER [*sadly*] X.X.

THE MAN. Aye, youre a thrue Irish grasshopper.

THE GRASSHOPPER [*loudly*] X.X.X.

THE MAN. Three cheers for ould Ireland, is it? That

helps you to face out the misery and the poverty and the torment, doesnt it?

THE GRASSHOPPER [*plaintively*] X.X.

THE MAN. Ah, it's no use, me poor little friend. If you could jump as far as a kangaroo you couldnt jump away from your own heart an its punishment. You can only look at Heaven from here: you cant reach it. There! [*pointing with his stick to the sunset*] thats the gate o glory, isnt it?

THE GRASSHOPPER [*assenting*] X.X.

THE MAN. Sure it's the wise grasshopper yar to know that. But tell me this, Misther Unworldly Wiseman: why does the sight of Heaven wring your heart an mine as the sight of holy wather wrings the heart o the divil? What wickedness have you done to bring that curse on you? Here! where are you jumpin to? Wheres your manners to go skyrocketin like that out o the box in the middle o your confession [*he threatens it with his stick*]?

THE GRASSHOPPER [*penitently*] X.

THE MAN [*lowering the stick*] I accept your apology; but dont do it again. And now tell me one thing before I let you go home to bed. Which would you say this counthry was: hell or purgatory?

THE GRASSHOPPER. X.

THE MAN. Hell! Faith I'm afraid youre right. I wondher what you and me did when we were alive to get sent here.

THE GRASSHOPPER [*shrilly*] X.X.

THE MAN [*nodding*] Well, as you say, it's a delicate subject; and I wont press it on you. Now off widja.

THE GRASSHOPPER. X.X. [*It springs away*].

THE MAN [*waving his stick*] God speed you! [*He walks away past the stone towards the brow of the hill. Immediately a young laborer, his face distorted with terror, slips round from behind the stone.*

THE LABORER [*crossing himself repeatedly*] Oh glory be to God! glory be to God! Oh Holy Mother an all the saints! Oh murdher! murdher! [*Beside himself, calling*] Fadher Keegan! Fadher Keegan!

THE MAN [*turning*] Who's there? Whats that? [*He comes back and finds the laborer, who clasps his knees*] Patsy Farrell! What are you doing here?

PATSY. Oh for the love o God dont lave me here wi dhe grasshopper. I hard it spakin to you. Dont let it do me any harm, Fadher darlint.

KEEGAN. Get up, you foolish man, get up. Are you afraid of a poor insect because I pretended it was talking to me?

PATSY. Oh, it was no pretendin, Fadher dear. Didnt it give three cheers n say it was a divil out o hell? Oh say youll see me safe home, Fadher; n put a blessin on me or somethin [*he moans with terror*].

KEEGAN. What were you doin there, Patsy, listnin? Were you spyin on me?

PATSY. No, Fadher: on me oath an soul I wasnt: I was waitn to meet Masther Larry n carry his luggage from the car; n I fell asleep on the grass; n you woke me talkin to the grasshopper; n I hard its wicked little voice. Oh, d'ye think I'll die before the year's out, Fadher?

KEEGAN. For shame, Patsy! Is that your religion, to be afraid of a little deeshy grasshopper? Suppose it was a divil, what call have you to fear it? If I could ketch it, I'd make you take it home widja in your hat for a penance.

PATSY. Sure, if you wont let it harm me, I'm not afraid, your riverence. [*He gets up, a little reassured. He is a callow, flaxen polled, smoothfaced, downy chinned lad, fully grown but not yet fully filled out, with blue eyes and an instinctively acquired air of helplessness and silliness, indicating, not his real character, but a cunning developed by his constant dread of a hostile dominance, which he habitually tries to disarm and tempt into unmasking by pretending to be a much greater fool than he really is. Englishmen think him half-witted, which is exactly what he intends them to think. He is clad in corduroy trousers, unbuttoned waistcoat, and coarse blue striped shirt*].

KEEGAN [*admonitorily*] Patsy: what did I tell you about callin me Father Keegan an your reverence? What did Father Dempsey tell you about it?

PATSY. Yis, Fadher.

KEEGAN. Father!

PATSY [*desperately*] Arra, hwat am I to call you? Fadher Dempsey sez youre not a priest; n we all know youre not a man; n how do we know what ud happen to us if we shewed any disrespect to you? N sure they say wanse a priest always a priest.

KEEGAN [*sternly*] It's not for the like of you, Patsy, to go behind the instruction of your parish priest and set yourself up to judge whether your Church is right or wrong.

PATSY. Sure I know that, sir.

KEEGAN. The Church let me be its priest as long as it thought me fit for its work. When it took away my papers it meant you to know that I was only a poor madman, unfit and unworthy to take charge of the souls of the people.

PATSY. But wasnt it only because you knew more Latn than Father Dempsey that he was jealous of you?

KEEGAN [*scolding him to keep himself from smiling*] How dar you, Patsy Farrell, put your own wicked little spites and foolishnesses into the heart of your priest? For two pins I'd tell him what you just said.

PATSY [*coaxing*] Sure you wouldnt—

KEEGAN. Wouldnt I? God forgive you! youre little better than a heathen.

PATSY. Deedn I am, Fadher: it's me bruddher the tinsmith in Dublin youre thinkin of. Sure he had to be a free-thinker when he larnt a thrade and went to live in the town.

KEEGAN. Well, he'll get to Heaven before you if youre not careful, Patsy. And now you listen to me, once and for all. Youll talk to me and pray for me by the name of Pether Keegan, so you will. And when youre angry and tempted to lift your hand agen the donkey or stamp your foot on the little grasshopper, remember that the donkey's Pether Keegan's brother, and the grasshopper Pether Keegan's friend. And when youre tempted to throw a stone at a sinner or a curse at a beggar, remember that Pether Keegan is a worse sinner and a worse beggar, and keep the stone and the curse for him the next time you meet him. Now say God bless you, Pether, to me before I go, just to practise you a bit.

PATSY. Sure it wouldnt be right, Fadher. I cant—

KEEGAN. Yes you can. Now out with it; or I'll put this stick into your hand an make you hit me with it.

PATSY [*throwing himself on his knees in an ecstasy of adoration*] Sure it's your blessin I want, Fadher Keegan. I'll have no luck widhout it.

KEEGAN [*shocked*] Get up out o that, man. Dont kneel to me: I'm not a saint.

PATSY [*with intense conviction*] Oh in throth yar, sir. [*The grasshopper chirps. Patsy, terrified, clutches at Keegan's hands*] Dont set it on me, Fadher: I'll do anythin you bid me.

KEEGAN [*pulling him up*] You bosthoon, you! Dont you see that it only whistled to tell me Miss Reilly's comin? There! Look at her and pull yourself together for shame. Off widja to the road: youll be late for the car if you dont make haste [*bustling him down the hill*]. I can see the dust of it in the gap already.

PATSY. The Lord save us! [*He goes down the hill towards the road like a haunted man*].

Nora Reilly comes down the hill. A slight weak woman in a pretty muslin print gown (her best), she is a figure commonplace enough to Irish eyes; but on the inhabitants of fatter-fed, crowded, hustling and bustling modern countries she makes a very different impression. The absence of any symptoms of coarseness or hardness or appetite in her, her comparative delicacy of manner and sensibility of apprehension, her fine hands and frail figure, her novel accent, with the caressing plaintive Irish melody of her speech, give her a charm which is all the more effective because, being untravelled, she is unconscious of it, and never dreams of deliberately dramatizing and exploiting it, as the Irishwomen in England do. For Tom Broadbent therefore, an attractive woman, whom he would even call ethereal. To Larry Doyle, an everyday woman fit only for the eighteenth century, helpless, useless, almost sexless, an invalid without the excuse of disease, an incarnation of everything in Ireland that drove him out of it. These judgments have little value and no finality; but they are the judgments on which her fate hangs just at present. Keegan touches his hat to her: he does not take it off.

NORA. Mr. Keegan: I want to speak to you a minute if you dont mind.

KEEGAN [*dropping the broad Irish vernacular of his speech to Patsy*] An hour if you like, Miss Reilly: youre always welcome. Shall we sit down?

NORA. Thank you. [*They sit on the heather. She is shy and anxious; but she comes to the point promptly because she can think of nothing else*]. They say you did a gradle o travelling at one time.

KEEGAN. Well, you see I'm not a Mnooth man [*he means that he was not a student at Maynooth College*]. When I was young I admired the older generation of priests that had been educated in Salamanca. So when I felt sure of my vocation I went to Salamanca. Then I walked from Salamanca to Rome, an sted in a monastery there for a year. My pilgrimage to Rome taught me that walking is a better way of travelling than the train; so I walked from Rome to the Sorbonne in Paris; and I wish I could have walked from Paris to Oxford; for I was very sick on the sea. After a year of Oxford I had to walk to Jerusalem to walk the Oxford feeling off me. From Jerusalem I came back to Patmos, and spent six months at the monastery of Mount Athos. From that I came to Ireland and settled down as a parish priest until I went mad.

NORA [*startled*] Oh dont say that.

KEEGAN. Why not? Dont you know the story ? how I confessed a black man and gave him absolution? and how he put a spell on me and drove me mad?

NORA. How can you talk such nonsense about yourself? For shame!

KEEGAN. It's not nonsense at all: it's true—in a way. But never mind the black man. Now that you know what a travelled man I am, what can I do for you? [*She hesitates and plucks nervously at the heather. He stays her hand gently*]. Dear Miss Nora: dont pluck the little flower. If it was a pretty baby you wouldnt want to pull its head off and stick it in a vawse o water to look at. [*The grasshopper chirps: Keegan turns his head and addresses it in the vernacular*]. Be aisy, me son: she wont spoil the swing-swong in your little three. [*To Nora, resuming his urbane style*] You see I'm quite cracked; but never mind: I'm harmless. Now what is it?

NORA [*embarrassed*] Oh, only idle curiosity. I wanted to know whether you found Ireland—I mean the country part of Ireland, of course—very small and backwardlike when you came back to it from Rome and Oxford and all the great cities.

KEEGAN. When I went to those great cities I saw wonders I had never seen in Ireland. But when I came back to Ireland I found all the wonders there waiting for me. You see they had been there all the time; but my eyes had never been opened to them. I did not know what my own house was like, because I had never been outside it.

NORA. D'ye think thats the same with everybody?

KEEGAN. With everybody who has eyes in his soul as well as in his head.

NORA. But really and truly now, werent the people rather disappointing? I should think the girls must have seemed rather coarse and dowdy after the foreign princesses and people? But I suppose a priest wouldnt notice that.

KEEGAN. It's a priest's business to notice everything. I wont tell you all I noticed about women; but I'll tell you this. The more a man knows, and the farther he travels, the more likely he is to marry a country girl afterwards.

NORA [*blushing with delight*] Youre joking, Mr Keegan: I'm sure yar.

KEEGAN. My way of joking is to tell the truth. It's the funniest joke in the world.

NORA [*incredulous*] Galong with you!

KEEGAN [*springing up actively*] Shall we go down to the road and meet the car? [*She gives him her hand and he helps her up*]. Patsy Farrell told me you were expecting young Doyle.

NORA [*tossing her chin up at once*] Oh, I'm not expecting him particularly. It's a wonder he's come back at all. After staying away eighteen years he can harly expect us to be very anxious to see him: can he now?

KEEGAN. Well, not anxious perhaps; but you will be curious to see how much he's changed in all these years.

NORA [*with a sudden bitter flush*] I suppose thats all that brings him back to look at us, just to see how much weve changed. Well, he can wait and see me be candlelight: I didnt come out to meet him: I'm going to walk to the Round Tower [*going west across the hill*].

KEEGAN. You couldnt do better this fine evening. [*Gravely*] I'll tell him where youve gone. [*She turns as if to forbid him; but the deep understanding in his eyes makes that impossible; and she only looks at him earnestly and goes. He watches her disappear on the other side of the hill; then says*] Aye, he's come to torment you; and youre driven already to torment him. [*He shakes his head, and goes slowly away across the hill in the opposite direction, lost in thought*].

By this time the car has arrived, and dropped three of its passengers on the high road at the foot of the hill. It is a monster jaunting car, black and dilapidated, one of the last survivors of the public vehicles known to earlier generations as Beeyankiny cars, the Irish having laid violent tongues on the name of their projector, one Bianconi, an enterprising Italian. The three passengers are the parish priest, Father Dempsey; Cornelius Doyle, Larry's father; and Broadbent, all in overcoats and as stiff as only an Irish car could make them.

The priest, stout and fatherly, falls far short of that finest type of countryside pastor which represents the genius of priesthood; but he is equally far above the base type in which a strongminded unscrupulous peasant uses the Church to extort money, power, and privilege. He is a priest neither by vocation nor ambition, but because the life suits him. He has boundless authority over his flock, and taxes them stiffly enough to be a rich man. The old Protestant ascendency is now too broken to gall him. On the whole, an easygoing, amiable, even modest man as long as his dues are paid and his authority and dignity fully admitted.

Cornelius Doyle is an elder of the small wiry type, with a hardskinned, rather worried face, clean shaven except for sandy whiskers blanching into a lustreless pale yellow and quite white at the roots. His dress is that of a country-town man of business: that is, an oldish shooting suit, with elastic sided boots quite unconnected with shooting. Feeling shy with Broadbent, he is hasty, which is his way of trying to appear genial.

Broadbent, for reasons which will appear later, has no luggage except a field glass and a guide book. The other two have left theirs to the unfortunate Patsy Farrell, who struggles up the hill after them, loaded with a sack of potatoes, a hamper, a fat goose, a colossal salmon, and several paper parcels.

Cornelius leads the way up the hill, with Broadbent at his heels. The priest follows. Patsy lags laboriously behind.

CORNELIUS. This is a bit of a climb, Mr Broadbent; but it's shorter than goin round be the road.

BROADBENT [*stopping to examine the great stone*] Just a moment, Mr Doyle: I want to look at this stone. It must be Finian's die-cast.

CORNELIUS [*in blank bewilderment*] Hwat?

BROADBENT. Murray describes it. One of your great national heroes—I cant pronounce the name—Finian Somebody, I think.

FATHER DEMPSEY [*also perplexed, and rather scandalized*] Is it Fin McCool you mean?

BROADBENT. I daresay it is. [*Referring to the guide book*] Murray says that a huge stone, probably of Druidic origin, is still pointed out as the die cast by Fin in his celebrated match with the devil.

CORNELIUS [*dubiously*] Jeuce a word I ever heard of it!

FATHER DEMPSEY [*very seriously indeed, and even a little severely*] Dont believe any such nonsense, sir. There never was any such thing. When people talk to you about Fin McCool and the like, take no notice of them. It's all idle stories and superstition.

BROADBENT [*somewhat indignantly; for to be rebuked by an Irish priest for superstition is more than he can stand*] You dont suppose I believe it, do you?

FATHER DEMPSEY. Oh, I thought you did. D'ye see the top o the Roun Tower there? thats an antiquity worth lookin at.

BROADBENT [*deeply interested*] Have you any theory as to what the Round Towers were for?

FATHER DEMPSEY [*a little offended*] A theory? Me! [*Theories are connected in his mind with the late Professor Tyndall, and with scientific scepticism generally: also perhaps with the view that the Round Towers are phallic symbols*].

CORNELIUS [*remonstrating*] Father Dempsey is the priest of the parish, Mr Broadbent. What would he be doing with a theory?

FATHER DEMPSEY [*with gentle emphasis*] I have a knowledge of what the Roun Towers were, if thats what you mean. They are the forefingers of the early Church, pointing us all to God.

Patsy, intolerably overburdened, loses his balance, and sits down involuntarily. His burdens are scattered over the hillside. Cornelius and Father Dempsey turn furiously on him, leaving Broadbent beaming at the stone and the tower with fatuous interest.

CORNELIUS. Oh, be the hokey, the sammin's broke in two! You schoopid ass, what d'ye mean?

FATHER DEMPSEY. Are you drunk, Patsy Farrell? Did I tell you to carry that hamper carefully or did I not?

PATSY [*rubbing the back of his head, which has almost dinted a slab of granite*] Sure me fut slipt. Howkn I carry three men's luggage at wanst?

FATHER DEMPSEY. You were told to leave behind what you couldnt carry, an go back for it.

PATSY. An whose things was I to lave behind? Hwat would your reverence think if I left your hamper behind in the wet grass; n hwat would the masther say if I left the sammin and the goose be the side o the road for annywan to pick up?

CORNELIUS. Oh, youve a dale to say for yourself, you butther-fingered omadhaun. Waitll Ant Judy sees the state o that sammin: she'll talk to you. Here! gimmy that birdn that fish there; an take Father Dempsey's hamper to his house for him; n them come back for the rest.

FATHER DEMPSEY. Do, Patsy. And mind you dont fall down again.

PATSY. Sure I—

CORNELIUS [*bustling him up the hill*] Whisht! heres Ant Judy. [*Patsy goes grumbling in disgrace, with Father Dempsey's hamper*].

Aunt Judy comes down the hill, a woman of 50, in no way remarkable, lively and busy without energy or grip, placid without tranquillity, kindly without concern for others indeed without much concern for herself: a contented product of a narrow, strainless life. She wears her hair parted in the middle and quite smooth, with a flattened bun at the back. Her dress is a plain brown frock, with a woollen pel-

erine of black and aniline mauve over her shoulders, all very trim in honor of the occasion. She looks round for Larry; is puzzled; then stares incredulously at Broadbent.

AUNT JUDY. Surely to goodness thats not you, Larry!

CORNELIUS. Arra how could he be Larry, woman alive? Larry's in no hurry home, it seems. I havnt set eyes on him. This is his friend, Mr Broadbent. Mr Broadbent: me sister Judy.

AUNT JUDY [*hospitably: going to Broadbent and shaking hands heartily*] Mr Broadbent! Fancy me takin you for Larry! Sure we havnt seen a sight of him for eighteen years, n he ony a lad when he left us.

BROADBENT. It's not Larry's fault: he was to have been here before me. He started in our motor an hour before Mr Doyle arrived, to meet us at Athenmullet, intending to get here long before me.

AUNT JUDY. Lord save us! do you think he's had n axidnt?

BROADBENT. No: he's wired to say he's had a break-down and will come on as soon as he can. He expects to be here at about ten.

AUNT JUDY. There now! Fancy him trustn himself in a motor and we all expectn him! Just like him! he'd never do anything like anybody else. Well, what cant be cured must be injoored. Come on in, all of you. You must be dyin for your tea, Mr Broadbent.

BROADBENT [*with a slight start*] Oh, I'm afraid it's too late for tea [*he looks at his watch*].

AUNT JUDY. Not a bit: we never have it airlier than this. I hope they gave you a good dinner at Athenmullet.

BROADBENT [*trying to conceal his consternation as he realizes that he is not going to get any dinner after his drive*] Oh—er—excellent, excellent. By the way, hadnt I better see about a room at the hotel? [*They stare at him*].

CORNELIUS. The hotel!

FATHER DEMPSEY. Hwat hotel?

AUNT JUDY. Indeed youre not goin to a hotel. Youll stay with us. I'd have put you into Larry's room, ony the boy's pallyass is too short for you; but we'll make a comfortable bed for you on the sofa in the parlor.

BROADBENT. Youre very kind, Miss Doyle; but really I'm ashamed to give you so much trouble unnecessarily. I shant mind the hotel in the least.

FATHER DEMPSEY. Man alive! theres no hotel in Rosscullen.

BROADBENT. No hotel! Why, the driver told me there was the finest hotel in Ireland here. [*They regard him joylessly*].

AUNT JUDY. Arra would you mind what the like of him would tell you? Sure he'd say hwatever was the least trouble to himself and the pleasantest to you, thinkin you might give him a thruppeny bit for himself or the like.

BROADBENT. Perhaps theres a public house.

FATHER DEMPSEY [*grimly*] Theres seventeen.

AUNT JUDY. Ah then, how could you stay at a public house? theyd have no place to put you even if it was a right place for you to go. Come! is it the sofa youre afraid of? If it is, you can have me own bed. I can sleep with Nora.

BROADBENT. Not at all, not at all: I should be only too delighted. But to upset your arrangements in this way—

CORNELIUS [*anxious to cut short the discussion, which makes him ashamed of his house; for he guesses Broadbent's standard of comfort a little more accurately than his sister does*] Thats all right: itll be no trouble at all. Hweres Nora?

AUNT JUDY. Oh, how do I know? She slipped out a little while ago: I thought she was goin to meet the car.

CORNELIUS [*dissatisfied*] It's a queer thing of her to run out o the way at such a time.

AUNT JUDY. Sure she's a queer girl altogether. Come. Come in: come in.

FATHER DEMPSEY. I'll say good-night, Mr Broadbent. If there is anything I can do for you in this parish, let me know. [*He shakes hands with Broadbent*].

BROADBENT [*effusively cordial*] Thank you, Father Dempsey. Delighted to have met you, sir.

FATHER DEMPSEY [*passing on to Aunt Judy*] Good-night, Miss Doyle.

AUNT JUDY. Wont you stay to tea?

FATHER DEMPSEY. Not to-night, thank you kindly: I have business to do at home. [*He turns to go, and meets Patsy Farrell returning unloaded*]. Have you left that hamper for me?

PATSY. Yis, your reverence.

FATHER DEMPSEY. Thats a good lad [*going*].

PATSY [*to Aunt Judy*] Fadher Keegan sez—

FATHER DEMPSEY [*turning sharply on him*] Whats that you say?

PATSY [*frightened*] Fadher Keegan—

FATHER DEMPSEY. How often have you heard me bid you call Mister Keegan in his proper name, the same as I do? Father Keegan indeed! Cant you tell the difference between your priest and any ole madman in a black coat?

PATSY. Sure I'm afraid he might put a spell on me.

FATHER DEMPSEY [*wrathfully*] You mind what I tell you or I'll put a spell on you thatll make you lep. D'ye mind that now? [*He goes home*].

Patsy goes down the hill to retrieve the fish, the bird, and the sack.

AUNT JUDY. Ah, hwy cant you hold your tongue, Patsy, before Father Dempsey?

PATSY. Well, hwat was I to do? Father Keegan bid me tell you Miss Nora was gone to the Roun Tower.

AUNT JUDY. An hwy couldnt you wait to tell us until Father Dempsey was gone?

PATSY. I was afeerd o forgetn it; and then may be he'd a sent the grasshopper or the little dark looker into me at night to remind me of it. [*The dark looker is the common grey lizard, which is supposed to walk down the throats of incautious sleepers and cause them to perish in a slow decline*].

CORNELIUS. Yah, you great gaum, you! Widjer grasshoppers and dark lookers! Here: take up them things and let me hear no more o your foolish lip. [*Patsy obeys*]. You can take the sammin under your oxther. [*He wedges the salmon into Patsy's axilla*].

PATSY. I can take the goose too, sir. Put it on me back n gimmy the neck of it in me mouth. [*Cornelius is about to comply thoughtlessly*].

AUNT JUDY [*feeling that Broadbent's presence demands special punctiliousness*] For shame, Patsy! to offer to take the goose in your mouth that we have to eat after you! The masterll bring it in for you.

PATSY. Arra what would a dead goose care for me mouth? [*He takes his load up the hill*].

CORNELIUS. Hwats Nora doin at the Roun Tower?

AUNT JUDY. Oh, the Lord knows! Romancin, I suppose. Praps she thinks Larry would go there to look for her and see her safe home.

BROADBENT. Miss Reilly must not be left to wait and walk home alone at night. Shall I go for her?

AUNT JUDY [*contemptuously*] Arra hwat ud happen to her? Hurry in now, Corny. Come, Mr Broadbent: I left the tea on the hob to draw; and itll be black if we dont go in an drink it.

They go up the hill. It is dusk by this time.

Broadbent does not fare so badly after all at Aunt Judy's board. He gets not only tea and bread-and-butter, but more mutton chops than he has ever conceived it possible to eat at one sitting. There is also a most filling substance called potato cake. Hardly have his fears of being starved been replaced by his first misgiving that he is eating too much and will be sorry for it tomorrow, when his appetite is revived by the production of a bottle of illicitly distilled whisky, called potcheen, which he has read and dreamed of (he calls it pottine) and is now at last to taste. His goodhumor rises almost to excitement before Cornelius shews signs of sleepiness. The contrast between Aunt Judy's table service and that of the south and east coast hotels at which he spends his Fridays-to-Tuesdays when he is in London, seems to him delightfully Irish. The almost total atrophy of any sense of enjoyment in Cornelius, or even any desire for it or toleration of the possibility of life being something better than a round of sordid worries, relieved by tobacco, punch, fine mornings, and petty successes in buying and selling, passes with his guest as the whimsical affectation of a shrewd Irish humorist and incorrigible spendthrift. Aunt Judy seems to him an incarnate joke. The likelihood that the joke will pall after a month or so, and is probably not apparent at any time to born Rossculleners, or that he himself unconsciously entertains Aunt Judy by his fantastic English personality and English mispronunciations, does not occur to him for a moment. In the end he is so charmed, and so loth to go to bed and perhaps dream of prosaic England, that he insists on going out to smoke a cigar and look for Nora Reilly at the Round Tower. Not that any special insistence is needed; for the English inhibitive instinct does not seem to exist in Rosscullen. Just as Nora's liking to miss a meal and stay out at the Round Tower is accepted as a sufficient reason for her doing it, and for the family going to bed and leaving the door open for her, so Broadbent's whim to go out for a late stroll provokes neither hospitable remonstrance nor surprise. Indeed Aunt Judy wants to get rid of him whilst she makes a bed for him on the sofa. So off he goes, full fed, happy and enthusiastic, to explore the valley by moonlight.

The Round Tower stands about half an Irish mile from Rosscullen, some fifty yards south of the road on a knoll with a circle of wild greensward on it. The road once ran over this knoll; but modern engineering has tempered the level to the Beeyankiny car by carrying the road partly round the knoll and partly through a cutting; so that the way from the road to the tower is a footpath up the embankment through furze and brambles.

On the edge of this slope, at the top of the path, Nora is straining her eyes in the moonlight, watching for Larry. At last she gives it up with a sob of impatience, and retreats to the hoary foot of the tower, where she sits down discouraged and cries a little. Then she settles herself resignedly to wait, and hums a song—not an Irish melody, but a hackneyed English drawing room ballad of the season before last—until some slight noise suggests a footstep, when she springs up eagerly and runs to the edge of the slope again. Some moments of silence and suspense follow, broken by unmistakable footsteps. She gives a little gasp as she sees a man approaching.

NORA. Is that you, Larry? [*Frightened a little*] Who's that?

BROADBENT'S *voice from below on the path.* Dont be alarmed.

NORA. Oh, what an English accent youve got!

BROADBENT [*rising into view*] I must introduce myself—

NORA [*violently startled, retreating*] It's not you! Who are you? What do you want?

BROADBENT [*advancing*] I'm really so sorry to have alarmed you, Miss Reilly. My name is Broadbent. Larry's friend, you know.

NORA [*chilled*] And has Mr Doyle not come with you?

BROADBENT. No. Ive come instead. I hope I am not unwelcome.

NORA [*deeply mortified*] I'm sorry Mr Doyle should have given you the trouble, I'm sure.

BROADBENT. You see, as a stranger and an Englishman, I thought it would be interesting to see the Round Tower by moonlight.

NORA. Oh, you came to see the tower. I thought— [*confused, trying to recover her manners*] Oh, of course. I was so startled. It's a beautiful night, isnt it?

BROADBENT. Lovely. I must explain why Larry has not come himself.

NORA. Why should he come? He's seen the tower often enough: it's no attraction to him. [*Genteelly*] An what do you think of Ireland, Mr Broadbent? Have you ever been here before?

BROADBENT. Never.

NORA. An how do you like it?

BROADBENT [*suddenly betraying a condition of extreme sentimentality*] I can hardly trust myself to say how much I like it. The magic of this Irish scene, and—I really dont want to be personal, Miss Reilly; but the charm of your Irish voice—

NORA [*quite accustomed to gallantry, and attaching no seriousness whatever to it*] Oh, get along with you, Mr Broadbent! Youre breaking your heart about me already, I daresay, after seeing me for two minutes in the dark.

BROADBENT. The voice is just as beautiful in the dark, you know. Besides, Ive heard a great deal about you from Larry.

NORA [*with bitter indifference*] Have you now? Well, thats a great honor, I'm sure.

BROADBENT. I have looked forward to meeting you more than to anything else in Ireland.

NORA [*ironically*] Dear me! did you now?

BROADBENT. I did really. I wish you had taken half as much interest in me.

NORA. Oh, I was dying to see you, of course. I daresay you can imagine the sensation an Englishman like you would make among us poor Irish people.

BROADBENT. Ah, now youre chaffing me, Miss Reilly: you know you are. You mustnt chaff me. I'm very much in earnest about Ireland and everything Irish. I'm very much in earnest about you and about Larry.

NORA. Larry has nothing to do with me, Mr Broadbent.

BROADBENT. If I really thought that, Miss Reilly, I should—well, I should let myself feel that charm of which I spoke just now more deeply than I—than I—

NORA. Is it making love to me you are?

BROADBENT [*scared and much upset*] On my word I believe I am, Miss Reilly. If you say that to me again I shant answer for myself: all the harps of Ireland are in your voice. [*She laughs at him. He suddenly loses his head and seizes her arms, to her great indignation*]. Stop laughing: do you hear? I am in earnest: in English earnest. When I say a thing like that to a woman, I mean it. [*Releasing her and trying to recover his ordinary manner in spite of his bewildering emotion*] I beg your pardon.

NORA. How dare you touch me?

BROADBENT. There are not many things I would not

dare for you. That does not sound right perhaps; but I really—[*he stops and passes his hand over his forehead, rather lost*].

NORA. I think you ought to be ashamed. I think if you were a gentleman, and me alone with you in this place at night, you would die rather than do such a thing.

BROADBENT. You mean that it's an act of treachery to Larry?

NORA. Deed I dont. What has Larry to do with it? It's an act of disrespect and rudeness to me: it shews what you take me for. You can go your way now; and I'll go mine. Goodnight, Mr Broadbent.

BROADBENT. No, please, Miss Reilly. One moment. Listen to me. I'm serious: I'm desperately serious. Tell me that I'm interfering with Larry; and I'll go straight from this spot back to London and never see you again. Thats on my honor: I will. Am I interfering with him?

NORA [*answering in spite of herself in a sudden spring of bitterness*] I should think you ought to know better than me whether youre interfering with him. Youve seen him oftener than I have. You know him better than I do, by this time. Youve come to me quicker than he has, havnt you?

BROADBENT. I'm bound to tell you, Miss Reilly, that Larry has not arrived in Rosscullen yet. He meant to get here before me; but his car broke down; and he may not arrive until to-morrow.

NORA [*her face lighting up*] Is that the truth?

BROADBENT. Yes: thats the truth. [*She gives a sigh of relief*]. Youre glad of that?

NORA [*up in arms at once*] Glad indeed! Why should I be glad? As weve waited eighteen years for him we can afford to wait a day longer, I should think.

BROADBENT. If you really feel like that about him, there may be a chance for another man yet. Eh?

NORA [*deeply offended*] I suppose people are different in England, Mr Broadbent; so perhaps you dont mean any harm. In Ireland nobody'd mind what a man'd say in fun, nor take advantage of what a woman might say in answer to it. If a woman couldnt talk to a man for two minutes at their first meeting without being treated the way youre treating me, no decent woman would ever talk to a man at all.

BROADBENT. I dont understand that. I dont admit that. I am sincere; and my intentions are perfectly honorable. I think you will accept the fact that I'm an Englishman as a guarantee that I am not a man to act hastily or romantically; though I confess that your voice had such an extraordinary effect on me just now when you asked me so quaintly whether I was making love to you—

NORA [*flushing*] I never thought—

BROADBENT [*quickly*] Of course you didnt: I'm not so stupid as that. But I couldnt bear your laughing at the feeling it gave me. You—[*again struggling with a surge of emotion*] you dont know what I—[*he chokes for a moment and then blurts out with unnatural steadiness*] Will you be my wife?

NORA [*promptly*] Deed I wont. The idea! [*Looking at him more carefully*] Arra, come home, Mr Broadbent; and get your senses back again. I think youre not accustomed to potcheen punch in the evening after your tea.

BROADBENT [*horrified*] Do you mean to say that I—I—I—my God! that I appear drunk to you, Miss Reilly?

NORA [*compassionately*] How many tumblers had you?

BROADBENT [*helplessly*] Two.

NORA. The flavor of the turf prevented you noticing the strength of it. Youd better come home to bed.

BROADBENT [*fearfully agitated*] But this is such a horrible doubt to put into my mind—to—to—For Heaven's sake, Miss Reilly, am I really drunk?

NORA [*soothingly*] Youll be able to judge better in the morning. Come on now back with me, an think no more about it. [*She takes his arm with motherly solicitude and urges him gently towards the path*].

BROADBENT [*yielding in despair*] I must be drunk: frightfully drunk; for your voice drove me out of my senses—[*he stumbles over a stone*]. No: on my word, on my most sacred word of honor, Miss Reilly, I tripped over that stone. It was an accident: it was indeed.

NORA. Yes, of course it was. Just take my arm, Mr Broadbent, while we're goin down the path to the road. Youll be all right then.

BROADBENT [*submissively taking it*] I cant sufficiently apologize, Miss Reilly, or express my sense of your kindness when I am in such a disgusting state. How could I be such a bea—[*he trips again*] damn the heather! my foot caught in it.

NORA. Steady now, steady. Come along: come. [*He is led down to the road in the character of a convicted drunkard. To him there is something divine in the sympathetic indulgence she substitutes for the angry disgust with which one of his own countrywomen would resent his supposed condition. And he has no suspicion of the fact, or of her ignorance of it, that when an Englishman is sentimental he behaves very much as an Irishman does when he is drunk*].

Act Three

Next morning Broadbent and Larry are sitting at the ends of a breakfast table in the middle of a small grass plot before Cornelius Doyle's house. They have finished their meal, and are buried in newspapers. Most of the crockery is crowded upon a large square black tray of japanned metal. The teapot is of brown delft ware. There is no silver; and the butter on a dinner plate, is en bloc. The background to this breakfast is the house, a small white slated building, accessible by a half-glazed door. A person coming out into the garden by this door would find the table straight in front of him, and a gate leading to the road half way down the garden on his right; or, if he turned sharp to his left, he could pass round the end of the house through an unkempt shrubbery. The mutilated remnant of a huge plaster statue, nearly dissolved by the rains of a century, and vaguely resembling a majestic female in Roman draperies, with a wreath in her hand, stands neglected amid the laurels. Such statues, though apparently works of art, grow naturally in Irish gardens. Their germination is a mystery to the oldest inhabitants, to whose means and tastes they are totally foreign.

There is a rustic bench, much soiled by the birds, and decorticated and split by the weather, near the little gate. At the opposite side, a basket lies unmolested because it might as well be there as anywhere else. An empty chair at the table was lately occupied by Cornelius, who has finished his breakfast and gone in to the room in which he receives rents and keeps his books and cash, known in the household as "the office." This chair, like the two occupied by Larry and Broadbent, has a mahogany frame and is upholstered in black horsehair.

Larry rises and goes off through the shrubbery with his newspaper. Hodson comes in through the garden gate, dis-

consolate. Broadbent, who sits facing the gate, augurs the worst from his expression.

BROADBENT. Have you been to the village?

HODSON. No use, sir. We'll have to get everything from London by parcel post.

BROADBENT. I hope they made you comfortable last night.

HODSON. I was no worse than you were on that sofa, sir. One expects to rough it here, sir.

BROADBENT. We shall have to look out for some other arrangement. [*Cheering up irrepressibly*] Still, it's no end of a joke. How do you like the Irish, Hodson?

HODSON. Well, sir, theyre all right anywhere but in their own country. Ive known lots of em in England, and generally liked em. But here, sir, I seem simply to hate em. The feeling come over me the moment we landed at Cork, sir. It's no use pretendin, sir: I cant bear em. My mind rises up agin their ways, somehow: they rub me the wrong way all over.

BROADBENT. Oh, their faults are on the surface: at heart they are one of the finest races on earth. [*Hodson turns away, without affecting to respond to his enthusiasm*]. By the way, Hodson—

HODSON [*turning*] Yes, sir.

BROADBENT. Did you notice anything about me last night when I came in with that lady?

HODSON [*surprised*] No, sir.

BROADBENT. Not any—er—? You may speak frankly.

HODSON. I didnt notice nothing, sir. What sort of thing did you mean, sir?

BROADBENT. Well—er—er—well, to put it plainly, was I drunk?

HODSON [*amazed*] No, sir.

BROADBENT. Quite sure?

HODSON. Well, I should a said rather the opposite, sir. Usually when youve been enjoying yourself, youre a bit hearty like. Last night you seemed rather low, if anything.

BROADBENT. I certainly have no headache. Did you try the pottine, Hodson?

HODSON. I just took a mouthful, sir. It tasted of peat: oh! something horrid, sir. The people here call peat turf. Potcheen and strong porter is what they like, sir. I'm sure I dont know how they can stand it. Give me beer, I say.

BROADBENT. By the way, you told me I couldnt have porridge for breakfast; but Mr Doyle had some.

HODSON. Yes, sir. Very sorry, sir. They call it stirabout, sir: thats how it was. They know no better, sir.

BROADBENT. All right: I'll have some tomorrow.

Hodson goes to the house. When he opens the door he finds Nora and Aunt Judy on the threshold. He stands aside to let them pass, with the air of a well trained servant oppressed by heavy trials. Then he goes in. Broadbent rises. Aunt Judy goes to the table and collects the plates and cups on the tray. Nora goes to the back of the rustic seat and looks out at the gate with the air of a woman accustomed to have nothing to do. Larry returns from the shrubbery.

BROADBENT. Good morning, Miss Doyle.

AUNT JUDY [*thinking it absurdly late in the day for such a salutation*] Oh, good morning. [*Before moving his plate*] Have you done?

BROADBENT. Quite, thank you. You must excuse us for not waiting for you. The country air tempted us to get up early.

AUNT JUDY. N d'ye call this airly, God help you?

LARRY. Aunt Judy probably breakfasted about half past six.

AUNT JUDY. Whisht, you! draggin the parlor chairs

out into the gardn n givin Mr Broadbent his death over his meals out here in the cold air. [*To Broadbent*] Why d'ye put up with his foolishness, Mr Broadbent?

BROADBENT. I assure you I like the open air.

AUNT JUDY. Ah galong! How can you like whats not natural? I hope you slept well.

NORA. Did anything wake yup with a thump at three o'clock? I thought the house was falling. But then I'm a very light sleeper.

LARRY. I seem to recollect that one of the legs of the sofa in the parlor had a way of coming out unexpectedly eighteen years ago. Was that it, Tom?

BROADBENT [*hastily*] Oh, it doesnt matter: I was not hurt—at least—er—

AUNT JUDY. Oh now what a shame! An I told Patsy Farrll to put a nail in it.

BROADBENT. He did, Miss Doyle. There was a nail, certainly.

AUNT JUDY. Dear oh dear!

An oldish peasant farmer, small, leathery, peat-faced, with a deep voice and a surliness that is meant to be aggressive, and is in effect pathetic—the voice of a man of hard life and many sorrows—comes in at the gate. He is old enough to have perhaps worn a long tailed frieze coat and knee breeches in his time; but now he is dressed respectably in a black frock coat, tall hat, and pollard colored trousers; and his face is as clean as washing can make it, though that is not saying much, as the habit is recently acquired and not yet congenial.

THE NEW-COMER [*at the gate*] God save all here! [*He comes a little way into the garden*].

LARRY [*patronizingly, speaking across the garden to him*] Is that yourself, Matt Haffigan? Do you remember me?

MATTHEW [*intentionally rude and blunt*] No. Who are you?

NORA. Oh, I'm sure you remember him, Mr Haffigan.

MATTHEW [*grudgingly admitting it*] I suppose he'll be young Larry Doyle that was.

LARRY. Yes.

MATTHEW [*to Larry*] I hear you done well in America.

LARRY. Fairly well.

MATTHEW. I suppose you saw me brother Andy out dhere.

LARRY. No. It's such a big place that looking for a man there is like looking for a needle in a bundle of hay. They tell me he's a great man out there.

MATTHEW. So he is, God be praised. Wheres your father?

AUNT JUDY. He's inside, in the office, Mr Haffigan, with Barney Doarn n Father Dempsey.

Matthew, without wasting further words on the company, goes curtly into the house.

LARRY [*staring after him*] Is anything wrong with old Matt?

NORA. No. He's the same as ever. Why?

LARRY. He's not the same to me. He used to be very civil to Masther Larry: a deal too civil, I used to think. Now he's as surly and stand-off as a bear.

AUNT JUDY. Oh sure he's bought his farm in the Land Purchase. He's independent now.

NORA. It's made a great change, Larry. Youd harly know the old tenants now. Youd think it was a liberty to speak t'dhem—some o dhem. [*She goes to the table, and helps to take off the cloth, which she and Aunt Judy fold up between them*].

AUNT JUDY. I wonder what he wants to see Corny for. He hasnt been here since he paid the last of his old rent; and then he as good as threw it in Corny's face, I thought.

LARRY. No wonder! Of course they all hated us like the devil. Ugh! [*Moodily*] Ive seen them in that office, telling my father what a fine boy I was, amd plastering him with compliments, with your honor here and your honor there, when all the time their fingers were itching to be at his throat.

AUNT JUDY. Deedn why should they want to hurt poor Corny? It was he that got Matt the lease of his farm, and stood up for him as an industrious decent man.

BROADBENT. Was he industrious? Thats remarkable, you know, in an Irishman.

LARRY. Industrious! That man's industry used to make me sick, even as a boy. I tell you, an Irish peasant's industry is not human: it's worse than the industry of a coral insect. An Englishman has some sense about working: he never does more than he can help—and hard enough to get him to do that without scamping it; but an Irishman will work as if he'd die the moment he stopped. That man Matthew Haffigan and his brother Andy made a farm out of a patch of stones on the hillside: cleared it and dug it with their own naked hands and bought their first spade out of their first crop of potatoes. Talk of making two blades of wheat grow where one grew before! those two men made a whole field of wheat grow where not even a furze bush had ever got its head up between the stones.

BROADBENT. That was magnificent, you know. Only a great race is capable of producing such men.

LARRY. Such fools, you mean! What good was it to them? The moment theyd done it, the landlord put a rent of £5 a year on them, and turned them out because they couldnt pay it.

AUNT JUDY. Why couldnt they pay as well as Billy Byrne that took it after them?

LARRY [*angrily*] You know very well that Billy Byrne never paid it. He only offered it to get possession. He never paid it.

AUNT JUDY. That was because Andy Haffigan hurt him with a brick so that he was never the same again. Andy had to run away to America for it.

BROADBENT [*glowing with indignation*] Who can blame him, Miss Doyle? Who can blame him?

LARRY [*impatiently*] Oh, rubbish! whats the good of the man thats starved out of a farm murdering the man thats starved into it? Would you have done such a thing?

BROADBENT. Yes. I—I—I—I—[*stammering with fury*] I should have shot the confounded landlord, and wrung the neck of the damned agent, and blown the farm up with dynamite, and Dublin Castle along with it.

LARRY. Oh yes: youd have done great things; and a fat lot of good youd have got out of it, too! Thats an Englishman all over! make bad laws and give away all the land, and then, when your economic incompetence produces its natural and inevitable results, get virtuously indignant and kill the people that carry out your laws.

AUNT JUDY. Sure never mind him, Mr Broadbent. It doesnt matter, anyhow, because theres harly any landlords left; and therll soon be none at all.

LARRY. On the contrary, therll soon be nothing else; and the Lord help Ireland then!

AUNT JUDY. Ah, youre never satisfied, Larry. [*To Nora*] Come on, alanna, an make the paste for the pie. We can leave them to their talk. They dont want us [*she takes up the tray and goes into the house*].

BROADBENT [*rising and gallantly protesting*] Oh, Miss Doyle! Really, really—

Nora, following Aunt Judy with the rolled up cloth in her hands, looks at him and strikes him dumb. He watches her until she disappears; then comes to Larry and addresses him with sudden intensity.

BROADBENT. Larry.

LARRY. What is it?

BROADBENT. I got drunk last night, and proposed to Miss Reilly.

LARRY. You hwat??? [*He screams with laughter in the falsetto Irish register unused for that purpose in England*].

BROADBENT. What are you laughing at?

LARRY [*stopping dead*] I dont know. Thats the sort of thing an Irishman laughs at. Has she accepted you?

BROADBENT. I shall never forget that with the chivalry of her nation, though I was utterly at her mercy, she refused me.

LARRY. That was extremely improvident of her. [*Beginning to reflect*] But look here: when were you drunk? You were sober enough when you came back from the Round Tower with her.

BROADBENT. No, Larry, I was drunk, I am sorry to say. I had two tumblers of punch. She had to lead me home. You must have noticed it.

LARRY. I did not.

BROADBENT. She did.

LARRY. May I ask how long it took you to come to business? You can hardly have known her for more than a couple of hours.

BROADBENT. I am afraid it was hardly a couple of minutes. She was not here when I arrived; and I saw her for the first time at the tower.

LARRY. Well, you are a nice infant to be let loose in this country! Fancy the potcheen going to your head like that!

BROADBENT. Not to my head, I think. I have no headache; and I could speak distinctly. No: potcheen goes to the heart, not to the head. What ought I to do?

LARRY. Nothing. What need you do?

BROADBENT. There is rather a delicate moral question involved. The point is, was I drunk enough not to be morally responsible for my proposal? Or was I sober enough to be bound to repeat it now that I am undoubtedly sober?

LARRY. I should see a little more of her before deciding.

BROADBENT. No, no. That would not be right. That would not be fair. I am either under a moral obligation or I am not. I wish I knew how drunk I was.

LARRY. Well, you were evidently in a state of blithering sentimentality, anyhow.

BROADBENT. That is true, Larry: I admit it. Her voice has a most extraordinary effect on me. That Irish voice!

LARRY [*sympathetically*] Yes, I know. When I first went to London I very nearly proposed to walk out with a waitress in an Aerated Bread shop because her Whitechapel accent was so distinguished, so quaintly touching, so pretty—

BROADBENT [*angrily*] Miss Reilly is not a waitress, is she?

LARRY. Oh, come! The waitress was a very nice girl.

BROADBENT. You think every Englishwoman an angel. You really have coarse tastes in that way, Larry. Miss Reilly is one of the finer types: a type rare in England, except perhaps in the best of the aristocracy.

LARRY. Aristocracy be blowed! Do you know what Nora eats?

BROADBENT. Eats! what do you mean?

LARRY. Breakfast: tea and bread-and-butter, with an occasional rasher, and an egg on special occasions: say on her birthday. Dinner in the middle of the day, one course and nothing else. In the evening, tea and bread-and-butter again. You compare her with your Englishwomen who wolf down from three to five meat meals a day; and naturally you find her a sylph. The difference is not a difference of type: it's the difference between the woman who eats not wisely but too well, and the woman who eats not wisely but too little.

BROADBENT [*furious*] Larry: you—you—you disgust me. You are a damned fool. [*He sits down angrily on the rustic seat, which sustains the shock with difficulty*].

LARRY. Steady! stead-eee! [*He laughs and seats himself on the table*].

Cornelius Doyle, Father Dempsey, Barney Doran, and Matthew Haffigan come from the house. Doran is a stout-bodied, short armed, roundheaded, red haired man on the verge of middle age, of sanguine temperament, with an enormous capacity for derisive, obscene, blasphemous, or merely cruel and senseless fun, and a violent and impetuous intolerance of other temperaments and other opinions, all this representing energy and capacity wasted and demoralized by want of sufficient training and social pressure to force it into beneficent activity and build a character with it; for Barney is by no means either stupid or weak. He is recklessly untidy as to his person; but the worst effects of his neglect are mitigated by a powdering of flour and mill dust; and his unbrushed clothes, made of a fashionable tailor's sackcloth, were evidently chosen regardless of expense for the sake of their appearance.

Matthew Haffigan, ill at ease, coasts the garden shyly on the shrubbery side until he anchors near the basket, where he feels least in the way. The priest comes to the table and slaps Larry on the shoulder. Larry, turning quickly, and recognizing Father Dempsey, alights from the table and shakes the priest's hand warmly. Doran comes down the garden between Father Dempsey and

Matt; and Cornelius, on the other side of the table, turns to Broadbent, who rises genially.

CORNELIUS. I think we all met las night.

DORAN. I hadnt that pleasure.

CORNELIUS. To be sure, Barney: I forgot. [*To Broadbent, introducing Barney*] Mr Doran. He owns that fine mill you noticed from the car.

BROADBENT [*delighted with them all*] Most happy, Mr Doran. Very pleased indeed.

Doran, not quite sure whether he is being courted or patronized, nods independently.

DORAN. Hows yourself, Larry?

LARRY. Finely, thank you. No need to ask you. [*Doran grins; and they shake hands*].

CORNELIUS. Give Father Dempsey a chair, Larry.

Matthew Haffigan runs to the nearest end of the table and takes the chair from it, placing it near the basket; but Larry has already taken the chair from the other end and placed it in front of the table. Father Dempsey accepts that more central position.

CORNELIUS. Sit down, Barney, will you; and you, Matt.

Doran takes the chair Matt is still offering to the priest; and poor Matthew, outfaced by the miller, humbly turns the basket upside down and sits on it. Cornelius brings his own breakfast chair from the table and sits down on Father Dempsey's right. Broadbent resumes his seat on the rustic bench. Larry crosses to the bench and is about to sit down beside him when Broadbent holds him off nervously.

BROADBENT. Do you think it will bear two, Larry?

LARRY. Perhaps not. Dont move. I'll stand. [*He posts himself behind the bench*].

They are all now seated, except Larry; and the session assumes a portentous air, as if something important were coming.

CORNELIUS. Praps youll explain, Father Dempsey.

FATHER DEMPSEY. No, no: go on, you: the Church has no politics.

CORNELIUS. Were yever thinkin o goin into parliament at all, Larry?

LARRY. Me!

FATHER DEMPSEY [*encouragingly*] Yes, you. Hwy not?

LARRY. I'm afraid my ideas would not be popular enough.

CORNELIUS. I dont know that. Do you, Barney?

DORAN. Theres too much blatherumskite in Irish politics: a dale too much.

LARRY. But what about your present member? Is he going to retire?

CORNELIUS. No: I dont know that he is.

LARRY [*interrogatively*] Well? then?

MATTHEW [*breaking out with surly bitterness*] Weve had enough of his foolish talk agen lanlords. Hwat call has he to talk about the lan, that never was outside of a city office in his life?

CORNELIUS. We're tired of him. He doesnt know where to stop. Every man cant own land; and some men must own it to employ them. It was all very well when solid men like Doran an Matt were kep from ownin land. But hwat man in his senses ever wanted to give land to Patsy Farrll an dhe like o him?

BROADBENT. But surely Irish landlordism was accountable for what Mr Haffigan suffered.

MATTHEW. Never mind hwat I suffered. I know what I suffered adhout you tellin me. But did I ever ask for more dhan the farm I made wid me own hans? tell me that, Corny Doyle, and you that knows. Was I fit for the responsibility or was I not? [*Snarling angrily at Cornelius*] Am I to be compared to Patsy Farrll, that doesnt harly know his right hand from his left? What did he ever suffer, I'd like to know?

CORNELIUS. Thats just what I say. I wasnt comparin you to your disadvantage.

MATTHEW [*implacable*] Then hwat did you mane be talkin about givin him lan?

DORAN. Aisy, Matt, aisy. Youre like a bear with a sore back.

MATTHEW [*trembling with rage*] An who are you, to offer to taitch me manners?

FATHER DEMPSEY [*admonitorily*] Now, now, now, Matt! none o dhat. How often have I told you youre too ready to take offence where none is meant? You dont understand: Corny Doyle is saying just what you want to have said. [*To Cornelius*] Go on, Mr Doyle; and never mind him.

MATTHEW [*rising*] Well, if me lan is to be given to Patsy and his like, I'm goin oura dhis. I—

DORAN [*with violent impatience*] Arra who's goin to give your lan to Patsy, yowl fool ye?

FATHER DEMPSEY. Aisy, Barney, aisy. [*Sternly, to Matt*] I told you, Matthew Haffigan, that Corny Doyle was sayin nothin against you. I'm sorry your priest's word is not good enough for you. I'll go, sooner than stay to make you commit a sin against the Church. Good morning, gentlemen. [*He rises. They all rise, except Broadbent*].

DORAN [*to Matt*] There! Sarve you dam well right, you cantankerous oul noodle.

MATTHEW [*appalled*] Dont say dhat, Fadher Dempsey. I never had a thought agen you or the Holy Church. I know I'm a bit hasty when I think about the lan. I ax your pardon for it.

FATHER DEMPSEY [*resuming his seat with dignified reserve*] Very well: I'll overlook it this time. [*He sits down.*

The others sit down, except Matthew. Father Dempsey, about to ask Corny to proceed, remembers Matthew and turns to him, giving him just a crumb of graciousness]. Sit down, Matt [*Matthew, crushed, sits down in disgrace, and is silent, his eyes shifting piteously from one speaker to another in an intensely mistrustful effort to understand them*]. Go on, Mr Doyle. We can make allowances. Go on.

CORNELIUS. Well, you see how it is, Larry. Round about here, weve got the land at last; and we want no more Goverment meddlin. We want a new class o man in parliament: one dhat knows dhat the farmer's the real backbone o the country, n doesnt care a snap of his fingers for the shoutn o the riff-raff in the towns, or for the foolishness of the laborers.

DORAN. Aye; an dhat can afford to live in London and pay his own way until Home Rule comes, instead o wantin subscriptions and the like.

FATHER DEMPSEY. Yes: thats a good point, Barney. When too much money goes to politics, it's the Church that has to starve for it. A member of parliament ought to be a help to the Church instead of a burden on it.

LARRY. Heres a chance for you, Tom. What do you say?

BROADBENT [*deprecatory, but important and smiling*] Oh, I have no claim whatever to the seat. Besides, I'm a Saxon.

DORAN. A hwat?

BROADBENT. A Saxon. An Englishman.

DORAN. An Englishman. Bedad I never heard it called dhat before.

MATTHEW [*cunningly*] If I might make so bould, Fadher, I wouldnt say but an English Prodestn mightnt have a more indepindent mind about the lan, an be less afeerd to spake out about it, dhan an Irish Catholic.

CORNELIUS. But sure Larry's as good as English: arnt you, Larry?

LARRY. You may put me out of your head, father, once for all.

CORNELIUS. Arra why?

LARRY. I have strong opinions which wouldnt suit you.

DORAN [*rallying him blatantly*] Is it still Larry the bould Fenian?

LARRY. No: the bold Fenian is now an older and possibly foolisher man.

CORNELIUS. Hwat does it matter to us hwat your opinions are? You know that your father's bought his place here, just the same as Matt's farm n Barney's mill. All we ask now is to be let alone. Youve nothin against that, have you?

LARRY. Certainly I have. I dont believe in letting anybody or anything alone.

CORNELIUS [*losing his temper*] Arra what d'ye mean, you young fool? Here Ive got you the offer of a good seat in parliament; n you think yourself mighty smart to stand there and talk foolishness to me. Will you take it or leave it?

LARRY. Very well: I'll take it with pleasure if youll give it to me.

CORNELIUS [*subsiding sulkily*] Well, why couldnt you say so at once? It's a good job youve made up your mind at last.

DORAN [*suspiciously*] Stop a bit: stop a bit.

MATTHEW [*writhing between his dissatisfaction and his fear of the priest*] It's not because he's your son that he's to get the sate. Fadher Dempsey: wouldnt you think well to ask him what he manes about the lan?

LARRY [*coming down on Matt promptly*] I'll tell you, Matt. I always thought it was a stupid, lazy, good-for-nothing sort of thing to leave the land in the hands of the old landlords without calling them to a strict account for the use they made of it, and the condition of the people on it. I could see for myself that they thought of nothing but what they could get out of it to spend in England; and that they mortgaged and mortgaged until hardly one of them owned his own property or could have afforded to keep it up decently if he'd wanted to. But I tell you plump and plain, Matt, that if anybody thinks things will be any better now that the land is handed over to a lot of little men like you, without calling you to account either, theyre mistaken.

MATTHEW [*sullenly*] What call have you to look down on me? I suppose you think youre everybody because your father was a land agent.

LARRY. What call have you to look down on Patsy Farrell? I suppose you think youre everybody because you own a few fields.

MATTHEW. Was Patsy Farrll ever ill used as I was ill used? tell me dhat.

LARRY. He will be, if ever he gets into your power as you were in the power of your old landlord. Do you think, because youre poor and ignorant and half-crazy with toiling and moiling morning noon and night, that youll be any less greedy and oppressive to them that have no land at all than old Nick Lestrange, who was an educated travelled gentleman that would not have been tempted as hard by a hundred pounds as youd be by five shillings? Nick was too high above Patsy Farrell to be jealous of him; but you, that are only one little step above him, would die sooner than let him come up that step; and well you know it.

MATTHEW [*black with rage, in a low growl*] Lemmy oura dhis. [*He tries to rise; but Doran catches his coat and drags him down again*] I'm goin, I say. [*Raising his voice*] Leggo me coat, Barney Doran.

DORAN. Sit down, yowl omadhaun, you. [*Whispering*] Dont you want to stay an vote agen him?

FATHER DEMPSEY [*holding up his finger*] Matt! [*Matt subsides*]. Now, now, now! come, come! Hwats all dhis about Patsy Farrll? Hwy need you fall out about him?

LARRY. Because it was by using Patsy's poverty to undersell England in the markets of the world that we drove England to ruin Ireland. And she'll ruin us again the moment we lift our heads from the dust if we trade in cheap labor; and serve us right too! If I get into parliament, I'll try to get an Act to prevent any of you from giving Patsy less than a pound a week [*they all start, hardly able to believe their ears*] or working him harder than youd work a horse that cost you fifty guineas.

DORAN. Hwat!!!

CORNELIUS [*aghast*] A pound a—God save us! the boy's mad.

Matthew, feeling that here is something quite beyond his powers, turns openmouthed to the priest, as if looking for nothing less than the summary excommunication of Larry.

LARRY. How is the man to marry and live a decent life on less?

FATHER DEMPSEY. Man alive, hwere have you been living all these years? and hwat have you been dreaming of? Why, some o dhese honest men here cant make that much out o the land for dhemselves, much less give it to a laborer.

LARRY [*now thoroughly roused*] Then let them make room for those who can. Is Ireland never to have a chance? First she was given to the rich; and now that they have gorged on her flesh, her bones are to be flung to the poor, that can do nothing but suck the marrow out of her. If we cant have men of honor own the land, lets have men of ability. If we cant have men with ability, let us at least have men with capital. Anybody's better than Matt, who has neither honor, nor ability, nor capital, nor anything but mere brute labor and greed in him, Heaven help him!

DORAN. Well, we're not all foostherin oul doddherers like Matt. [*Pleasantly, to the subject of this description*] Are we, Matt?

LARRY. For modern industrial purposes you might just as well be, Barney. Youre all children: the big world that I belong to has gone past you and left you. Anyhow, we Irishmen were never made to be farmers; and we'll never do any good at it. We're like the Jews: the Almighty gave us brains, and bid us farm them, and leave the clay and the worms alone.

FATHER DEMPSEY [*with gentle irony*] Oh! is it Jews you want to make of us? I must catechize you a bit meself, I think. The next thing youll be proposing is to repeal the disestablishment of the so-called Irish Church.

LARRY. Yes: why not? [*Sensation*].

MATTHEW [*rancorously*] He's a turncoat.

LARRY. St Peter, the rock on which our Church was built, was crucified head downwards for being a turncoat.

FATHER DEMPSEY [*with a quiet authoritative dignity which checks Doran, who is on the point of breaking out*] Thats true. You hold your tongue as befits your ignorance, Matthew Haffigan; and trust your priest to deal with this young man. Now, Larry Doyle, whatever the blessed St Peter was crucified for, it was not for being a Prodestan. Are you one?

LARRY. No. I am a Catholic intelligent enough to see that the Protestants are never more dangerous to us than when they are free from all alliances with the

State. The so-called Irish Church is stronger today than ever it was.

MATTHEW. Fadher Dempsey: will you tell him dhat me mother's ant was shot and kilt dead in the sthreet o Rosscullen be a soljer in the tithe war? [*Frantically*] He wants to put the tithes on us again. He—

LARRY [*interrupting him with overbearing contempt*] Put the tithes on you again! Did the tithes ever come off you? Was your land any dearer when you paid the tithe to the parson than it was when you paid the same money to Nick Lestrange as rent, and he handed it over to the Church Sustentation Fund? Will you always be duped by Acts of Parliament that change nothing but the necktie of the man that picks your pocket? I'll tell you what I'd do with you, Matt Haffigan: I'd make you pay tithes to your own Church. I want the Catholic Church established in Ireland: thats what I want. Do you think that I, brought up to regard myself as the son of a great and holy Church, can bear to see her begging her bread from the ignorance and superstition of men like you? I would have her as high above worldly want as I would have her above worldly pride or ambition. Aye; and I would have Ireland compete with Rome itself for the chair of St Peter and the citadel of the Church; for Rome, in spite of all the blood of the martyrs, is pagan at heart to this day, while in Ireland the people is the Church and the Church the people.

FATHER DEMPSEY [*startled, but not at all displeased*] Whisht, man! youre worse than mad Pether Keegan himself.

BROADBENT [*who has listened in the greatest astonishment*] You amaze me, Larry. Who would have thought of your coming out like this! [*Solemnly*] But much as I appreciate your really brilliant eloquence, I implore you not to desert the great Liberal principle of Disestablishment.

LARRY. I am not a Liberal: Heaven forbid! A disestablished Church is the worst tyranny a nation can groan under.

BROADBENT [*making a wry face*] Dont be paradoxical, Larry. It really gives me a pain in my stomach.

LARRY. Youll soon find out the truth of it here. Look at Father Dempsey! he is disestablished: he has nothing to hope or fear from the State; and the result is that he's the most powerful man in Rosscullen. The member for Rosscullen would shake in his shoes if Father Dempsey looked crooked at him. [*Father Dempsey smiles, by no means averse to this acknowledgment of his authority*]. Look at yourself! you would defy the established Archbishop of Canterbury ten times a day; but catch you daring to say a word that would shock a Nonconformist! not you. The Conservative party today is the only one thats not priestridden—excuse the expression, Father [*Father Dempsey nods tolerantly*]—because it's the only one that has established its Church and can prevent a clergyman becoming a bishop if he's not a Statesman as well as a Churchman.

He stops. They stare at him dumbfounded, and leave it to the priest to answer him.

FATHER DEMPSEY [*judicially*] Young man: youll not be the member for Rosscullen; but dheres more in your head than the comb will take out.

LARRY. I'm sorry to disappoint you, father; but I told you it would be no use. And now I think the candidate had better retire and leave you to discuss his successor. [*He takes a newspaper from the table and goes away through the shrubbery amid dead silence, all turning to watch him until he passes out of sight round the corner of the house*].

DORAN [*dazed*] Hwat sort of a fella is he at all at all?

FATHER DEMPSEY. He's a clever lad: dheres the making of a man in him yet.

MATTHEW [*in consternation*] D'ye mane to say dhat yll put him into parliament to bring back Nick Lesthrange on me, and to put tithes on me, and to rob me for the like o Patsy Farrll, because he's Corny Doyle's son?

DORAN [*brutally*] Arra hould your whisht: who's goin to send him into parliament? Maybe youd like us to send you dhere to thrate dhem to a little o your anxiety about dhat dirty little podato patch o yours.

MATTHEW [*plaintively*] Am I to be towld dhis afther all me sufferins?

DORAN. Och, I'm tired o your sufferins. Weve been hearin nothin else ever since we was childher but sufferins. Hwen it wasnt yours it was somebody else's; and hwen it was nobody else's it was ould Irelan's. How the divil are we to live on wan anodher's sufferins?

FATHER DEMPSEY. Thats a thrue word, Barney Doarn; only your tongue's a little too familiar wi dhe divil. [*To Matt*] If youd think a little more o the sufferins of the blessed saints, Matt, an a little less o your own, youd find the way shorter from your farm to heaven [*Matt is about to reply*] Dhere now! dhats enough! we know you mean well; an I'm not angry with you.

BROADBENT. Surely, Mr Haffigan, you can see the simple explanation of all this. My friend Larry Doyle is a most brilliant speaker; but he's a Tory: an ingrained old-fashioned Tory.

CORNELIUS. N how d'ye make dhat out, if I might ask you, Mr Broadbent?

BROADBENT [*collecting himself for a political deliverance*] Well, you know, Mr Doyle, theres a strong dash of Toryism in the Irish character. Larry himself says that the great Duke of Wellington was the most typical Irishman that ever lived. Of course, thats an absurd paradox; but still theres a great deal of truth in it. Now I am a Liberal. You know the great principles of the Liberal Party. Peace—

FATHER DEMPSEY [*piously*] Hear! hear!

BROADBENT [*encouraged*] Thank you. Retrenchment—[*he waits for further applause*].

MATTHEW [*timidly*] What might rethrenchment mane now?

BROADBENT. It means an immense reduction in the burden of the rates and taxes.

MATTHEW [*respectfully approving*] Dhats right. Dhats right, sir.

BROADBENT [*perfunctorily*] And, of course, Reform.

CORNELIUS
FATHER DEMPSEY
DORAN } [*conventionally*] Of course.

MATTHEW [*still suspicious*] Hwat does Reform mane, sir? Does it mane altherin annythin dhats as it is now?

BROADBENT [*impressively*] It means, Mr Haffigan, maintaining those reforms which have already been conferred on humanity by the Liberal Party, and trusting for future developments to the free activity of a free people on the basis of those reforms.

DORAN. Dhats right. No more meddlin. We're all right now: all we want is to be let alone.

CORNELIUS. Hwat about Home Rule?

BROADBENT [*rising so as to address them more imposingly*] I really cannot tell you what I feel about Home Rule without using the language of hyperbole.

DORAN. Savin Fadher Dempsey's presence, eh?

BROADBENT [*not understanding him*] Quite so—er—oh yes. All I can say is that as an Englishman I blush for the Union. It is the blackest stain on our national history. I look forward to the time—and it cannot be far distant, gentlemen, because Humanity is looking forward to it too, and insisting on it with no uncertain voice—I look forward to the time when an Irish legislature shall arise once more on the emerald pasture of College Green, and the Union Jack—that detestable symbol of a decadent Imperialism—be replaced by a flag as green as the island over which it waves: a flag on which we shall ask for England only a modest quartering in memory of our great party and of the immortal name of our grand old leader.

DORAN [*enthusiastically*] Dhats the style, begob! [*He smites his knee, and winks at Matt*].

MATTHEW. More power to you, sir!

BROADBENT. I shall leave you now, gentlemen, to your deliberations. I should like to have enlarged on the services rendered by the Liberal Party to the religious faith of the great majority of the people of Ireland; but I shall content myself with saying that in my opinion you should choose no representative who—no matter what his personal creed may be—is not an ardent supporter of freedom of conscience, and is not prepared to prove it by contributions, as lavish as his means will allow, to the great and beneficent work which you, Father Dempsey [*Father Dempsey bows*], are doing for the people of Rosscullen. Nor should the lighter, but still most important question of the sports of the people be forgotten. The local cricket club—

CORNELIUS. The hwat!

DORAN. Nobody plays bat n ball here, if dhats what you mane.

BROADBENT. Well, let us say quoits. I saw two men, I think, last night—but after all, these are questions of detail. The main thing is that your candidate, whoever he may be, shall be a man of some means, able to help the locality instead of burdening it. And if he were a countryman of my own, the moral effect on the House of Commons would be immense! tremendous! Pardon my saying these few words: nobody feels their impertinence more than I do. Good morning, gentlemen.

He turns impressively to the gate, and trots away, congratulating himself, with a little twist of his head and cock of his eye on having done a good stroke of political business.

HAFFIGAN [*awestruck*] Good morning, sir.

THE REST. Good morning. [*They watch him vacantly until he is out of earshot*].

CORNELIUS. Hwat d'ye think, Father Dempsey?

FATHER DEMPSEY [*indulgently*] Well, he hasnt much sense, God help him; but for the matter o that, neether has our present member.

DORAN. Arra musha he's good enough for parliament: what is there to do there but gas a bit, an chivy the Goverment, an vote wi dh Irish party?

CORNELIUS [*ruminatively*] He's the queerest Englishman *I* ever met. When he opened the paper dhis mornin the first thing he saw was that an English expedition had been bet in a battle in Inja somewhere; an he was as pleased as Punch! Larry told him that if he'd been alive when the news o Waterloo came, he'd a died o grief over it. Bedad I dont think he's quite right in his head.

DORAN. Divil a matther if he has plenty o money. He'll do for us right enough.

MATTHEW [*deeply impressed by Broadbent, and unable to understand their levity concerning him*] Did you mind what he said about rethrenchment? That was very good, I thought.

FATHER DEMPSEY. You might find out from Larry, Corny, what his means are. God forgive us all! it's poor work spoiling the Egyptians, though we have good warrant for it; so I'd like to know how much spoil there is before I commit meself. [*He rises. They all rise respectfully*].

CORNELIUS [*ruefully*] I'd set me mind on Larry himself for the seat; but I suppose it cant be helped.

FATHER DEMPSEY [*consoling him*] Well, the boy's young yet; an he has a head on him. Goodbye, all. [*He goes out through the gate*].

DORAN. I must be goin, too. [*He directs Cornelius's attention to what is passing in the road*]. Look at me bould Englishman shakin hans wid Fadher Dempsey for all the world like a candidate on election day. And look at Fadher Dempsey givin him a squeeze an a wink as much as to say It's all right, me boy. You watch him shakin hans with me too: he's waitn for me. I'll tell him he's as good as elected. [*He goes, chuckling mischievously*].

CORNELIUS. Come in with me, Matt. I think I'll sell you the pig after all. Come in an wet the bargain.

MATTHEW [*instantly dropping into the old whine of the tenant*] I'm afeerd I cant afford the price, sir. [*He follows Cornelius into the house*].

Larry, newspaper still in hand, comes back through the shrubbery. Broadbent returns through the gate.

LARRY. Well? What has happened?

BROADBENT [*hugely self-satisfied*] I think Ive done the trick this time. I just gave them a bit of straight talk; and it went home. They were greatly impressed: everyone of those men believes in me and will vote for me when the question of selecting a candidate comes up. After all, whatever you say, Larry, they like an Englishman. They feel they can trust him, I suppose.

LARRY. Oh! theyve transferred the honor to you, have they?

BROADBENT [*complacently*] Well, it was a pretty obvious move, I should think. You know, these fellows have plenty of shrewdness in spite of their Irish oddity. [*Hodson comes from the house. Larry sits in Doran's chair and reads.*] Oh, by the way, Hodson—

HODSON [*coming between Broadbent and Larry*] Yes, sir?

BROADBENT. I want you to be rather particular as to how you treat the people here.

HODSON. I havnt treated any of em yet, sir. If I was to accept all the treats they offer me I shouldnt be able to stand at this present moment, sir.

BROADBENT. Oh well, dont be too stand-offish, you know, Hodson. I should like you to be popular. If it costs anything I'll make it up to you. It doesnt matter if you get a bit upset at first: theyll like you all the better for it.

HODSON. I'm sure youre very kind, sir; but it dont seem to matter to me whether they like me or not. I'm not going to stand for parliament here, sir.

BROADBENT. Well, I am. Now do you understand?

HODSON [*waking up at once*] Oh, I beg your pardon, sir, I'm sure. I understand, sir.

CORNELIUS [*appearing at the house door with Matt*] Patsy'll drive the pig over this evenin, Matt. Goodbye. [*He goes back into the house. Matt makes for the gate. Broadbent stops him. Hodson, pained by the derelict basket, picks it up and carries it away behind the house*].

BROADBENT [*beaming candidatorially*] I must thank you very particularly, Mr Haffigan, for your support this morning. I value it because I know that the real heart of a nation is the class you represent, the yeomanry.

MATTHEW [*aghast*] The yeomanry!!!

LARRY [*looking up from his paper*] Take care, Tom! In Rosscullen a yeoman means a sort of Orange Bashi-

Bazouk. In England, Matt, they call a freehold farmer a yeoman.

MATTHEW [*huffily*] I dont need to be insthructed be you, Larry Doyle. Some people think no one knows anythin but dhemselves. [*To Broadbent, deferentially*] Of course I know a gentleman like you would not compare me to the yeomanry. Me own granfather was flogged in the sthreets of Athenmullet be them when they put a gun in the thatch of his house an then went and found it there, bad cess to them!

BROADBENT [*with sympathetic interest*] Then you are not the first martyr of your family, Mr Haffigan?

MATTHEW. They turned me out o the farm I made out of the stones o Little Rosscullen hill wid me own hans.

BROADBENT. I have heard about it; and my blood still boils at the thought. [*Calling*] Hodson—

HODSON [*behind the corner of the house*] Yes, sir. [*He hurries forward*].

BROADBENT. Hodson: this gentleman's sufferings should make every Englishman think. It is want of thought rather than want of heart that allows such iniquities to disgrace society.

HODSON [*prosaically*] Yes, sir.

MATTHEW. Well, I'll be goin. Good mornin to you kindly, sir.

BROADBENT. You have some distance to go, Mr Haffigan: will you allow me to drive you home?

MATTHEW. Oh sure it'd be throublin your honor.

BROADBENT. I insist: it will give me the greatest pleasure, I assure you. My car is in the stable: I can get it round in five minutes.

MATTHEW. Well, sir, if you wouldnt mind, we could bring the pig Ive just bought from Corny—

BROADBENT [*with enthusiasm*] Certainly, Mr Haffigan: it will be quite delightful to drive with a pig in the car: I shall feel quite like an Irishman. Hodson: stay with Mr Haffigan; and give him a hand with the pig if necessary. Come, Larry; and help me. [*He rushes away through the shrubbery*].

LARRY [*throwing the paper ill-humoredly on the chair*] Look here, Tom! here, I say! confound it!—[*he runs after him*].

MATTHEW [*glowering disdainfully at Hodson, and sitting down on Cornelius's chair as an act of social self-assertion*] N are you the valley?

HODSON. The valley? Oh, I follow you: yes: I'm Mr Broadbent's valet.

MATTHEW. Ye have an aisy time of it: you look purty sleek. [*With suppressed ferocity*] Look at me! Do *I* look sleek?

HODSON [*sadly*] I wish I ad your ealth: you look as ard as nails. I suffer from an excess of uric acid.

MATTHEW. Musha what sort o disease is zhouragassid? Didjever suffer from injustice and starvation? Dhats the Irish disease. It's aisy for you to talk o sufferin, an you livin on the fat o the land wid money wrung from us.

HODSON [*suddenly dropping the well-spoken valet, and breaking out in his native cockney*] Wots wrong with you, aold chep? Ez ennybody been doin ennythink to you?

MATTHEW. Anythin timmy! Didnt your English masther say that the blood biled in him to hear the way they put a rint on me for the farm I made wid me own hans, and turned me out of it to give it to Billy Byrne?

HODSON. Ow, Tom Broadbent's blad boils pretty easy over ennything that eppens aht of his aown cantry. Downt you be tiken in by my aowl men, Peddy.

MATTHEW [*indignantly*] Paddy yourself! How dar you call me Paddy?

HODSON [*unmoved*] You jast keep your air on and listen to me. You Awrish people are too well off: thets wots the metter with you. [*With sudden passion*] You talk of your rotten little fawm cause you mide it by chackin a few stowns dahn a ill! Well, wot prawce maw grenfawther, Oi should lawk to knaow, that fitted ap a fust clawss shop and built ap a fust clawss dripery business in Landon by sixty years work, and then was chacked aht of it on is ed at the end of is lease withaht a penny for his goodwill. You talk of evictions! you that cawnt be moved until youve ran ap ighteen months rent. Oi once ran ap four weeks in Lembeth wen Oi was aht of a job in winter. They took the door off its inges and the winder aht of its seshes on me, an gev maw wawf pnoomownia. Oi'm a widower nah. [*Between his teeth*] Gawd! when Oi think of the things we Englishmen as to pat ap with, and eah you Awrish ahlin abaht your silly little grievances, and see the wy you mike it worse for haz by the rotten wiges youll cam over and tike and the rotten plices youll sleep in, I jast feel that I could tike the aowl bloomin British awland and mike you a present of it, jast to let you fawnd aht wot reel awdship's lawk.

MATTHEW [*starting up, more in scandalized incredulity than in anger*] D'ye have the face to set up England agen Ireland for injustices an wrongs an disthress an sufferin?

HODSON [*with intense disgust and contempt*] Ow, chack it, Paddy. Cheese it. You danno wot awdship is owver eah: all you knaow is ah to ahl abaht it. You tike the biscuit at thet, you do. Oi'm a Owm Ruler, Oi em. Do you knaow woy?

MATTHEW [*equally contemptuous*] D'ye know, yourself?

HODSON. Yus Oi do. It's because Oi want a little attention pide to my aown cantry; and thetll never be as long as your cheps are ollerin at Wesminister as if nowbody mettered but your own bloomin selves. Send em beck to ell or C'naught, as good aowld English Cramwell said. I'm jast sick of Awrland. Let it gow. Cat the caible. Mike it a present to Germany to keep the aowl Kyzer busy for a wawl; and give poor aowld England a chawnce: thets wot Oi sy.

MATTHEW [*full of scorn for a man so ignorant as to be unable to pronounce the word Connaught, which practically rhymes with bonnet in Ireland, though in Hodson's dialect it rhymes with untaught*] Take care we dont cut the cable ourselves some day, bad scran to you! An tell me dhis: have yanny Coercion Acs in England? Have yanny Removable magisthruts? Have you Dublin Castle to suppress every newspaper dhat takes the part o your own counthry?

HODSON. We can beyive ahrselves withaht sich things.

MATTHEW. Bedad youre right. It'd ony be waste o time to muzzle a sheep. Here! wheres me pig? God forgimmy for talkin to a poor ignorant craycher like you!

HODSON [*grinning with good-humored malice, too convinced of his own superiority to feel his withers wrung*] Your pig'll ev a rare doin in that car, Peddy. Forty mawl an ahr dahn that rocky line will strawk it pretty pink, you bet.

MATTHEW [*scornfully*] Hwy cant you tell a raisonable lie when youre about it? What horse can go forty mile an hour?

HODSON. Orse! Wy, you silly aowl rotter, it's not a orse: it's a mowtor. Do you spowse Tom Broadbent ud gow himself to fetch a orse?

MATTHEW [*in consternation*] Holy Moses! dont tell me it's the ingine he wants to take me on.

HODSON. Wot else?

MATTHEW. Your sowl to Morris Kelly! why didnt you tell me that before? The divil an ingine he'll get me on this day. [*His ear catches an approaching teuf-teuf*] Oh murdher! it's comin afther me: I hear the puff-puff of it. [*He runs away through the gate, much to Hodson's amusement. The noise of the motor ceases; and Hodson, anticipating Broadbent's return, throws off the cockney and recomposes himself as a valet. Broadbent and Larry come through the shrubbery. Hodson moves aside to the gate*].

BROADBENT. Where is Mr Haffigan? Has he gone for the pig?

HODSON. Bolted, sir? Afraid of the motor, sir.

BROADBENT [*much disappointed*] Oh, thats very tiresome. Did he leave any message?

HODSON. He was in too great a hurry, sir. Started to run home, sir, and left his pig behind him.

BROADBENT [*eagerly*] Left the pig! Then it's all right. The pig's the thing: the pig will win over every Irish heart to me. We'll take the pig home to Haffigan's farm in the motor: it will have a tremendous effect. Hodson!

HODSON. Yes, sir?

BROADBENT. Do you think you could collect a crowd to see the motor?

HODSON. Well, I'll try, sir.

BROADBENT. Thank you, Hodson: do.

Hodson goes out through the gate.

LARRY [*desperately*] Once more, Tom, will you listen to me?

BROADBENT. Rubbish! I tell you it will be all right.

LARRY. Only this morning you confessed how surprised you were to find that the people here shewed no sense of humor.

BROADBENT [*suddenly very solemn*] Yes: their sense of humor is in abeyance: I noticed it the moment we landed. Think of that in a country where every man is a born humorist! Think of what it means! [*Impressively*] Larry: we are in the presence of a great national grief.

LARRY. Whats to grieve them?

BROADBENT. I divined it, Larry: I saw it in their faces. Ireland has never smiled since her hopes were buried in the grave of Gladstone.

LARRY. Oh, whats the use of talking to such a man? Now look here, Tom. Be serious for a moment if you can.

BROADBENT [*stupent*] Serious! I!!!

LARRY. Yes, you. You say the Irish sense of humor is in abeyance. Well, if you drive through Rosscullen in a motor car with Haffigan's pig, it wont stay in abeyance. Now I warn you.

BROADBENT [*breezily*] Why, so much the better! I shall enjoy the joke myself more than any of them. [*Shouting*] Hallo, Patsy Farrell, where are you?

PATSY [*appearing in the shrubbery*] Here I am, your honor.

BROADBENT. Go and catch the pig and put it into the car: we're going to take it to Mr Haffigan's. [*He gives Larry a slap on the shoulders that sends him staggering off through the gate, and follows him buoyantly, exclaiming*] Come on, you old croaker! I'll shew you how to win an Irish seat.

PATSY [*meditatively*] Bedad, if dhat pig gets a howlt o the handle o the machine—[*He shakes his head ominously and drifts away to the pigsty*].

Act Four

The parlor in Cornelius Doyle's house. It communicates with the garden by a half glazed door. The fireplace is at the other side of the room, opposite the door and windows, the architect not having been sensitive to draughts. The table, rescued from the garden, is in the middle; and at it sits Keegan, the central figure in a rather crowded apartment. Nora, sitting with her back to the fire at the end of the table, is playing backgammon across its corner with him, on his left hand. Aunt Judy, a little further back, sits facing the fire knitting, with her feet on the fender. A little to Keegan's right, in front of the table, and almost sitting on it, is Barney Doran. Half a dozen friends of his, all men, are between him and the open door, supported by others outside. In the corner behind them is the sofa, of mahogany and horsehair, made up as a bed for Broadbent. Against the wall behind Keegan stands a mahogany sideboard. A door leading to the interior of the house is near the fireplace, behind Aunt Judy. There are chairs against the wall, one at each end of the sideboard. Keegan's hat is on the one nearest the inner door; and his stick is leaning against it. A third chair, also against the wall, is near the garden door.

There is a strong contrast of emotional atmosphere between the two sides of the room. Keegan is extraordinarily stern: no game of backgammon could possibly make a man's face so grim. Aunt Judy is quietly busy. Nora is trying to ignore Doran and attend to her game.

On the other hand Doran is reeling in an ecstasy of mischievous mirth which has infected all his friends. They are screaming with laughter, doubled up, leaning on the furniture and against the walls, shouting, screeching, crying.

AUNT JUDY [*as the noise lulls for a moment*] Arra hold your noise, Barney. What is there to laugh at?

DORAN. It got its fut into the little hweel—[*he is overcome afresh; and the rest collapse again*].

AUNT JUDY. Ah, have some sense: youre like a parcel o childher. Nora: hit him a thump on the back: he'll have a fit.

DORAN [*with squeezed eyes, exsufflicate with cachinnation*] Frens, he sez to dhem outside Doolan's: I'm takin the gintleman that pays the rint for a dhrive.

AUNT JUDY. Who did he mean be that?

DORAN. They call a pig that in England. Thats their notion of a joke.

AUNT JUDY. Musha God help them if they can joke no better than that!

DORAN [*with renewed symptoms*] Thin—

AUNT JUDY. Ah now dont be tellin it all over and settin yourself off again, Barney.

NORA. Youve told us three times, Mr Doran.

DORAN. Well but whin I think of it—!

AUNT JUDY. Then dont think of it, alanna.

DORAN. Dhere was Patsy Farrll in the back sate wi dhe pig between his knees, n me bould English boyoh in front at the machinery, n Larry Doyle in the road startin the injine wid a bed winch. At the first puff of it the pig lep out of its skin and bled Patsy's nose wi dhe ring in its snout. [*Roars of laughter: Keegan glares at them*]. Before Broadbint knew hwere he was, the pig was up his back and over into his lap; and bedad the poor baste did credit to Corny's thrainin of it; for it put in the fourth speed wid its right crubeen as if it was enthered for the Gordn Bennett [auto race].

NORA [*reproachfully*] And Larry in front of it and all! It's nothin to laugh at, Mr Doran.

DORAN. Bedad, Miss Reilly, Larry cleared six yards sideways at wan jump if he cleared an inch; and he'd a cleared seven if Doolan's granmother hadnt cotch him in her apern widhout intindin to. [*Immense merriment*].

AUNT JUDY. Ah, for shame, Barney! the poor old woman! An she was hurt before, too, when she slipped on the stairs.

DORAN. Bedad, maam, she's hurt behind now; for Larry bouled her over like a skittle. [*General delight at this typical stroke of Irish Rabelaisianism*].

NORA. It's well Mr Doyle wasnt killed.

DORAN. Faith it wasnt o Larry we were thinkin jus dhen, wi dhe pig takin the main sthreet o Rosscullen on market day at a mile a minnit. Dh ony thing Broadbint could get at wi dhe pig in front of him was a fut brake; n the pig's tail was undher dhat; so that whin he thought he was putn non the brake he was ony squeezin the life out o the pig's tail. The more he put the brake on the more the pig squealed n the fasther he dhruv.

AUNT JUDY. Why couldnt he throw the pig out into the road?

DORAN. Sure he couldnt stand up to it, because he was spanchelled-like between his seat and dhat thing like a wheel on top of a stick between his knees.

AUNT JUDY. Lord have mercy on us!

NORA. I dont know how you can laugh. Do you, Mr Keegan?

KEEGAN [*grimly*] Why not? There is danger, destruction, torment! What more do we need to make us merry? Go on, Barney: the last drops of joy are not squeezed from the story yet. Tell us again how our brother was torn asunder.

DORAN [*puzzled*] Whose bruddher?

KEEGAN. Mine.

NORA. He means the pig, Mr Doran. You know his way.

DORAN [*rising gallantly to the occasion*] Bedad I'm sorry for your poor bruddher, Misther Keegan; but I recommend you to thry him wid a couple o fried eggs for your breakfast tomorrow. It was a case of Excelsior wi dhat ambitious baste; for not content wid jumping from the back seat into the front wan, he jumped from the front wan into the road in front of the car. And—

KEEGAN. And everybody laughed!

NORA. Dont go over that again, please, Mr. Doran.

DORAN. Faith be the time the car went over the poor pig dhere was little left for me or anywan else to go over except wid a knife an fork.

AUNT JUDY. Why didnt Mr Broadbent stop the car when the pig was gone?

DORAN. Stop the car! He might as well ha thried to stop a mad bull. First it went wan way an made fireworks o Molly Ryan's crockery stall; an dhen it slewed round an ripped ten fut o wall out o the corner o the pound. [*With enormous enjoyment*] Begob, it just tore the town in two and sent the whole dam market to blazes. [*Nora, offended, rises*].

KEEGAN [*indignantly*] Sir!

DORAN [*quickly*] Savin your presence, Miss Reilly, and Misther Keegan's. Dhere! I wont say anuddher word.

NORA. I'm surprised at you, Mr Doran. [*She sits down again*].

DORAN [*reflectively*] He has the divil's own luck, that Englishman, annyway; for hwen they picked him up he hadnt a scratch on him, barrn hwat the pig did to his cloes. Patsy had two fingers out o jynt; but the smith pulled them sthraight for him. Oh, you never heard such a hullaballoo as there was. There was Molly cryin Me chaney, me beautyful chaney! n oul Matt shoutin Me pig, me pig! n the polus takin the number o the car, n not a man in the town able to speak for laughin—

KEEGAN [*with intense emphasis*] It is hell: it is hell. Nowhere else could such a scene be a burst of happiness for the people.

Cornelius comes in hastily from the garden, pushing his way through the little crowd.

CORNELIUS. Whisht your laughin, boys! Here he is. [*He puts his hat on the sideboard, and goes to the fireplace, where he posts himself with his back to the chimneypiece*].

AUNT JUDY. Remember your behavior, now.

Everybody becomes silent, solemn, concerned, sympathetic. Broadbent enters, soiled and disordered as to his motoring coat: immensely important and serious as to himself. He makes his way to the end of the table nearest the garden door, whilst Larry, who accompanies him, throws his motoring coat on the sofa bed, and sits down, watching the proceedings.

BROADBENT [*taking off his leather cap with dignity and placing it on the table*] I hope you have not been anxious about me.

AUNT JUDY. Deedn we have, Mr Broadbent. It's a mercy you werent killed.

DORAN. Kilt! It's a mercy dheres two bones of you left houldin together. How dijjescape at all at all? Well, I never thought I'd be so glad to see you safe and sound again. Not a man in the town would say less [*murmurs of kindly assent*]. Wont you come down to Doolan's and have a dhrop o brandy to take the shock off?

BROADBENT. Youre all really too kind; but the shock has quite passed off.

DORAN [*jovially*] Never mind. Come along all the same and tell us about it over a frenly glass.

BROADBENT. May I say how deeply I feel the kindness with which I have been overwhelmed since my accident? I can truthfully declare that I am glad it happened, because it has brought out the kindness and sympathy of the Irish character to an extent I had no conception of.

SEVERAL PRESENT. { Oh, sure youre welcome!
Sure it's only natural.
Sure you might have been kilt.

A young man, feeling that he must laugh or burst, hurries out. Barney puts an iron constraint on his features.

BROADBENT. All I can say is that I wish I could drink the health of everyone of you.

DORAN. Dhen come an do it.

BROADBENT [*very solemnly*] No: I am a teetotaller.

AUNT JUDY [*incredulously*] Arra since when?

BROADBENT. Since this morning, Miss Doyle. I have had a lesson [*he looks at Nora significantly*] that I shall not forget. It may be that total abstinence has already saved my life; for I was astonished at the steadiness of my nerves when death stared me in the face today. So I will ask you to excuse me. [*He collects himself for a speech*] Gentlemen: I hope the gravity of the peril through which we have all passed—for I know that the danger to the bystanders was as great as to the occupants of the car—will prove an earnest of closer and more serious relations between us in the future. We have had a somewhat agitating day: a valuable and innocent animal has lost its life: a public building has been wrecked: an aged and infirm lady has suffered an impact for which I feel personally responsible, though my old friend Mr Laurence Doyle unfortunately incurred the first effects of her very natural resentment. I greatly regret the damage to Mr Patrick Farrell's fingers; and I have of course taken care that he shall not suffer pecuniarily by his mishap. [*Murmurs of admiration at his magnanimity, and A Voice* "Youre a gentleman, sir"]. I am glad to say that Patsy took it like an Irishman, and, far from expressing any vindictive feeling, declared his willingness to break all his fingers and toes for me on the same terms [*subdued applause, and* "More power to Patsy!"]. Gentlemen: I felt at home in Ireland from the first [*rising excitement among his hearers*]. In every Irish breast I have found that spirit of liberty [*A cheery voice* "Hear Hear"], that instinctive mistrust of the Government [*A small pious voice, with intense expression,* "God bless you, sir!"], that love of independence [*A defiant voice,* "Thats it! Independence!"], that indignant sympathy with the cause of oppressed nationalities abroad. [*A threatening growl from all: the ground-swell of patriotic passion*] and with the resolute assertion of personal rights at home, which is all but extinct in my own country. If it were legally possible I should become a naturalized Irishman; and if ever it be my good fortune to represent an Irish constituency in parliament, it shall be my first care to introduce a Bill legalizing such an operation. I believe a large section of the Liberal party would avail themselves of it. [*Momentary scepticism*]. I do. [*Convulsive cheering*]. Gentlemen: I have said enough. [*Cries of* "Go on"]. No: I have as yet no right to address you at all on political subjects; and we must not abuse the warm-hearted Irish hospitality of Miss Doyle by turning her sitting room into a public meeting.

DORAN [*energetically*] Three cheers for Tom Broadbent, the future member for Rosscullen!

AUNT JUDY [*waving a half knitted sock*] Hip hip hurray!

The cheers are given with great heartiness, as it is by this time, for the more humorous spirits present, a question of vociferation or internal rupture.

BROADBENT. Thank you from the bottom of my heart, friends.

NORA [*whispering to Doran*] Take them away, Mr Doran [*Doran nods*].

DORAN. Well, good evenin, Mr Broadbent; an may you never regret the day you wint dhrivin wid Haffigan's pig! [*They shake hands*]. Good evenin, Miss Doyle.

General handshaking, Broadbent shaking hands with everybody effusively. He accompanies them to the garden and can be heard outside saying Goodnight in every inflexion known to parliamentary candidates. Nora, Aunt Judy, Keegan, Larry, and Cornelius are left in the parlor. Larry goes to the threshold and watches the scene in the garden.

NORA. It's a shame to make game of him like that. He's a gradle more good in him than Barney Doran.

CORNELIUS. It's all up with his candidature. He'll be laughed out o the town.

LARRY [*turning quickly from the doorway*] Oh no he wont: he's not an Irishman. He'll never know theyre laughing at him; and while theyre laughing he'll win the seat.

CORNELIUS. But he cant prevent the story getting about.

LARRY. He wont want to. He'll tell it himself as one of the most providential episodes in the history of England and Ireland.

AUNT JUDY. Sure he wouldnt make a fool of himself like that.

LARRY. Are you sure he's such a fool after all, Aunt Judy? Suppose you had a vote! which would you rather give it to? the man that told the story of Haffigan's pig Barney Doran's way or Broadbent's way?

AUNT JUDY. Faith I wouldnt give it to a man at all. It's a few women they want in parliament to stop their foolish blather.

BROADBENT [*bustling into the room, and taking off his damaged motoring overcoat, which he puts down on the sofa*] Well, thats over. I must apologize for making a speech, Miss Doyle; but they like it, you know. Everything helps in electioneering.

Larry takes the chair near the door; draws it near the table; and sits astride it, with his elbows folded on the back.

AUNT JUDY. I'd no notion you were such an orator, Mr Broadbent.

BROADBENT. Oh, it's only a knack. One picks it up on the platform. It stokes up their enthusiasm.

AUNT JUDY. Oh, I forgot. Youve not met Mr Keegan. Let me introjoosha.

BROADBENT [*shaking hands effusively*] Most happy to meet you, Mr Keegan. I have heard of you, though I have not had the pleasure of shaking your hand before. And now may I ask you—for I value no man's opinion more—what you think of my chances here.

KEEGAN [*coldly*] Your chances, sir, are excellent. You will get into parliament.

BROADBENT [*delighted*] I hope so. I think so. [*Fluctuating*] You really think so? You are sure you are not allowing your enthusiasm for our principles to get the better of your judgment?

KEEGAN. I have no enthusiasm for your principles, sir. You will get into parliament because you want to get into it enough to be prepared to take the necessary steps to induce the people to vote for you. That is how people usually get into that fantastic assembly.

BROADBENT [*puzzled*] Of course. [*Pause*]. Quite so. [*pause*]. Er—yes. [*Buoyant again*] I think they will vote for me. Eh? Yes?

AUNT JUDY. Arra why shouldnt they? Look at the people they do vote for!

BROADBENT [*encouraged*] Thats true: thats very true.

When I see the windbags, the carpet-baggers, the charlatans, the—the—the fools and ignoramuses who corrupt the multitude by their wealth, or seduce them by spouting balderdash to them, I cannot help thinking that an Englishman with no humbug about him, who will talk straight common sense and take his stand on the solid ground of principle and public duty, must win his way with men of all classes.

KEEGAN [*quietly*] Sir: there was a time, in my ignorant youth, when I should have called you a hypocrite.

BROADBENT [*reddening*] A hypocrite!

NORA [*hastily*] Oh I'm sure you dont think anything of the sort, Mr Keegan.

BROADBENT [*emphatically*] Thank you, Miss Reilly: thank you.

CORNELIUS [*gloomily*] We all have to stretch it a bit in politics: hwats the use o pretendin we dont?

BROADBENT [*stiffly*] I hope I have said or done nothing that calls for any such observation, Mr Doyle. If there is a vice I detest—or against which my whole public life has been a protest—it is the vice of hypocrisy. I would almost rather be inconsistent than insincere.

KEEGAN. Do not be offended, sir: I know that you are quite sincere. There is a saying in the Scripture which runs—so far as the memory of an oldish man can carry the words—Let not the right side of your brain know what the left side doeth. I learnt at Oxford that this is the secret of the Englishman's strange power of making the best of both worlds.

BROADBENT. Surely the text refers to our right and left hands. I am somewhat surprised to hear a member of your Church quote so essentially Protestant a document as the Bible; but at least you might quote it accurately.

LARRY. Tom: with the best intentions youre making an ass of yourself. You dont understand Mr Keegan's peculiar vein of humor.

BROADBENT [*instantly recovering his confidence*] Ah! it was only your delightful Irish humor, Mr Keegan. Of course, of course. How stupid of me! I'm so sorry. [*He pats Keegan consolingly on the back*]. John Bull's wits are still slow, you see. Besides, calling me a hypocrite was too big a joke to swallow all at once, you know.

KEEGAN. You must also allow for the fact that I am mad.

NORA. Ah, dont talk like that, Mr Keegan.

BROADBENT [*encouragingly*] Not at all, not at all. Only a whimsical Irishman, eh?

LARRY. Are you really mad, Mr Keegan?

AUNT JUDY [*shocked*] Oh, Larry, how could you ask him such a thing?

LARRY. I dont think Mr Keegan minds. [*To Keegan*] Whats the true version of the story of that black man you confessed on his deathbed?

KEEGAN. What story have you heard about that?

LARRY. I am informed that when the devil came for the black heathen, he took off your head and turned it three times round before putting it on again; and that your head's been turned ever since.

NORA [*reproachfully*] Larry!

KEEGAN [*blandly*] That is not quite what occurred. [*He collects himself for a serious utterance: they attend involuntarily*]. I heard that a black man was dying, and that the people were afraid to go near him. When I went to the place I found an elderly Hindoo, who told me one of those tales of unmerited misfortune, of cruel ill luck, of relentless persecution by destiny, which sometimes wither the commonplaces of consolation on the lips of a priest. But this man did not complain of his misfortunes. They were brought upon him, he said, by sins committed in a former existence. Then, without a word of comfort from me, he died with a clear-eyed resignation that my most earnest exhortations have rarely produced in a Christian, and left me sitting there by his bedside with the mystery of this world suddenly revealed to me.

BROADBENT. That is a remarkable tribute to the liberty of conscience enjoyed by the subjects of our Indian Empire.

LARRY. No doubt; but may we venture to ask what is the mystery of this world?

KEEGAN. This world, sir, is very clearly a place of torment and penance, a place where the fool flourishes and the good and wise are hated and persecuted, a place where men and women torture one another in the name of love; where children are scourged and enslaved in the name of parental duty and education; where the weak in body are poisoned and mutilated in the name of healing, and the weak in character are put to the horrible torture of imprisonment, not for hours but for years, in the name of justice. It is a place where the hardest toil is a welcome refuge from the horror and tedium of pleasure, and where charity and good works are done only for hire to ransom the souls of the spoiler and the sybarite. Now, sir, there is only one place of horror and torment known to my religion; and that place is hell. Therefore it is plain to me that this earth of ours must be hell, and that we are all here, as the Indian revealed to me—perhaps he was sent to reveal it to me—to expiate crimes committed by us in a former existence.

AUNT JUDY [*awestruck*] Heaven save us, what a thing to say!

CORNELIUS [*sighing*] It's a queer world: thats certain.

BROADBENT. Your idea is a very clever one, Mr Keegan: really most brilliant: *I* should never have thought of it. But it seems to me—if I may say so—that you are overlooking the fact that, of the evils you describe, some are absolutely necessary for the preservation of society, and others are encouraged only when the Tories are in office.

LARRY. I expect you were a Tory in a former existence; and that is why you are here.

BROADBENT [*with conviction*] Never, Larry, never. But leaving politics out of the question, I find the world quite good enough for me: rather a jolly place, in fact.

KEEGAN [*looking at him with quiet wonder*] You are satisfied?

BROADBENT. As a reasonable man, yes. I see no evils in the world—except, of course, natural evils—that cannot be remedied by freedom, self-government, and English institutions. I think so, not because I am an Englishman, but as a matter of common sense.

KEEGAN. You feel at home in the world, then?

BROADBENT. Of course. Dont you?

KEEGAN [*from the very depths of his nature*] No.

BROADBENT [*breezily*] Try phosphorus pills. I always take them when my brain is overworked. I'll give you the address in Oxford Street.

KEEGAN [*enigmatically: rising*] Miss Doyle: my wandering fit has come on me: will you excuse me?

AUNT JUDY. To be sure: you know you can come in n nout as you like.

KEEGAN. We can finish the game some other time, Miss Reilly. [*He goes for his hat and stick*].

NORA. No: I'm out with you [*she disarranges the pieces and rises*]. I was too wicked in a former existence to play backgammon with a good man like you.

AUNT JUDY [*whispering to her*] Whisht, whisht, child! Dont set him back on that again.

KEEGAN [*to Nora*] When I look at you, I think that perhaps Ireland is only purgatory, after all. [*He passes on to the garden door*].

NORA. Galong with you!

BROADBENT [*whispering to Cornelius*] Has he a vote?

CORNELIUS [*nodding*] Yes. An theres lotsle vote the way he tells them.

KEEGAN [*at the garden door, with gentle gravity*] Good evening, Mr Broadbent. You have set me thinking. Thank you.

BROADBENT [*delighted, hurrying across to him to shake hands*] No, really? You find that contact with English ideas is stimulating, eh?

KEEGAN. I am never tired of hearing you talk, Mr Broadbent.

BROADBENT [*modestly remonstrating*] Oh come! come!

KEEGAN. Yes, I assure you. You are an extremely interesting man. [*He goes out*].

BROADBENT [*enthusiastically*] What a nice chap! What an intelligent, broadminded character, considering his cloth! By the way, I'd better have a wash. [*He takes up his coat and cap, and leaves the room through the inner door*].

Nora returns to her chair and shuts up the backgammon board.

AUNT JUDY. Keegan's very queer today. He has his mad fit on him.

CORNELIUS [*worried and bitter*] I wouldnt say but he's right after all. It's a contrairy world. [*To Larry*] Why would you be such a fool as to let Broadbent take the seat in parliament from you?

LARRY [*glancing at Nora*] He will take more than that from me before he's done here.

CORNELIUS. I wish he'd never set foot in my house, bad luck to his fat face! D'ye think he'd lend me £300 on the farm, Larry? When I'm so hard up, it seems a waste o money not to mortgage it now it's me own.

LARRY. *I* can lend you £300 on it.

CORNELIUS. No, no; I wasnt putn in for that. When I die and leave you the farm I should like to be able to feel that it was all me own, and not half yours to start with. Now I'll take me oath Barney Doarn's going to ask Broadbent to lend him £500 on the mill to put in a new hweel; for the old one'll harly hol together. An Haffigan cant sleep with covetn that corner o land at the foot of his medda that belongs to Doolan. He'll have to mortgage to buy it. I may as well be first as last. D'ye think Broadbent'd len me a little?

LARRY. I'm quite sure he will.

CORNELIUS. Is he as ready as that? Would he len me five hunderd, d'ye think?

LARRY. He'll lend you more than the landll ever be worth to you; so for Heaven's sake be prudent.

CORNELIUS [*judicially*] All right, all right, me son: I'll be careful. I'm goin into the office for a bit. [*He withdraws through the inner door, obviously to prepare his application to Broadbent*].

AUNT JUDY [*indignantly*] As if he hadnt seen enough o borryin when he was an agent without beginnin borryin himself! [*She rises*]. I'll borry him, so I will. [*She puts her knitting on the table and follows him out, with a resolute air that bodes trouble for Cornelius*].

Larry and Nora are left together for the first time since his arrival. She looks at him with a smile that perishes as she sees him aimlessly rocking his chair, and reflecting, evidently not about her, with his lips pursed as if he were whistling. With a catch in her throat she takes up Aunt Judy's knitting, and makes a pretence of going on with it.

NORA. I suppose it didnt seem very long to you.

LARRY [*starting*] Eh? What didnt?

NORA. The eighteen years youve been away.

LARRY. Oh, that! No: it seems hardly more than a week. I've been so busy—had so little time to think.

NORA. Ive had nothin else to do but think.

LARRY. That was very bad for you. Why didnt you give it up? Why did you stay here?

NORA. Because nobody sent for me to go anywhere else, I suppose. Thats why.

LARRY. Yes: one does stick frightfully in the same place, unless some external force comes and routs one out. [*He yawns slightly; but as she looks up quickly at him, he pulls himself together and rises with an air of waking up and setting to work cheerfully to make himself agreeable*]. And how have you been all this time?

NORA. Quite well, thank you.

LARRY. Thats right. [*Suddenly finding that he has nothing else to say, and being ill at ease in consequence, he strolls about the room humming distractedly*].

NORA [*struggling with her tears*] Is that all you have to say to me, Larry?

LARRY. Well, what is there to say? You see, we know each other so well.

NORA [*a little consoled*] Yes: of course we do. [*He does not reply*]. I wonder you came back at all.

LARRY. I couldnt help it. [*She looks up affectionately*]. Tom made me. [*She looks down again quickly to conceal the effect of this blow. He whistles another stave; then resumes*] I had a sort of dread of returning to Ireland. I felt somehow that my luck would turn if I came back. And now here I am, none the worse.

NORA. Praps it's a little dull for you.

LARRY. No: I havnt exhausted the interest of strolling

about the old places and remembering and romancing about them.

NORA [*hopefully*] Oh! You do remember the places, then?

LARRY. Of course. They have associations.

NORA [*not doubting that the associations are with her*] I suppose so.

LARRY. M'yes. I can remember particular spots where I had long fits of thinking about the countries I meant to get to when I escaped from Ireland. America and London, and sometimes Rome and the east.

NORA [*deeply mortified*] Was that all you used to be thinking about?

LARRY. Well, there was precious little else to think about here, my dear Nora, except sometimes at sunset, when one got maudlin and called Ireland Erin, and imagined one was remembering the days of old, and so forth. [*He whistles Let Erin Remember*].

NORA. Did jever get a letter I wrote you last February?

LARRY. Oh yes; and I really intended to answer it. But I havnt had a moment; and I knew you wouldnt mind. You see, I am so afraid of boring you by writing about affairs you dont understand and people you dont know! And yet what else have I to write about? I begin a letter; and then I tear it up again. The fact is, fond as we are of one another, Nora, we have so little in common—I mean of course the things one can put in a letter—that correspondence is apt to become the hardest of hard work.

NORA. Yes: it's hard for me to know anything about you if you never tell me anything.

LARRY [*pettishly*] Nora: a man cant sit down and write his life day by day when he's tired enough with having lived it.

NORA. I'm not blaming you.

LARRY [*looking at her with some concern*] You seem rather out of spirits. [*Going closer to her, anxiously and tenderly*] You havnt got neuralgia, have you?

NORA. No.

LARRY [*reassured*] I get a touch of it sometimes when I am below par. [*Absently, again strolling about*] Yes, yes. [*He gazes through the doorway at the Irish landscape, and sings, almost unconsciously, but very expressively, an air from Offenbach's Whittington*].

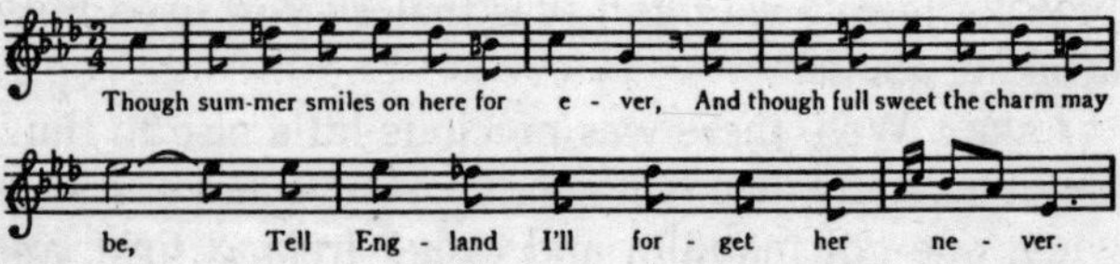

[*Nora, who has been at first touched by the tenderness of his singing, puts down her knitting at this very unexpected sentiment, and stares at him. He continues until the melody soars out of his range, when he trails off into whistling Let Erin Remember*].

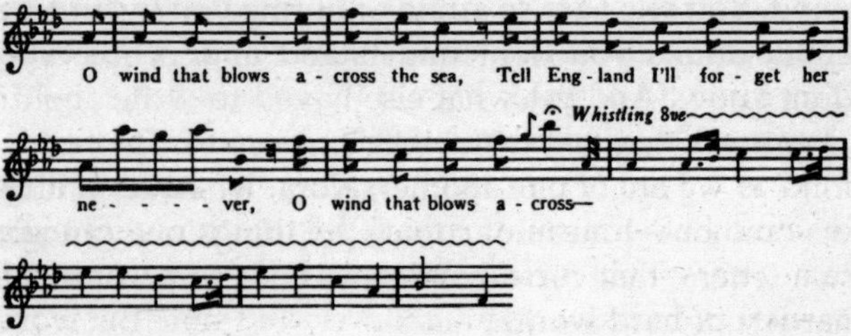

I'm afraid I'm boring you, Nora, though youre too kind to say so.

NORA. Are you wanting to get back to England already?

LARRY. Not at all. Not at all.

NORA. Thats a queer song to sing to me if youre not.

LARRY. The song! Oh, it doesnt mean anything: it's by a German Jew, like most English patriotic sentiment. Never mind me, my dear: go on with your work; and dont let me bore you.

NORA [*bitterly*] Rosscullen isnt such a lively place that I am likely to be bored by you at our first talk together after eighteen years, though you dont seem to have much to say to me after all.

LARRY. Eighteen years is a devilish long time, Nora. Now if it had been eighteen minutes, or even eighteen months, we should be able to pick up the interrupted thread, and chatter like two magpies. But as it is, I have simply nothing to say; and you seem to have less.

NORA. I—[*her tears choke her; but she keeps up appearances desperately*].

LARRY [*quite unconscious of his cruelty*] In a week or so we shall be quite old friends again. Meanwhile, as I feel that I am not making myself particularly entertaining, I'll take myself off. Tell Tom Ive gone for a stroll over the hill.

NORA. You seem very fond of Tom, as you call him.

LARRY [*the triviality going suddenly out of his voice*] Yes: I'm fond of Tom.

NORA. Oh, well, dont let me keep you from him.

LARRY. I know quite well that my departure will be a relief. Rather a failure, this first meeting after eighteen years, eh? Well, never mind: these great sentimental events always are failures; and now the worst of it's over anyhow. [*He goes out through the garden door*].

Nora, left alone, struggles wildly to save herself from breaking down, and then drops her face on the table and gives way to a convulsion of crying. Her sobs shake her so that she can hear nothing; and she has no suspicion that she is no longer alone until her head and breast are raised by Broadbent, who, returning newly washed and combed through the inner door, has seen her condition, first with surprise and concern, and then with an emotional disturbance that quite upsets him.

BROADBENT. Miss Reilly. Miss Reilly. Whats the matter? Dont cry: I cant stand it: you mustnt cry. [*She makes a choked effort to speak, so painful that he continues with impulsive sympathy*] No: dont try to speak: it's all right now. Have your cry out: never mind me: trust me. [*Gathering her to him, and babbling consolatorily*] Cry on my chest: the only really comfortable place for a woman to cry is a man's chest: a real man, a real friend. A good broad chest, eh? not less than forty-two inches—no: dont fuss: never mind the conventions: we're two friends, arnt we? Come now, come, come! It's all right and comfortable and happy now, isnt it?

NORA [*through her tears*] Let me go. I want me hankerchief.

BROADBENT [*holding her with one arm and producing a large silk handkerchief from his breast pocket*] Heres a handkerchief. Let me [*he dabs her tears dry with it*]. Never mind your own: it's too small: it's one of those wretched little cambric handkerchiefs—

NORA [*sobbing*] Indeed it's a common cotton one.

BROADBENT. Of course it's a common cotton one—silly little cotton one—not good enough for the dear eyes of Nora Cryna—

NORA [*spluttering into a hysterical laugh and clutching him convulsively with her fingers while she tries to stifle her laughter against his collar bone*] Oh dont make me laugh: please dont make me laugh.

BROADBENT [*terrified*] I didnt mean to, on my soul. What is it? What is it?

NORA. Nora Creena, Nora Creena.

BROADBENT [*patting her*] Yes, yes, of course, Nora Creena, Nora acushla [*he makes cush rhyme to plush*]—

NORA. Acushla [*she makes cush rhyme to bush*].

BROADBENT. Oh, confound the language! Nora darling—my Nora—the Nora I love—

NORA [*shocked into propriety*] You mustnt talk like that to me.

BROADBENT [*suddenly becoming prodigiously solemn and letting her go*] No, of course not. I dont mean it. At least I do mean it; but I know it's premature. I had no right to take advantage of your being a little upset; but I lost my self-control for a moment.

NORA [*wondering at him*] I think youre a very kind-hearted man, Mr Broadbent; but you seem to me to have no self-control at all [*she turns her face away with a keen pang of shame and adds*] no more than myself.

BROADBENT [*resolutely*] Oh yes, I have: you should see me when I am really roused: then I have TREMENDOUS self-control. Remember: we have been alone together only once before; and then, I regret to say, I was in a disgusting state.

NORA. Ah no, Mr Broadbent: you wernt disgusting.

BROADBENT [*mercilessly*] Yes I was: nothing can excuse it: perfectly beastly. It must have made a most unfavorable impression on you.

NORA. Oh, sure it's all right. Say no more about that.

BROADBENT. I must, Miss Reilly: it is my duty. I shall not detain you long. May I ask you to sit down. [*He indicates her chair with oppressive solemnity. She sits down wondering. He then, with the same portentous gravity, places a chair for himself near her; sits down; and proceeds to explain*]. First, Miss Reilly, may I say that I have tasted nothing of an alcoholic nature today.

NORA. It doesnt seem to make as much difference in you as it would in an Irishman, somehow.

BROADBENT. Perhaps not. Perhaps not. I never quite lose myself.

NORA [*consolingly*] Well, anyhow, youre all right now.

BROADBENT [*fervently*] Thank you, Miss Reilly: I am. Now we shall get along. [*Tenderly, lowering his voice*] Nora: I was in earnest last night. [*Nora moves as if to rise*]. No: one moment. You must not think I am going to press you for an answer before you have known me for 24 hours. I am a reasonable man, I hope; and I am prepared to wait as long as you like, provided you will give me some small assurance that the answer will not be unfavorable.

NORA. How could I go back from it if I did? I sometimes think youre not quite right in your head, Mr Broadbent, you say such funny things.

BROADBENT. Yes: I know I have a strong sense of humor which sometimes makes people doubt whether I am quite serious. That is why I have always thought I should like to marry an Irishwoman. She would always understand my jokes. For instance, you would understand them, eh?

NORA [*uneasily*] Mr Broadbent: I couldnt.

BROADBENT [*soothingly*] Wait: let me break this to you gently, Miss Reilly: hear me out. I daresay you have noticed that in speaking to you I have been putting a very strong constraint on myself, so as to avoid wounding your delicacy by too abrupt an avowal of my feelings. Well, I feel now that the time has come to be open, to be frank, to be explicit. Miss Reilly: you have inspired in me a very strong attachment. Perhaps, with a woman's intuition, you have already guessed that.

NORA [*rising distractedly*] Why do you talk to me in that unfeeling nonsensical way?

BROADBENT [*rising also, much astonished*] Unfeeling! Nonsensical!

NORA. Dont you know that you have said things to me that no man ought to say unless—unless—[*she suddenly breaks down again and hides her face on the table as before*] Oh, go away from me: I wont get married at all: what is it but heartbreak and disappointment?

BROADBENT [*developing the most formidable symptoms of rage and grief*] Do you mean to say that you are going to refuse me? that you dont care for me?

NORA [*looking at him in consternation*] Oh, dont take it to heart, Mr Br—

BROADBENT [*flushed and almost choking*] I dont want to be petted and blarneyed. [*With childish rage*] I love you. I want you for my wife. [*In despair*] I cant help your refusing. I'm helpless: I can do nothing. You have no right to ruin my whole life. You—[*a hysterical convulsion stops him*].

NORA [*almost awestruck*] Youre not going to cry, are you? I never thought a man could cry. Dont.

BROADBENT. I'm not crying. I—I—I leave that sort of thing to your damned sentimental Irishmen. You think I have no feeling because I am a plain unemotional Englishman, with no powers of expression.

NORA. I dont think you know the sort of man you are at all. Whatever may be the matter with you, it's not want of feeling.

BROADBENT [*hurt and petulant*] It's you who have no feeling. Youre as heartless as Larry.

NORA. What do you expect me to do? Is it to throw meself at your head the minute the word is out o your mouth?

BROADBENT [*striking his silly head with his fists*] Oh,

what a fool! what a brute I am! It's only your Irish delicacy: of course, of course. You mean Yes. Eh? What? Yes? yes? yes?

NORA. I think you might understand that though I might choose to be an old maid, I could never marry anybody but you now.

BROADBENT [*clasping her violently to his breast, with a crow of immense relief and triumph*] Ah, thats right, thats right: thats magnificent. I knew you would see what a first-rate thing this will be for both of us.

NORA [*incommoded and not at all enraptured by his ardor*] Youre dreadfully strong, an a gradle too free with your strength. An I never thought o whether it'd be a good thing for us or not. But when you found me here that time, I let you be kind to me, and cried in your arms, because I was too wretched to think of anything but the comfort of it. An how could I let any other man touch me after that?

BROADBENT [*moved*] Now thats very nice of you, Nora: thats really most delicately womanly [*he kisses her hand chivalrously*].

NORA [*looking earnestly and a little doubtfully at him*] Surely if you let one woman cry on you like that youd never let another touch you.

BROADBENT [*conscientiously*] One should not. One ought not, my dear girl. But the honest truth is, if a chap is at all a pleasant sort of chap, his chest becomes a fortification that has to stand many assaults: at least it is so in England.

NORA [*curtly, much disgusted*] Then youd better marry an Englishwoman.

BROADBENT [*making a wry face*] No, no: the Englishwoman is too prosaic for my taste, too material, too much of the animated beefsteak about her. The ideal is what I like. Now Larry's taste is just the opposite:

he likes em solid and bouncing and rather keen about him. It's a very convenient difference; for weve never been in love with the same woman.

NORA. An d'ye mean to tell me to me face that youve ever been in love before?

BROADBENT. Lord! yes.

NORA. I'm not your first love!

BROADBENT. First love is only a little foolishness and a lot of curiosity: no really self-respecting woman would take advantage of it. No, my dear Nora: Ive done with all that long ago. Love affairs always end in rows. We're not going to have any rows: we're going to have a solid four-square home: man and wife: comfort and common sense. And plenty of affection, eh [*he puts his arm round her with confident proprietorship*]?

NORA [*coldly, trying to get away*] I dont want any other woman's leavings.

BROADBENT [*holding her*] Nobody asked you to, maam. I never asked any woman to marry me before.

NORA [*severely*] Then why didnt you if youre an honorable man?

BROADBENT. Well, to tell you the truth, they were mostly married already. But never mind! there was nothing wrong. Come! dont take a mean advantage of me. After all, you must have had a fancy or two yourself, eh?

NORA [*conscience-stricken*] Yes. I suppose Ive no right to be particular.

BROADBENT [*humbly*] I know I'm not good enough for you, Nora. But no man is, you know, when the woman is a really nice woman.

NORA. Oh, I'm no better than yourself. I may as well tell you about it.

BROADBENT. No, no: lets have no telling: much better not. *I* shant tell you anything: dont you tell me anything. Perfect confidence in one another and no tellings: thats the way to avoid rows.

NORA. Dont think it was anything I need be ashamed of.

BROADBENT. I dont.

NORA. It was only that I'd never known anybody else that I could care for; and I was foolish enough once to think that Larry—

BROADBENT [*disposing of the idea at once*] Larry! Oh, that wouldnt have done at all, not at all. You dont know Larry as I do, my dear. He has absolutely no capacity for enjoyment: he couldnt make any woman happy. He's as clever as be-blowed; but life's too earthly for him: he doesnt really care for anything or anybody.

NORA. Ive found that out.

BROADBENT. Of course you have. No, my dear: take my word for it, youre jolly well out of that. There! [*swinging her round against his breast*] thats much more comfortable for you.

NORA [*with Irish peevishness*] Ah, you mustnt go on like that. I dont like it.

BROADBENT [*unabashed*] Youll acquire the taste by degrees. You mustnt mind me: it's an absolute necessity of my nature that I should have somebody to hug occasionally. Besides, it's good for you: it'll plump out your muscles and make em elastic and set up your figure.

NORA. Well, I'm sure! if this is English manners! Arnt you ashamed to talk about such things?

BROADBENT [*in the highest feather*] Not a bit. By George, Nora, it's a tremendous thing to be able to enjoy oneself. Lets go off for a walk out of this stuffy little room. I want the open air to expand in, Come along. Co-o-ome along. [*He puts her arm into his and sweeps her out into the garden as an equinoctial gale might sweep a dry leaf*].

Later in the evening, the grasshopper is again enjoying the sunset by the great stone on the hill; but this time he enjoys neither the stimulus of Keegan's conversation nor the pleasure of terrifying Patsy Farrell. He is alone until Nora and Broadbent come up the hill arm in arm. Broadbent is still breezy and confident; but she has her head averted from him and is almost in tears.

BROADBENT [*stopping to snuff up the hillside air*] Ah! I like this spot. I like this view. This would be a jolly good place for a hotel and a golf links. Friday to Tuesday, railway ticket and hotel all inclusive. I tell you Nora, I'm going to develop this place. [*Looking at her*] Hallo! Whats the matter? Tired?

NORA [*unable to restrain her tears*] I'm ashamed out o me life.

BROADBENT [*astonished*] Ashamed! What of?

NORA. Oh, how could you drag me all round the place like that, telling everybody that we're going to be married, and introjoocing me to the lowest of the low, and letting them shake hans with me, and encouraging them to make free with us? I little thought I should live to shaken hans with be Doolan in broad daylight in the public street of Rosscullen.

BROADBENT. But, my dear, Doolan's a publican: a most influential man. By the way, I asked him if his wife would be at home tomorrow. He said she would; so you must take the motor car round and call on her.

NORA [*aghast*] Is it me call on Doolan's wife!

BROADBENT. Yes, of course: call on all their wives. We must get a copy of the register and a supply of canvassing cards. No use calling on people who havent votes. Youll be a great success as a canvasser, Nora: they call you the heiress; and theyll be flattered no end by your calling, especially as youve never cheapened yourself by speaking to them before—have you?

NORA [*indignantly*] Not likely, indeed.

BROADBENT. Well, we mustnt be stiff and stand-off, you know. We must be thoroughly democratic, and patronize everybody without distinction of class. I tell you I'm a jolly lucky man, Nora Cryna. I get engaged to the most delightful woman in Ireland; and it turns out that I couldnt have done a smarter stroke of electioneering.

NORA. An would you let me demean meself like that, just to get yourself into parliament?

BROADBENT [*buoyantly*] Aha! Wait til you find out what an exciting game electioneering is: youll be mad to get me in. Besides, youd like people to say that Tom Broadbent's wife had been the making of him? that she got him into parliament? into the Cabinet, perhaps, eh?

NORA. God knows I dont grudge you me money! But to lower meself to the level of common people—

BROADBENT. To a member's wife, Nora, nobody is common provided he's on the register. Come, my dear! it's all right: do you think I'd let you do it if it wasnt? The best people do it. Everybody does it.

NORA [*who has been biting her lip and looking over the hill, disconsolate and unconvinced*] Well, praps you know best what they do in England. They must have very little respect for themselves. I think I'll go in now. I see Larry and Mr Keegan coming up the hill; and I'm not fit to talk to them.

BROADBENT. Just wait and say something nice to Keegan. They tell me he controls nearly as many votes as Father Dempsey himself.

NORA. You little know Peter Keegan. He'd see through me as if I was a pane o glass.

BROADBENT. Oh, he wont like it any the less for that.

What really flatters a man is that you think him worth flattering. Not that I would flatter any man: dont think that. I'll just go and meet him. [*He goes down the hill with the eager forward look of a man about to greet a valued acquaintance. Nora dries her eyes, and turns to go as Larry strolls up the hill to her*].

LARRY. Nora. [*She turns and looks at him hardly, without a word. He continues anxiously, in his most conciliatory tone*] When I left you that time, I was just as wretched as you. I didnt rightly know what I wanted to say; and my tongue kept clacking to cover the loss I was at. Well, Ive been thinking ever since; and now I know what I ought to have said. Ive come back to say it.

NORA. Youve come too late, then. You thought eighteen years was not long enough, and that you might keep me waiting a day longer. Well, you were mistaken. I'm engaged to your friend Mr Broadbent; and I'm done with you.

LARRY [*naïvely*] But that was the very thing I was going to advise you to do.

NORA [*involuntarily*] Oh you brute! to tell me that to me face!

LARRY [*nervously relapsing into his most Irish manner*] Nora, dear, dont you understand that I'm an Irishman, and he's an Englishman. He wants you; and he grabs you. *I* want you; and I quarrel with you and have to go on wanting you.

NORA. So you may. Youd better go back to England to the animated beefsteaks youre so fond of.

LARRY [*amazed*] Nora! [*Guessing where she got the metaphor*] He's been talking about me, I see. Well, never mind: we must be friends, you and I. I dont want his marriage to you to be his divorce from me.

NORA. You care more for him than you ever did for me.

LARRY [*with curt sincerity*] Yes of course I do: why should I tell you lies about it? Nora Reilly was a person of very little consequence to me or anyone else outside this miserable little hole. But Mrs Tom Broadbent will be a person of very considerable consequence indeed. Play your new part well, and there will be no more neglect, no more loneliness, no more idle regrettings and vain-hopings in the evenings by the Round Tower, but real life and real work and real cares and real joys among real people: solid English life in London, the very centre of the world. You will find your work cut out for you keeping Tom's house and entertaining Tom's friends and getting Tom into parliament; but it will be worth the effort.

NORA. You talk as if I was under an obligation to him for marrying me.

LARRY. I talk as I think. Youve made a very good match, let me tell you.

NORA. Indeed! Well, some people might say he's not done so badly himself.

LARRY. If you mean that you will be a treasure to him, he thinks so now; and you can keep him thinking so if you like.

NORA. I wasnt thinking o meself at all.

LARRY. Were you thinking of your money, Nora?

NORA. I didnt say so.

LARRY. Your money will not pay your cook's wages in London.

NORA [*flaming up*] If thats true—and the more shame for you to throw it in me face if it is true—at all events itll make us independent; for if the worst comes to the worst, we can always come back here an live on it. An if I have to keep his house for him, at all events I can keep you out of it; for Ive done with you; and I wish

I'd never seen you. So goodbye to you, Mister Larry Doyle. [*She turns her back on him and goes home*].

LARRY [*watching her as she goes*] Goodbye. Goodbye. Oh, thats so Irish! Irish both of us to the backbone: Irish! Irish! Iri—

Broadbent arrives, conversing energetically with Keegan.

BROADBENT. Nothing pays like a golfing hotel, if you hold the land instead of the shares, and if the furniture people stand in with you, and if you are a good man of business.

LARRY. Nora's gone home.

BROADBENT [*with conviction*] You were right this morning, Larry. I must feed up Nora. She's weak; and it makes her fanciful. Oh, by the way, did I tell you that we're engaged?

LARRY. She told me herself.

BROADBENT [*complacently*] She's rather full of it, as you may imagine. Poor Nora! Well, Mr Keegan, as I said, I begin to see my way here. I begin to see my way.

KEEGAN [*with a courteous inclination*] The conquering Englishman, sir. Within 24 hours of your arrival you have carried off our only heiress, and practically secured the parliamentary seat. And you have promised me that when I come here in the evenings to meditate on my madness; to watch the shadow of the Round Tower lengthening in the sunset; to break my heart uselessly in the curtained gloaming over the dead heart and blinded soul of the island of the saints, you will comfort me with the bustle of a great hotel, and the sight of the little children carrying the golf clubs of your tourists as a preparation for the life to come.

BROADBENT [*quite touched, mutely offering him a cigar to console him, at which he smiles and shakes his head*] Yes, Mr Keegan: youre quite right. Theres poetry in everything, even [*looking absently into the cigar case*] in the most modern prosaic things, if you know how to extract it [*he extracts a cigar for himself and offers one to Larry, who takes it*]. If I was to be shot for it I couldnt extract it myself; but thats where you come in, you see. [*Roguishly, waking up from his reverie and bustling Keegan goodhumoredly*] And then *I* shall wake you up a bit. Thats where *I* come in: eh? d'ye see? Eh? eh? [*He pats him very pleasantly on the shoulder, half admiringly, half pityingly*]. Just so, just so. [*Coming back to business*] By the way, I believe I can do better than a light railway here. There seems to be no question now that the motor boat has come to stay. Well, look at your magnificent river there, going to waste.

KEEGAN [*closing his eyes*] "Silent, O Moyle, be the roar of thy waters."

BROADBENT. You know, the roar of a motor boat is quite pretty.

KEEGAN. Provided it does not drown the Angelus.

BROADBENT [*reassuringly*] Oh no: it wont do that: not the least danger. You know, a church bell can make a devil of a noise when it likes.

KEEGAN. You have an answer for everything, sir. But your plans leave one question still unanswered: how to get butter out of a dog's throat.

BROADBENT. Eh?

KEEGAN. You cannot build your golf links and hotels in the air. For that you must own our land. And how will you drag our acres from the ferret's grip of Matthew Haffigan? How will you persuade Cornelius Doyle to forego the pride of being a small landowner? How will Barney Doran's millrace agree with your motor boats? Will Doolan help you to get a license for your hotel?

BROADBENT. My dear sir: to all intents and purposes

the syndicate I represent already owns half Rosscullen. Doolan's is a tied house; and the brewers are in the syndicate. As to Haffigan's farm and Doran's mill and Mr Doyle's place and half a dozen others, they will be mortgaged to me before a month is out.

KEEGAN. But pardon me, you will not lend them more on their land than the land is worth; so they will be able to pay you the interest.

BROADBENT. Ah, you are a poet, Mr Keegan, not a man of business.

LARRY. We will lend everyone of these men half as much again on their land as it is worth, or ever can be worth, to them.

BROADBENT. You forget, sir, that we, with our capital, our knowledge, our organization, and may I say our English business habits, can make or lose ten pounds out of land that Haffigan, with all his industry, could not make or lose ten shillings out of. Doran's mill is a superannuated folly: I shall want it for electric lighting.

LARRY. What is the use of giving land to such men? they are too small, too poor, too ignorant, too simple-minded to hold it against us: you might as well give a dukedom to a crossing sweeper.

BROADBENT. Yes, Mr Keegan: this place may have an industrial future, or it may have a residential future: I cant tell yet; but it's not going to be a future in the hands of your Dorans and Haffigans, poor devils!

KEEGAN. It may have no future at all. Have you thought of that?

BROADBENT. Oh, I'm not afraid of that. I have faith in Ireland. Great faith, Mr Keegan.

KEEGAN. And we have none: only empty enthusiasms and patriotisms, and emptier memories and regrets. Ah yes: you have some excuse for believing that if there be any future, it will be yours; for our faith seems dead, and our hearts cold and cowed. An island of dreamers who wake up in your jails, of critics and cowards whom you buy and tame for your own service, of bold rogues who help you to plunder us that they may plunder you afterwards.

BROADBENT [*a little impatient of this unbusinesslike view*] Yes, yes; but you know you might say that of any country. The fact is, there are only two qualities in the world: efficiency and inefficiency, and only two sorts of people: the efficient and the inefficient. It dont matter whether theyre English or Irish. I shall collar this place, not because I'm an Englishman and Haffigan and Co are Irishmen, but because theyre duffers, and I know my way about.

KEEGAN. Have you considered what is to become of Haffigan?

LARRY. Oh, we'll employ him in some capacity or other, and probably pay him more than he makes for himself now.

BROADBENT [*dubiously*] Do you think so? No no: Haffigan's too old. It really doesnt pay now to take on men over forty even for unskilled labor, which I suppose is all Haffigan would be good for. No: Haffigan had better go to America, or into the Union, poor old chap! He's worked out, you know: you can see it.

KEEGAN. Poor lost soul, so cunningly fenced in with invisible bars!

LARRY. Haffigan doesnt matter much. He'll die presently.

BROADBENT [*shocked*] Oh come, Larry! Don't be unfeeling. It's hard on Haffigan. It's always hard on the inefficient.

LARRY. Pah! what does it matter where an old and broken man spends his last days, or whether he has a million at the bank or only the workhouse dole? It's the young men, the able men, that matter. The real tragedy of Haffigan is the tragedy of his wasted youth, his stunted mind, his drudging over his clods and pigs until he has become a clod and a pig himself—until the soul within him has smouldered into nothing but a dull temper that hurts himself and all around him. I say let him die, and let us have no more of his like. And let young Ireland take care that it doesnt share his fate, instead of making another empty grievance of it. Let your syndicate come—

BROADBENT. Your syndicate too, old chap. You have your bit of the stock.

LARRY. Yes: mine if you like. Well, our syndicate has no conscience: it has no more regard for your Haffigans and Doolans and Dorans than it has for a gang of Chinese coolies. It will use your patriotic blatherskite and balderdash to get parliamentary powers over you as cynically as it would bait a mousetrap with toasted cheese. It will plan, and organize, and find capital while you slave like bees for it and revenge yourselves by paying politicians and penny newspapers out of your small wages to write articles and report speeches against its wickedness and tyranny, and to crack up your own Irish heroism, just as Haffigan once paid a witch a penny to put a spell on Billy Byrne's cow. In the end it will grind the nonsense out of you, and grind strength and sense into you.

BROADBENT [*out of patience*] Why cant you say a simple thing simply, Larry, without all that Irish exaggeration and talky-talky? The syndicate is a perfectly respectable body of responsible men of good position. We'll take Ireland in hand, and by straightforward business habits teach it efficiency and self-help on sound Liberal principles. You agree with me, Mr Keegan, dont you?

KEEGAN. Sir: I may even vote for you.

BROADBENT [*sincerely moved, shaking his hand warmly*] You shall never regret it, Mr Keegan: I give you my word for that. I shall bring money here: I shall raise wages: I shall found public institutions: a library, a Polytechnic (undenominational, of course), a gymnasium, a cricket club, perhaps an art school. I shall make a Garden city of Rosscullen: the round tower shall be thoroughly repaired and restored.

KEEGAN. And our place of torment shall be as clean and orderly as the cleanest and most orderly place I know in Ireland, which is our poetically named Mountjoy prison. Well, perhaps I had better vote for an efficient devil that knows his own mind and his own business than for a foolish patriot who has no mind and no business.

BROADBENT [*stiffly*] Devil is rather a strong expression in that connexion, Mr Keegan.

KEEGAN. Not from a man who knows that this world is hell. But since the word offends you, let me soften it, and compare you simply to an ass. [*Larry whitens with anger*].

BROADBENT [*reddening*] An ass!

KEEGAN [*gently*] You may take it without offence from a madman who calls the ass his brother—and a very honest, useful and faithful brother too. The ass, sir, is the most efficient of beasts, matter-of-fact, hardy, friendly when you treat him as a fellow-creature, stubborn when you abuse him, ridiculous only in love, which sets him braying, and in politics, which move him to roll about in the public road and raise a dust about nothing. Can you deny these qualities and habits in yourself, sir?

BROADBENT [*goodhumoredly*] Well, yes, I'm afraid I do, you know.

KEEGAN. Then perhaps you will confess to the ass's one fault.

BROADBENT. Perhaps so: what is it?

KEEGAN. That he wastes all his virtues—his efficiency, as you call it—in doing the will of his greedy masters instead of doing the will of Heaven that is in himself. He is efficient in the service of Mammon, mighty in mischief, skilful in ruin, heroic in destruction. But he comes to browse here without knowing that the soil his hoof touches is holy ground. Ireland, sir, for good or evil, is like no other place under heaven; and no man can touch its sod or breathe its air without becoming better or worse. It produces two kinds of men in strange perfection: saints and traitors. It is called the island of the saints; but indeed in these later years it might be more fitly called the island of the traitors; for our harvest of these is the fine flower of the world's crop of infamy. But the day may come when these islands shall live by the quality of their men rather than by the abundance of their minerals; and then we shall see.

LARRY. Mr Keegan: if you are going to be sentimental about Ireland, I shall bid you good evening. We have had enough of that, and more than enough of cleverly proving that everybody who is not an Irishman is an ass. It is neither good sense nor good manners. It will not stop the syndicate; and it will not interest young Ireland so much as my friend's gospel of efficiency.

BROADBENT. Ah, yes, yes: efficiency is the thing. I dont in the least mind your chaff, Mr Keegan; but Larry's right on the main point. The world belongs to the efficient.

KEEGAN [*with polished irony*] I stand rebuked, gentlemen. But believe me, I do every justice to the efficiency of you and your syndicate. You are both, I am told, thoroughly efficient civil engineers; and I have no doubt the golf links will be a triumph of your art. Mr Broadbent will get into parliament most efficiently, which is more than St Patrick could do if he were alive now. You may even build the hotel efficiently if you can find enough efficient masons, carpenters, and plumbers, which I rather doubt. [*Dropping his irony, and beginning to fall into the attitude of the priest rebuking sin*] When the hotel becomes insolvent [*Broadbent takes his cigar out of his mouth, a little taken aback*] your English business habits will secure the thorough efficiency of the liquidation. You will reorganize the scheme efficiently; you will liquidate its second bankruptcy efficiently [*Broadbent and Larry look quickly at one another; for this, unless the priest is an old financial hand, must be inspiration*]; you will get rid of its original shareholders efficiently after efficiently ruining them; and you will finally profit very efficiently by getting that hotel for a few shillings in the pound. [*More and more sternly*] Besides these efficient operations, you will foreclose your mortgages most efficiently [*his rebuking forefinger goes up in spite of himself*]; you will drive Haffigan to America very efficiently; you will find a use for Barney Doran's foul mouth and bullying temper by employing him to slave-drive your laborers very efficiently; and [*low and bitter*] when at last this poor desolate countryside becomes a busy mint in which we shall all slave to make money for you, with our Polytechnic to teach us how to do it efficiently, and our library to fuddle the few imaginations your distilleries will spare, and our repaired Round Tower with admission sixpence, and refreshments and penny-in-the-slot mutoscopes to make it interesting, then no doubt your

English and American shareholders will spend all the money we make for them very efficiently in shooting and hunting, in operations for cancer and appendicitis, in gluttony and gambling; and you will devote what they save to fresh land development schemes. For four wicked centuries the world has dreamed this foolish dream of efficiency; and the end is not yet. But the end will come.

BROADBENT [*seriously*] Too true, Mr Keegan, only too true. And most eloquently put. It reminds me of poor Ruskin: a great man, you know. I sympathize. Believe me, I'm on your side. Dont sneer, Larry: I used to read a lot of Shelley years ago. Let us be faithful to the dreams of our youth [*he wafts a wreath of cigar smoke at large across the hill*].

KEEGAN. Come, Mr Doyle! is this English sentiment so much more efficient than our Irish sentiment, after all? Mr Broadbent spends his life inefficiently admiring the thoughts of great men, and efficiently serving the cupidity of base money hunters. We spend our lives efficiently sneering at him and doing nothing. Which of us has any right to reproach the other?

BROADBENT [*coming down the hill again to Keegan's right hand*] But you know, something must be done.

KEEGAN. Yes: when we cease to do, we cease to live. Well, what shall we do?

BROADBENT. Why, what lies to our hand.

KEEGAN. Which is the making of golf links and hotels to bring idlers to a country which workers have left in millions because it is a hungry land, a naked land, an ignorant and oppressed land.

BROADBENT. But, hang it all, the idlers will bring money from England to Ireland!

KEEGAN. Just as our idlers have for so many generations taken money from Ireland to England. Has that saved England from poverty and degradation more horrible than we have ever dreamed of? When I went to England, sir, I hated England. Now I pity it. [*Broadbent can hardly conceive an Irishman pitying England; but as Larry intervenes angrily, he gives up and takes to the hill and his cigar again*].

LARRY. Much good your pity will do it!

KEEGAN. In the accounts kept in heaven, Mr Doyle, a heart purified of hatred may be worth more than even a Land Development Syndicate of Anglicized Irishmen and Gladstonized Englishmen.

LARRY. Oh, in heaven, no doubt. I have never been there. Can you tell me where it is?

KEEGAN. Could you have told me this morning where hell is? Yet you know now that it is here. Do not despair of finding heaven: it may be no farther off.

LARRY [*ironically*] On this holy ground, as you call it, eh?

KEEGAN [*with fierce intensity*] Yes, perhaps, even on this holy ground which such Irishmen as you have turned into a Land of Derision.

BROADBENT [*coming between them*] Take care! you will be quarrelling presently. Oh, you Irishmen, you Irishmen! Toujours Ballyhooly, eh? [*Larry, with a shrug, half comic, half impatient, turns away up the hill, but presently strolls back on Keegan's right. Broadbent adds, confidentially to Keegan*] Stick to the Englishman, Mr Keegan: he has a bad name here; but at least he can forgive you for being an Irishman.

KEEGAN. Sir: when you speak to me of English and Irish you forget that I am a Catholic. My country is not Ireland nor England, but the whole mighty realm of my Church. For me there are but two countries: heaven and hell; but two conditions of men: salvation and damnation. Standing here between you the Englishman, so clever in your foolishness, and this Irishman, so foolish in his cleverness, I cannot in my ignorance be sure which of you is the more deeply damned; but I should be unfaithful to my calling if I opened the gates of my heart less widely to one than to the other.

LARRY. In either case it would be an impertinence, Mr Keegan, as your approval is not of the slightest consequence to us. What use do you suppose all this drivel is to men with serious practical business in hand?

BROADBENT. I dont agree with that, Larry. I think these things cannot be said too often: they keep up the moral tone of the community. As you know, I claim the right to think for myself in religious matters: in fact, I am ready to avow myself a bit of a—of a—well, I dont care who knows it—a bit of a Unitarian; but if the Church of England contained a few men like Mr Keegan, I should certainly join it.

KEEGAN. You do me too much honor, sir. [*With priestly humility to Larry*] Mr Doyle: I am to blame for having unintentionally set your mind somewhat on edge against me. I beg your pardon.

LARRY [*unimpressed and hostile*] I didnt stand on ceremony with you: you neednt stand on it with me. Fine manners and fine words are cheap in Ireland: you can keep both for my friend here, who is still imposed on by them. *I* know their value.

KEEGAN. You mean you dont know their value.

LARRY [*angrily*] I mean what I say.

KEEGAN [*turning quietly to the Englishman*] You see, Mr Broadbent, I only make the hearts of my countrymen harder when I preach to them: the gates of hell still prevail against me. I shall wish you good evening. I am better alone, at the Round Tower, dreaming of heaven. [*He goes up the hill*].

LARRY. Aye, thats it! there you are! dreaming! dreaming! dreaming! dreaming!

KEEGAN [*halting and turning to them for the last time*] Every dream is a prophecy: every jest is an earnest in the womb of Time.

BROADBENT [*reflectively*] Once, when I was a small kid, I dreamt I was in heaven. [*They both stare at him*]. It was a sort of pale blue satin place, with all the pious old ladies in our congregation sitting as if they were at a service; and there was some awful person in the study at the other side of the hall. I didnt enjoy it, you know. What is it like in your dreams?

KEEGAN. In my dreams it is a country where the State is the Church and the Church the people: three in one and one in three. It is a commonwealth in which work is play and play is life: three in one and one in three. It is a temple in which the priest is the worshipper and the worshipper the worshipped: three in one and one in three. It is a godhead in which all life is human and all humanity divine: three in one and one in three. It is, in short, the dream of a madman. [*He goes away across the hill*].

BROADBENT [*looking after him affectionately*] What a regular old Church and State Tory he is! He's a character: he'll be an attraction here. Really almost equal to Ruskin and Carlyle.

LARRY. Yes; and much good they did with all their talk!

BROADBENT. Oh tut, tut, Larry! They improved my mind: they raised my tone enormously. I feel sincerely obliged to Keegan: he has made me feel a better man: distinctly better. [*With sincere elevation*] I feel now as I never did before that I am right in devoting my life to the cause of Ireland. Come along and help me to choose the site for the hotel.